PIERRE-SIMON BALLANCHE
Precursor of Romanticism

by

Albert Joseph George

SYRACUSE UNIVERSITY PRESS

SYRACUSE, NEW YORK

For
GEORGE DAVIS CHASE
Gentleman and Scholar

ACKNOWLEDGMENTS

MANY people have helped to make this book, through their advice or encouragement. I should especially like to express my gratitude to Wharton Miller, Librarian of Syracuse University, for his consistent faith in this work. Professor Albert D. Menut of Syracuse not only aided with much-needed counsel, but also with the loan of a microfilm projector. Thanks to him and to Professor Fernand Baldensperger, of the University of California at Los Angeles, who unbegrudgingly gave of his precious time to read the manuscript and offer valued criticism. Professor Jean-Albert Bédé, of Columbia University, time and again set aside his own work to come to my rescue with advice and suggestions for improvements. I should also like to acknowledge the kindness of the American Council of Learned Societies in granting me financial aid to finish my research. And last, but not least, thanks to my wife, whose pencil ruthlessly obliterated some of my most passionate prose.

ALBERT JOSEPH GEORGE

Syracuse University

FOREWORD

MEDIEVAL Lyons, as a trading and banking center of international importance, was a meeting-place for people from every Western country. At the same time, its Catholic traditions, uniting the oldest ties of Gaul with the Christian faith, struggled for preservation. Hence the rigid law, I suppose, which prevented any resident from acquiring citizenship unless he had spent ten years in the city. The present writer, having, in more modern times, passed ten years teaching at the University of Lyons and having married there, may boast of intellectual, artistic and social contacts with that somewhat reticent community, antagonistic in many ways to the brilliant capital, Paris.

Michelet, the historian, simplified the complexity of the city's personality with the formula: "a hill that works, a hill that prays," thus giving to La Croix-Rousse and to Fourvières a kind of polarity dominating the city at their feet. Georges Duhamel, when in charge of the book chronicle section of the *Mercure de France,* wondered whether "there still was a Lyonese school," an allusion to Renaissance days when, partly under Italian influence, Maurice Scève and other poets revealed an inspiration quite different from that of Paris and Tourangeau. As a matter of fact, despite French centralization, some characteristics quite different from the versatility of Paris and the virtuosity of our Southern countrymen have remained inherent in a city that can boast of Puvis de Chavannes in modern painting, and of many contributions to community life, such as the creation of department stores and banking complexes.

Such peculiarities were still more marked during the years following the downfall of Napoleon, in the strange era of "Restoration," and Professor George's study of Ballanche will greatly help to cast more light on the stream of ideas that surged into view after twenty-five years of unprecedented events. Had France to make amends for her "regicide" movements of 1793? Many "Prophets of the Past" advocated that a repentant France return to the ancient order of things. What a derision of so many sacrifices and brave struggles for an ideal! On the other hand, was the ancient history of France, with its religious traditions, to be rejected as contrary to the trend of modern thought? If the middle class really had won the Revolution, was money to become the sole criterion of the times, now that the peasantry had gained independent possession of the soil?

Many, then, were the programs and ideologies connected with such issues and, from 1815 to 1830 (and even after), the wavering policies of the government reflected dogmas which literature, busy with another struggle, did not always represent in their true light. Romantic aspirations and Classical devotions were often connected with reverse ideas in the political field. How much more was this the case in Lyons, where mysticism eventually gave a characteristic tinge to the dominant faith of a city that celebrates in May the martyrdom of Saint Blandine, the virgin slave of unblemished devotion, and, in December, the "fête de la Sainte Vierge," with lights on every window casement.

"Civilization is initiation" seems to have been the inner conviction of a solitary writer, working in the shadow, not for success but simply for the true expression of beliefs acquired during a life of retired, but nevertheless watchful, experience. "Woman has to play a part in keeping the real torch aflame, and womanly innocence and sacrifice is the highest form of ideal." Hidden truths, more than open appeals to the public, are to be expected from those writers who have at heart, not their own glory, but the welfare of their countrymen. Just as in prehistoric times, a kind of "symbolism" is bound to be associated with the sayings of the mentally gifted.

To what extent was the spirit of Lyons reflected in Ballanche's case? It would be a dangerous simplification of problems, a "Geoliteratur" of the poorest quality, to explain the peculiarities of a man with far-reaching relations, intimate with Chateaubriand and many returned French emigrés, by the simple fact that he had early been transplanted between Saône and Rhône from the picturesque village of Morteau in the Franche-Comté, and witnessed there the extremities of Jacobinism. But there is no doubt that Ballanche, to anybody familiar with even the modern Lyonnais, suggests a quaint and remote flavor of intrinsic, modest, even clumsy, merits not always associated in the mind of the general public with things French. Professor George's biography will help greatly to bring that flavor to life again.

FERNAND BALDENSPERGER

Los Angeles, 1945

INTRODUCTION

P IERRE-SIMON BALLANCHE is not a famous man. Even in his day
no excited crowds milled around book stores to buy his works,
nor did enthusiastic young men seek battle with balding classicists
in defense of his ideas. He was of second rank, as he himself
suspected.

But Pierre-Simon has his importance. In considering the development of French romanticism, critics most frequently turn to
the extremists. Rarely is notice taken of the large group of educated
citizens who bridged the gap between the neo-classicists and the
romanticists. They formed the middle group, and they ultimately
picked the winner. They bought the books, attended the theaters,
and voted for the victorious candidates. Ballanche came from this
stratum of society and, like his kind, he was mildly liberal in
politics, in religion a Catholic. He worried over the effects of the
Revolution on civil rights, particularly property, and sought an
explanation for contemporary social changes that would enable
him to face the future with confidence. He believed in progress,
but with reservations: traditions ought to be discarded only when
new ones could be established. Occultism was not foreign to him,
but he preferred the church of his fathers, though he wished it
more favorable to social innovations and separated from the state.
He was, in short, an excellent example of the more enlightened
bourgeoisie.

Despite this coating of common clay, Ballanche stood out from
the mass of his fellow citizens. As an exceedingly thoughtful individual, he had more to offer than the ideas of his class. He became
one of the principal Catholic lay philosophers of his times, a leading
philosopher of history and an eminent sociologist; his inquiries into
the development of institutions did much to foster the growth of

this new social science. Though acquiring sufficient fame to win a seat in the Académie Française, his real literary importance lies in the many ways in which he helped prepare French romanticism. His works contain almost all the ideas later to be gathered together loosely in the romantic "philosophy."

For all these contributions, Pierre-Simon Ballanche has received little attention from critics and scholars. During his life, Sainte-Beuve singled him out for study as a writer of rare talent,[1] but since then little has appeared except for some short studies. About the middle of the century, Jean-Jacques Ampère wrote a sketch of his friend,[2] as did Victor de Laprade,[3] Charles Lenormant,[4] and Louis de Loménie.[5] Emile Faguet later included Ballanche in the Politiques et moralistes,[6] but treated him with marked hostility and condescension. Though a few articles have been published on special aspects of Ballanche,[7] these lie for the most part buried in obscure periodicals or received little circulation. Ballanche remained known principally as the friend of Madame Récamier and Chateaubriand until the turn of the twentieth century, when Charles Huit[8] and Gaston Frainnet[9] published biographies of him. Of the two, the former is principally a defense of orthodoxy, while the latter has been made incomplete by the more recent publication of Edouard Herriot's Madame Récamier[10] and Alfred Marquiset's collection of Ballanche's letters.[11] These have increased Ballanche's stature and have indicated more clearly his place in the history of French literature. There exists, therefore, no complete modern biography of Ballanche and, more especially, only H. J. Hunt's chapter on him in English.[12] The present study hopes to remedy somewhat both these lacunae.

Insofar as possible, the plan of the work follows a chronological sequence. Since it has not been in the interest of clarity and concision to follow this plan strictly in some instances, certain aspects of his career are treated in a block. Simultaneously with the account of Ballanche's life, an effort has been made to explain his works in relation to the times and the literary situation of a given moment, as well as to the development of his thought. Since Ballanche was a provincial, it has thus been necessary to inquire into the literary life of Lyon in the early nineteenth century and to discuss the evolution of certain ideas in the second city of France. Occasionally, this has also involved consideration of other than literary topics, of the Industrial Revolution or of French penal systems, but it is hoped that the added background material will clarify to some extent Ballanche's contribution to the century and to indicate the true value of the gentle philosopher who was known to his age as "le bon Ballanche."

CONTENTS

PIERRE-SIMON BALLANCHE

CHAPTER I

The early years—Du Sentiment

I

1776. The year had been a bad one for France. Louis XVI, barely two years on the throne, had already alienated most of those who had greeted him as an enlightened despot. The year before, Turgot had valiantly attempted to realize the doctrines of the Physiocrats. To establish *laissez-faire,* he had abolished restrictions on the grain trade, curtailed the privileges of the ancient guilds, even presented the king with a mémoire on religious tolerance, but, as quickly as France's hopes grew, disillusionment sprouted. Louis squirmed when the Church, the court and the Parliament of Paris objected to the policies of his minister, hesitated, then dismissed Turgot in May, 1776. The date marked the end of Louis' flirtation with liberalism. Over the protests of the *philosophes,* Clugny assumed power and wastefulness again flourished in the ministries. Prices rose; pamphleteers dared attack even the royal family; and here and there could be heard the grumbles of the coming insurrections.

Into this growing revolt against the maintenance of a static society Pierre-Simon Ballanche was born, in Lyon, on August 4, 1776. He was the youngest of three children, of whom Anne, the eldest, lived but a short time.[1] Aimée, the second child, had preceded Pierre-Simon by little more than a year.[2] Since the Ballanche home lay in the shadow of Saint-Nizier, one of the twelve houses composing the short, dark rue des Trois-Carreaux,[3] the baby was taken there for baptism. On August 7 he was named Pierre-Simon in honor of an uncle, priest of the diocese of Besançon.[4]

Neither of his parents came from Lyon. His mother, Claudine Poulat, was from Grigny-sur-Rhône, in the *baillage* of Givors;[5] his father, Hugues-Jean Ballanche, from Morteau, in the Franche-Comté, not far from Besançon. Not much is known of Claudine

Poulat or of Hugues-Jean except that the Ballanche family seems to have inhabited Morteau for a long time.[6] Hugues-Jean had been born there January 21, 1748, the son of Gertrude Jolis and Guillaume-François Ballanche-Jacquot. The latter, in accordance with local custom, had assumed his mother's name to prevent confusion among the numerous branches of the family.

Hugues-Jean did not remain long at Morteau, for there remains no trace of him at the village after 1759, at which time he appeared as witness at a wedding. Probably he stayed there until the death of his mother on April 6, 1762, then left the province in search of broader opportunities.[7] Ten years later, August 9, 1772, his name reappears on the registers of Saint-Nizier as a grain merchant of Lyon. Apparently he had become the protégé of Aimé Delaroche, a printer of the Halles de la Grenette, for it was the latter who authorized Hugues' marriage. Delaroche and his wife also stood as godparents for Anne, the first child.

Hugues-Jean experienced some difficulty settling on the choice of a career. In turn he had been grain merchant in 1772, draper in 1776, and it was probably while exercising the latter profession he met Claudine Poulat, herself the daughter of a draper.[8] Finally Delaroche, head of the printing house in the Halles de la Grenette, 66, accepted him as an associate in one of the most important publishing concerns in France's second city.

The position with Delaroche lifted the Ballanche family into the ranks of a rich and proud bourgeoisie. At the end of the eighteenth century, Lyon was making a determined effort to replace Paris as the most important city of the realm. In some respects it had succeeded. The Académie de Lyon could boast of experiments and discoveries more venturesome than any Paris could offer. On August 19, 1783, the Marquis de Jouffroy ran trials with one of the first steamboats, and, a few months later, January 19, 1784, Montgolfier electrified the world with his first balloon ascension. Nor did Lyon defer to Paris in other matters. One of the centers of Free-Masonry and occult thought, it could point with pride to the fact that Saint-Martin, *le philosophe inconnu,* was living there: R ∴ L ∴ la Bienfaisance, à l'o ∴ de Lyon.[9]

Since a city so responsive to ideas offered full opportunity to brilliant young men, Hugues-Jean quickly gained a solid reputation among his fellow bourgeois. They came to think of him as an humble and just man who "joignait à une profonde intelligence de la profession d'imprimeur, les convictions et la pratique d'une vie religieuse." Madame Ballanche they considered "un modèle accompli de piété." In this center of Catholicism the sincere practice of religion counted almost as much as a reputation for probity in business.[10]

II

Pierre-Simon grew up in an atmosphere of piety and success and, by all rights, his should have been a happy childhood. Unfortunately, poor health robbed him of a normal life. While others of his age played and ran about, Pierre-Simon led a sedentary existence, too feeble for games. His worried parents often sent him to Grigny, to his mother's home, away from the gloomy, sunless house, in the hope that the quiet life of the country would give strength to a weak body. Here in Grigny, fifteen kilometers from Lyon, Pierre-Simon grew up unaware of the cracks edging across the pompous façade of French monarchy. His parents attempted to hide from him the sequence of events that was burning revolution into the minds of the people. He heard little of Danton, Marat, Robespierre, or Talleyrand, new actors who had usurped the principal rôles in the tremendous drama.

Slowly the storm crept over Lyon, somewhat milder than at Paris. Lyon at first welcomed the abolition of privilege, her bourgeoisie feeling that only the socially useful deserved special prerogatives. Thus, when in 1789 Parisians demolished the Bastille, the Lyonnais matched them by tearing down their own symbol of oppression, the Château de Pierre-Scise.[11] Liberty, equality, and fraternity were celebrated as aids to the commerce of the thriving city, and Lyon fell solidly in back of the Girondins. The Girondin policy of moderation appealed to business men with an eye on property rights. As fervent Catholics they had cause to distrust the attitude of the extremist Montagne. Lyon hoped that the Revolution would end soon, leaving the moderates in power. It frowned at the gambling craze that swept over France. The bewildering rise of prostitution in 1791-92 offended the middle-class sense of morality, while the rapid rise in the incidence of crime made the burghers voluble in their demands for stability.[12]

This wholesale support of the Girondins constituted a grave miscalculation on the part of the Lyonnais. Events soon conspired to show the city its error in choosing sides so definitely before the pendulum of revolution had travelled its full course. Catholics realized their predicament when, on the night of September 2, 1792, Paris mobs stormed Saint-Firmin, les Carmes and l'Abbaye. The Archbishop of Arles, and the Bishops of Saintes and Beauvais were summarily executed. The following day the Conciergerie, the Châtelet and l'Hôtel de la Force were sacked by the Parisians and most of the prisoners butchered. The order of the selection of the victims made many a thoughtful citizen pause: priests first, then men like Luce de Montmorin, governor of Fontainebleau, next, the court ladies and, finally, common criminals. The Lyonnais answered the attacks by backing the Girondins more vigorously, thus wringing from the Montagnards accusations of *modérantisme,* a word then synonymous with counter-revolution.

The coup d'état of June 2, 1793, in which the Montagne decimated the Gironde, convinced the city that in civil war lay the only solution to its predicament. Accordingly, Lyon joined Bordeaux and Toulon in the Federalist uprising against the Paris terrorists; whereupon the Convention retaliated on July 3 and 12, 1793, with decrees menacing the rebels. On July 16, Lyon answered insolently by guillotining Chalier, the local chief of the Montagne, and the citizens formed an enthusiastic, if untrained, army to defend themselves against inevitable attack.

The Montagne struck swiftly and so harshly that even forty years later Lyon remembered with shudders the treatment accorded it.[13] The Committee of Public Safety, on the 18th day of the first month, year II, signed the death warrant of an entire city:

Art. 3.   La ville de Lyon sera détruite.
Art. 4.   Il n'y sera conservé que la maison du pauvre, les manufactures, les ateliers des arts, les hôpitaux, les monuments publics et ceux de l'instruction.
Art. 5.   Cette ville cessera de s'appeler Lyon. Elle s'appellera *Commune Affranchie.*
Art. 6.   Sur les débris de Lyon sera élevé un monument où seront lus ces mots: *Lyon fit la guerre à la liberté; Lyon n'est plus.*[14]

Troops were dispatched under the leadership of Dubois de Crancé. The siege was laid August 9, 1793, and sixty thousand soldiers systematically began the destruction by bombardment of a city defended by seven or eight thousand amateur rebels. For almost two months the terrible shelling continued, and General Saudon reported to the Society of Jacobins: "Nos canonniers ont l'air de s'amuser en détruisant les maisons; et la ville de Lyon est déjà comme une écumoire."[15] A record of the military operations involved reveals the methodical manner of the besiegers:

> le 10 août 1793, canonnade depuis cinq heures du matin jusqu'à quatre heures du soir. . . .
> le 23, canonnade de Montessuy, depuis 6 heures du soir, jusqu'à sept heures du matin. . . .
> le 7 [septembre], bombardement et canonnade à boulets rouges, pendant huit heures. . . .
> du 15 au 21, bombardement continuel, nuit et jour.[16]

Finally the defense cracked. In a desperate sortie, Précy, chief of the insurgents, escaped on October 8. The next day the republican troops entered without opposition and the last item on the *Etat des opérations militaires . . . contre Lyon* ominously read: "Le 9 [octobre], fusillade des plus vives. . . ."[17]

Although the Montagnard army avoided fulfilling the letter of its instructions, the insurgents paid dearly for their resistance. A military tribunal promptly sentenced a hundred of the principal rebels. A *Commission de justice populaire* followed suit by condemning over a hundred more. Finally the famous *Commission révolutionnaire* assumed control of the city, with a guillotine to be fed constantly. For four months the commission indiscriminately plucked moderates and counter-revolutionaries from all strata of society: soldiers, priests, artisans, nobles or servants. Couthon, in charge but a short time, was replaced by the terrible Collot d'Herbois, even more pitiless than his predecessor, to whom he sarcastically referred as "le respectable Couthon." Fouché followed Collot d'Herbois, bringing new zeal to his office but even less kindness. From all the regions surrounding Lyon suspects were dragged in. One day, January 1, 1794, thirty-two notables arrived from Moulins, to be led to the guillotine in a group. The winter passed in a

continuous agony of killings, until the commission had beheaded
almost two thousand victims.[18]

Pierre-Simon escaped the wrath of the Federalists, but his father
was less fortunate. At the first sign of trouble, Hugues-Jean had
whisked his family away to Grigny, then returned alone to the city
to be trapped by the invaders. The printing house made his position
vulnerable. It had been founded by Aimé Delaroche in 1736, the
same Delaroche who had taken in Hugues-Jean as an associate.
Aimé Delaroche died in 1792, leaving a flourishing business to his
son Vatar, but the latter had been killed during the siege, on
September 4, 1793.[19] With a friend, Charles-François Millanois,
Hugues-Jean bought the interest of the heirs of Vatar Delaroche
and became head of the firm. Unfortunately, Millanois had also
played a prominent part in the insurgent army. A lieutenant-colonel
of the artillery that had kept the angry Montagne at bay for almost
two months, he could escape retribution only by a miracle. Furthermore, the conclusion of such an important contract smacked of
subterfuge to the Commission, perhaps an attempt to evade the
confiscation of the citizens' property. The Commission's suspicions
seemed justified when, tempted by Barrère's decree awarding the
property of counter-revolutionaries to their denouncers, one of the
printers, Gian Giuseppe Destefani, accused Millanois and Hugues-
Jean of being royalists. The Commission eyed the sale of the press,
considered Millanois' military record, and jailed both partners.
The trial was summary; Millanois was shot November 18, 1793,
and Hugues-Jean left in jail.[20] By a decree of the *Commission
temporaire* of December 13, 1793, the business was given to Destefani, sans-culotte, of Piedmont. In further reward, he was also named
government printer for the district.[21]

Hugues-Jean seemed doomed to a firing squad, too, but the
workers in the printing house came to his rescue. They appealed to
the Commission for leniency, pointing out that Hugues-Jean had
always treated them well, and demonstrating such affection for him
that the Commission relented. Hugues-Jean went free, but not until
the year V (1795), did he regain his business.

Hugues-Jean walked out of prison to find Lyon a shambles.
Fouché had rounded up the unemployed to demolish some of the

city's most beautiful buildings. Moreover, many of his friends had perished on the day that the ex-Oratorian had two hundred insurgents attached to the willows of the Place des Brotteaux and sabered as a reminder of the Montagne's displeasure.

The world he had known had perished with the Fête de la Raison, November 10, 1793. His position in the city became even more precarious when the victories and defeats of the Catholic Army sharpened anti-Church sentiment. Little by little, in the face of expropriations, terrorism, and the state adoption of the cult of the Supreme Being, the church went underground, helpless to aid the faithful who were caught attending secret masses. For Catholics like Hugues-Jean, Lyon was to remain the city of the cursed until opposition to Robespierre finally culminated in the Thermidorian *coup d'état* of July 9, 1794. For a short time, at least, respite was granted.

III

Pierre-Simon returned from Grigny in time to celebrate the fall of Robespierre, but the sight of the blackened walls and the gutted buildings unnerved him all the more because his parents had falsified the situation. He was still a sickly child, much given to brooding, sensitive, and deeply religious. They had, therefore, spoken little of the fate of the city to avoid exciting him, and, as a consequence, the sight was staggering. Friends had disappeared because their ideas were considered anti-social; landmarks were missing; and his father's business, the pride of the Ballanche household, had been handed to an informer.

It was probably the sight of the debris left by the holocaust that caused Pierre-Simon to worry himself into worse health. At any rate, shortly after the 9 thermidor, he fell desperately ill. Seeking a cure for the raging headaches that tormented his son, Hugues-Jean unfortunately permitted a charlatan to experiment on Pierre-Simon. The remedies prescribed not only aggravated the headaches, but induced caries of the jaw and lower skull.[22] Other physicians were then consulted, and, to save the boy, Hugues-Jean decided to follow their advice. What they recommended meant terrible agony, but offered the only possibility of life. Pierre-Simon was therefore prepared for the terrible operation of trepanning, placed in a chair, and the surgeons set to work. Some ladies remained in the room, curious to witness the operation, eager to help if needed. As the doctors labored, the women chattered near the fireplace at one end of the room. And so great was the courage of the young boy that not a whimper escaped him throughout the whole ordeal.[23]

The cure was not complete. For three years Pierre-Simon remained an invalid during a convalescence even harsher and more cruel than the malady. Because the technique of the surgeons had been hesitant, the left side of his face puckered from the hideous scars streaking it. Pierre-Simon was to carry these all his life and to become so conscious of them that he deliberately tried to keep his right profile towards the people with whom he conversed. What few portraits exist of him show only the right side of his face.[24] The trepanning also cut its impression on his mind. The illness, the pain, together with the knowledge of the horror that surrounded his home, made him nervous and sensitive. Always given to introversion, he kept to himself with books for his principal companions. Pierre-Simon avoided the society of all men, distrustful of their good will and, shut up in his room, he would experience hallucinations, not knowing whether he dreamed or read, but seeing visions come from another world.[25]

Deprived of the usual schooling afforded the young men of his age, Pierre-Simon took advantage of the extensive library of his father. He came to know authors of all nationalities in the course of his unguided reading. Epictetus and Camoëns followed Klopstock and Pythagoras; Milton and Young were put aside in favor of Ariosto. There were moments, too, when he curiously fingered translations from the Chinese, many more in which he avidly studied the illuminists and occult philosophers, Charles Bonnet or the Lyonnais Delisle-Desalle. But most of all he turned to the classics of antiquity or of France's golden age, to Fénelon, his favorite, to Pascal, Jean-Jacques Rousseau, Racine, and even to Ronsard and Rabelais.[26]

Constant converse with the great, especially with Fénelon, kindled in Pierre-Simon the urge to write his own book. He dreamed of joining their company, even of belonging to the French Academy.[27] A subject readily presented itself in the recent revolt at Lyon over which he brooded so much. He had begun an epic after the days of the Lyon Terror, and now he continued this in an effort to drive the nightmare from his mind. The epic never did reach publication, but some indication of its contents may be gained from references made in later works. The action takes place several centuries before the Revolution. The martyrs of a massacre similar to that of les Brotteaux have become the object of a cult; their ashes are venerated; and each year the city celebrates the anniversary of their death before the monument raised to them.[28] One day a traveller arrives from a distant region, and, seeing the festivities, asks the reason for the celebration. For his benefit the history of the siege is unrolled. The entire poem told as much about the author as about the city. Bewildered by the sudden changes taking place in contemporary society, Pierre-Simon strove to fathom the logic behind the Revolution. For the rest of his life he was to pursue the same course, inquiring in one way or another, into the causes and effects of this great event. Subsequent events prevent any attempt to point to this as the sole key to Ballanche's complex personality, but, unquestionably, it was an important facet of his character.

IV

Progressively as Ballanche convalesced, he ventured more into the company of young men of his age, finding fellowship in a literary society, which he promptly joined. The society, boasting the proud device *Amicitiae et litteris,* had been founded May 9, 1778, by a group of ambitious young writers: Riboud, Delandine, Béraud, Gerson, and Geoffroy.[29] In deference to Ballanche's inability to go out, the junior members of the group met at his home. Here gathered Dugas-Montbel, the future translator of Homer, Barret, later to become a brilliant Jesuit, Lenoir, André-Marie Ampère, still unaware of his genius, and Camille Jordan, just back from emigration. Avid to seize all knowledge, capable of great versatility, the members wrote verse, recited their own epics, tragedies, madrigals, or chansons. Together they read *la Chimie* of Lavoisier, marvelled at the wonders of his science, and were spurred to draw up a classification of all human knowledge.[30] Each brought to the meeting his manuscripts and plans for masterpieces. André-Marie Ampère, for instance, discussed his tragedies, *Agis, Conradin* and *Iphigénie en Aulide* or the epic he was weaving around Columbus, *l'Américide*. Ballanche recited fragments of his own epic or discussed literature in general until, one day in the year V, he surprised the membership by reading from the *Essai sur le sentiment,* a book on which he had been working for some time.[31] The young writers clung together for mutual support, complimented and encouraged each other in the common pursuit of literary glory. They enlivened the long hours Ballanche had to spend indoors, meeting faithfully at his house until his health improved, when the society appropriately moved to the Palais des Arts. Here they continued to investigate all questions but, above all, they searched for reasons why the Revolution should have appeared so suddenly to affect their lives.

Religion furnished another recurring theme for discussion. Since their world had tumbled about them, their former standards made useless, these young men floundered in search of beliefs to which they might anchor a new set of values. Ampère, for instance, had lost his father, a *juge de paix,* to the guillotine during the repressions following the siege. A perplexed Ballanche needed assurance that some form of reason guided the universe. All Catholics, though of varying degrees of intensity, they felt little attraction to the state church, rather, they were drawn closer to their faith by the intense persecution of Catholicism.

Revolution and religion, these two themes absorbed Ballanche, and he carried his preoccupation with them into the essay on which he continually worked. The Revolution seemed to be changing in spite of the continued restriction on religion. The Directory managed to turn a magnificent uprising into a second Regency, tolerant of all things but a code of morals. A weak regime, arbitrary, dissolute, and incapable of governing, it scorned opinion and was scorned in turn. Unskilled lawyers, finding too heavy the power that had fallen into their hands, worshipped only the persuasive importance of force.[32] Once hope came to the Catholics of Lyon when Camille Jordan was asked to report for the commission charged with revising the laws governing public worship. On July 17, 1797, he boldly voiced the opinion that tolerance was justified, but, before his report passed the discussion stage, the *coup d'état* of 18 fructidor ended the liberal republic and began a second terror. Catholics were again harried into secret masses.

Control of the new government rapidly passed into the hands of Napoleon Bonaparte and, with his eyes on the future, the ambitious Consul carefully considered the matter of religious tolerance. The roots of the Church went too deep to be disturbed by superficial measures. At least three courses lay open: he could ruthlessly continue the campaign against the Church in a determined effort to stamp it out in France; he could abrogate the decrees concerning the deportation of ecclesiastics, return the churches, and let the Church restore itself gradually, without pay, preeminence or official prerogatives, protected only by common right; or he could negotiate with the Pope, limiting, in the interests of both Church and State, the reciprocal rights of each. The first course was politically suicidal. The temper of France had changed greatly since the first days of the Revolution and the people shunned the state religion for that of their fathers. Constant war, too, had awakened in France a need for divine solace and assurance; the nation's desire for religion rose with the casualty lists. Nor did Bonaparte like the second choice. Traditionally the Church and the State had for centuries been inextricably intermingled. Many in France considered this a normal state of affairs, and the Consul was inclined to agree with them, but for different reasons. As a potential dictator, he wanted to absorb all sources of power. A free church constituted a free power, and any free power, even a moral one, was suspect. Any uncontrolled agency might sometime threaten his dreams of conquest. Furthermore, the Revolution had divided the Church itself into *constitutionnels* and *insermentés*. Since liberty granted to the Church meant the possibility of factional quarrels that might destroy Catholic and federal unity, Bonaparte chose to snip off this unwanted offshoot of the Revolution by negotiating with the Pope.[33]

The Consul moved with caution. The first sign of amelioration in the restrictions placed on Catholicism came the 8 frimaire an VIII (November 29, 1799), when a consular decree freed some of the priests emprisoned earlier in the Revolution. The next year watchful citizens noted signs of the future in the arrival of papal

legates, who immediately began bargaining with Bonaparte on how
to maintain the respective rights of Church and State. For eight long
months Catholic France held its breath while nine successive projects
were discarded. Twice there occurred memorable menaces of rupture
before July 15, 1801, when a compromise treaty was promulgated
which, in the official style of the times, was called *la convention du
26 messidor an IX*. Posterity was to rename it the Concordat. The
Pope ratified the convention August 15, 1801, and the Corps Légis-
latif followed suit April 8, 1802, over the opposition of Talleyrand
and many members of the Assemblée.

While these events had been promising religious peace, Ballanche
worked steadily on his essay, jotting down thoughts on the ultimate
meaning of the Revolution, or assaying the value of Christianity.
By attempting to fit these thoughts into the confines of literature
he gradually approached a personal art. Often he thought of publishing but, ever timid and sensitive, he worried over the reception
of a book into which he had put so much of himself. His new æsthetics, too, might receive rough handling from critics who considered any innovation an insult to their beloved classicism. His
point of view differed radically from that of most of his contemporaries:

> La littérature toute seule, c'est-à-dire, la littérature qui est son propre
> but à elle-même, il faut bien que je l'avoue, ne me parut jamais devoir
> être qu'un délassement. Nos facultés réelles . . . s'élèvent dans une
> région plus haute.
>   Oui, . . . il est des choses plus grandes . . . que la littérature . . .
> Ces grandes choses sont . . . la contexture même de l'esprit humain,
> et se nomment . . . la poésie, la philosophie, la religion.[34]

The members of the literary society had encouraged him, applauded
more than criticized, and assured him that he could expect no ill of
the public.[35] Hugues-Jean, too, insisted that the book should be
published. He swelled with pride at the thought of setting up on
his presses the work of his son.[36] But, for Pierre-Simon, there was a
weightier reason. France under Bonaparte seemed ready to hear
what he had to say, now that a concordat seemed about to close an
era of persecution. Therefore, in the year IX (1801), he turned the
manuscript over to his father and there appeared *Du sentiment considéré dans ses rapports avec la littérature et les arts*.[37]

V

The book had been long in preparation, but the subject matter was nevertheless chaotically arranged. No plan seems to have guided the selection of material. A glance at the table of contents reveals an interesting pot-pourri of ingredients: *De la sensibilité, Du goût de la campagne et des charmes du sol natal, De la mélancolie, Des institutions sociales, Des institutions religieuses, De la religion catholique, Etudes des modèles.*

Some of the apparent confusion, however, is dispelled by Ballanche's definition of the word *sentiment.* For him it meant not the result of sensation, nor the *sensibilité* of the eighteenth century, but

> . . . la puissance morale qui juge par instinct et sans délibération ce qui est conforme aux lois de notre nature considérées sous le triple rapport de notre *animalité,* de notre *personnalité,* et de notre *spiritualité.* Le sentiment ne sépare jamais ces trois rapports; il les aperçoit dans un instant indivisible. Le premier rapport établit l'empire de la sensibilité physique ou des sensations; le second, celui de l'individualité ou de la conscience; et le troisieme, celui de nos facultés intellectuelles ou de notre âme. Par le premier, nous sommes en contact avec toute la nature visible; par le second, nous parvenons à la connaissance de nous mêmes, et nous devenons susceptibles de mérite ou de démérite; par le troisième, nous concevons un ordre supérieur dont notre existence actuelle semble être une nuance, et c'est par-là que notre domaine s'étend dans des espaces infinis. De ces trois rapports, il en résulte un quatrième, qui est précisément l'ensemble des trois premiers, celui de notre humanité.[38]

In other words, *Du Sentiment* was to be concerned with the study of man's emotions, his taste in literature and his thoughts of a hereafter, or, more simply, with revolution, religion, and the art of personal literature, three topics that were to provide the entire nineteenth century with material for memorable thoughts and actions. Pierre-Simon was unwittingly firing one of the first shots of a long campaign.

The Revolution, to be sure, weighed most heavily on his mind, for not only had his father been jailed as suspect, but an exiled relative had died abroad.[39] Like many Frenchmen who regretted the abrupt denial of the past, Ballanche could write:

> J'ai vu la révolution française, devenue le fruit de cette guerre cruelle à toutes les illusions; j'ai vu des philosophes, forts de la supériorité

de leur raison, vouloir fixer l'empire de la vérité et de l'erreur, et dire au peuple: Ce colosse de soixante siècles est un fantôme.[40]

He reacted toward the Revolution as might be expected of a member of the class most hard hit, the wealthy bourgeoisie. Disregarding the benefits derived from the revolution, he invoked only the memory of former brutalities, heated shot crashing through houses, fusillades on the squares of Lyon, and the swishing rush of the guillotine. "Tout ce que l'imagination pouvait concevoir de crimes a été commis; tout ce qu'elle a pu inviter de monstrueux a été exécuté: en dix années se sont accumulés assez de forfaits pour que dix siècles en fussent encore souillés."[41]

By 1801, however, the most violent stage of the Revolution had passed. Bonaparte began to gather together the various sources of authority, carefully schooling France to respond to his firm grip. Delighted that an able administrator had checked the elements of violence, Ballanche sang the strong man's praises, helping thereby to lay the foundations for a legend that was to swell and grow in later years. Like many of his compatriots he saw Bonaparte as a divine instrument sent to enforce the will of Providence:

Du sein de ces grandes calamités, il s'est élevé un homme qui a été vu s'avançant dans le chemin obscur des plus hautes destinées, sans se douter de la grande mission dont il était investi. La Providence qui veillait, à l'insu des mortels ignorants et ingrats, la Providence avait dit: "J'ai choisi celui-ci pour qu'il rende aux institutions sociales leur garantie et l'appui des idées religieuses; mais pour que les peuples croient en lui, il exécutera de grandes choses, qui exciteront sa propre admiration.[42]

After this obeisance to the Consul, Ballanche paid tribute to the victims of the Terror. He appointed himself the poet of Lyon's suffering in a burst of lyric and oratorical prose:

Terre, terre barbare, qui as englouti ce que notre siècle eut de plus pur, qui as rendu une ville entière veuve, orpheline de ses plus illustres citoyens! terre, ouvre-toi, et laisse-nous voir nos amis! . . . O! si l'amitié, l'amour de la vertu, le patriotisme, le sentiment, suffisent pour une si grande entreprise, héros de Lyon, je suis votre barde![43]

With an eye to publicity, he reminded readers that he had already fixed in epic form scenes from the siege of Lyon. Some day, he hinted, this manuscript might appear but, in the meantime, he advised the city to raise a monument to its heroes, not an ornate and tawdry mausoleum, but a small park surrounded by "arbres mélancoliques," in which might be read touching inscriptions. Here fathers would teach sons to hate crime; and each year a day of commemoration would recall to the citizenry their glorious past. Then Ballanche dug into his epic to find a *Chant funèbre sur les héros de Lyon* which could be used on the suggested memorial day:

> Barde délaissé, prends ta lyre,
> Chante le malheur des héros;
> Et que ta faible voix soupire
> L'hymne funèbre des tombeaux:
> Et vous, Naïades du Permesse,
> Répondez à mes chants de deuil;
> Tous les amis de ma jeunesse
> Dorment dans le cercueil.[44]

Though a conservative politically, Ballanche was radical in his æsthetics. For most who claimed similar politics, Jean-Jacques Rousseau had already become anathema. But not for Ballanche. He liked Rousseau's teachings, especially the adoration of nature. Furthermore, he disliked heartily the neo-classic dictum that a set of precepts could substitute for genius.

> Froids didacticiens, si vous croyez que des préceptes donnent du génie, enseignez donc à cet artisan dont la tête est sans inspiration, enseignez-lui de faire onduler cette ligne voluptueuse qui forme les contours de la Vénus pudique . . . il fera la Phèdre de Pradon, au lieu du chef d'œuvre de tous les théâtres, la Phèdre de l'immortel Racine.[45]

On the contrary, genius superseded any artificial rules. Poets had sung of nature and of heroes long before grammarians and rhetoricians had begun to make the Muses yawn. The neo-classic rules had been formulated by unimaginative technicians from the works of their superiors, and these had served imitators in their travesties of genius. A pox on the usurper, shouted Ballanche, "qu'il reste dans la poussière, qu'il rampe à jamais."[46]

The only acceptable models for a writer were nature and the human heart. As Hugo was to repeat more than a quarter of a century later, Ballanche stated categorically that all art imitates nature, but added that this imitation should be tempered with *sentiment,* the only source of the true and the beautiful. "Dans les arts comme dans la nature, il n'est qu'une ligne: l'étude et le travail ne suffisent pas pour apercevoir cette ligne invariable; rien ne supplée à l'instinct du sentiment."[47]

His insistence fell as much on the true as on the beautiful. By truth he meant morality and virtue, a point on which his romantic offspring could not necessarily concur. But true to his principle that art should be socially useful, he considered literature coldly ornamental if it did not produce "cette morale universelle qui est indépendante des gouvernements et des opinions."[48]

As a guide for measuring the dose of *sentiment* required as a literary ingredient, Ballanche submitted his own poetics, based primarily on the inspiration received from solitude.

> La solitude plaît surtout à l'homme de génie, dont l'âme se courbe avec volupté sous le souffle élyséen de la mélancolie, comme une riche moisson qu'un léger zéphyr fait doucement onduler; c'est dans la solitude que ses idées s'élaborent, que ses sensations lui deviennent distinctes, que des pensées originales s'élancent de son cerveau avec facilité et sans confusion: c'est dans la solitude qu'il peut étudier avec succès les replis de son coeur; c'est dans la solitude enfin qu'il reçoit les plus belles inspirations.[49]

In the tradition of the eighteenth century pre-romanticists, he counselled for those interested in elegiac verse the silence of the night, a walk in the light of an uncertain moon. The advice was later to be *sine qua non* for the *Jeune-France:* to bewail, late at night, the friend whom a pitiless death had snatched away, or to meditate on a tender Eurydice who triumphantly leaves her tomb, vanishing at dawn from the last embraces of a lover. Like Young, poets should appeal to the muse of sadness. And, in a manner reminiscent of Ossian, he issued decrees for a new literature:

> Cherchez quelquefois l'orage; ne craignez pas les météores précurseurs de la tempête. Que la foudre déchire la nue, descende en sillons tortueux, brise un chêne vieux de plusieurs générations d'hommes, et vienne mourir à vos pieds; que l'aquilon mugisse dans les anfractuosités des rochers . . . que la nuit vous surprenne aux prises avec tous ces phénomènes terribles; que l'obscurité enveloppe ces sites menaçants; n'ayez d'autre lumière que la torche instantanée et intermittente de l'éclair. Ainsi perdu dans les ténèbres, fatigué par l'apparition des fantômes gigantesques qui se jouent d'une imagination épouvantée, attendez le retour de l'aurore.[50]

But nature constituted only one of the poet's models; there still remained the question of religion, not the worn-out mythology advocated by Boileau, but Catholicism in all the majesty of its mysteries. For the painter of scenes, Ballanche followed Fénelon in pointing out the *sentiment* latent in the Old Testament, the life of Christ, the resignation and courage of the martyrs, and the diffusion of Christianity. Since unguided man was only "un vermisseau qui rampe, et dont l'anéantissement ne ferait aucun vide dans l'univers,"[51] one of the artist's functions was to show him his place in the great chain of beings, to point out how he fits into the general harmony of nature. The benefit accruing to the artist for this labor lay in the fact that he thereby travelled the only road to greatness. "J'ose dire . . . que les grandes pensées ont pour origine les idées religieuses: en effet, sans elle, tout est mesquin, tout est fragile, tout avorte."[52] The genius, then, would unveil something beyond the vicissitudes of change, a new Jerusalem where nothing was to be desired or feared. In this way Ballanche linked up his growing need for religion with his fear of revolution, both of which he expressed in the poetics.

Ballanche's first book was decidedly not a success. It sinned lavishly in the manner of first books. Not only did it smack of the literary society, but, as Sainte-Beuve later pointed out, Ballanche's style verged on the pontifical.[53] The young author lectured his readers too strenuously and, in some places where he sensed himself on dangerous ground, attempted to carry his point by sheer audacity. Erudition there was aplenty, perhaps too much, for Ballanche sprinkled references lavishly, *Les douze surprises de Pythagore* neighboring with Pascal and Amyot. Furthermore, though Ballanche had admitted his book would be a "jardin anglais," his candid independence of all precept neither strengthened his arguments nor relieved the essay of its brashness.

And yet, with all its faults, there was much in this brave new book. Ballanche had managed to repeat a great many of the ideas that had been bruited in literary circles for years. His advocacy of a back-to-nature movement, for instance, held little novelty, but he had codified a great many of these clichés into a doctrine of sorts and thus earned the distinction of giving the nineteenth century one of its first unembarrassed manifestoes. Hugo's *Préface de Cromwell* would echo many of the statements of *Du Sentiment*. The first romanticists would mistrust the Revolution, favor the politics of the upper classes. They, too, would espouse the cause of the Church with violence and work towards a personal literature. Parts of his essay even contain the very elements of romanticism for which the *Figaro* would jeer at the *Jeune-France:* the wanderer in the moonlight, the poet meditating in the thunder storm, the writer finding inspiration beside a fresh grave.[54] Though Ballanche was probably unaware of it, he had become a full-fledged ancestor of a yet-unborn literary movement.

More than that, Ballanche's essay held the suggestion of a number of future books. Much of Lamartine lies in germ here, especially the *Méditations*. And would not Gautier's *La Cafetière* apparently follow the author's advice to dance with a young wraith in the small hours of the night? Benjamin Constant and others could read here the outline for a history of religions:

> . . . j'ai pensé que, pour tracer le tableau de l'esprit humain, il suffirait peut-être de faire l'histoire des différentes opinions religieuses qui ont successivement régné sur la terre. . . .
>
> Les cérémonies religieuses, l'architecture des temples, le choix des jours consacrés, les habillements des prêtres, les formes même que l'art prête aux divinités, seraient un riche accessoire de ce tableau général; car tour les détails du culte ne sont qu'un langage figuré de la croyance elle-même.[55]

Chateaubriand, too. All his themes were mentioned in *Du Sentiment*, even the title of *le Génie du Christianisme*. Probably the two men were independently arriving at the same æsthetics but, at times, it almost seems as if another had penned parts of Ballanche's essay:

> Une croix dans un cimetière, une chapelle au fond d'un bois, un hermitage sur le sommet d'un rocher; l'asile d'une hospitalité chrétienne au milieu d'un désert . . . ; des chaumières groupées autour d'un clocher de hameau; une sainte Vierge tenant un enfant dans ses bras, sculptée à l'angle de deux chemins, et qu'invoque l'homme égaré dans sa route, sont des images pittoresques, qui vivifient un paysage car c'est un tableau fait pour plaire éternellement, que celui de la Religion animant toute la nature, se plaçant parmi les sites les plus sauvages, réunissant les hommes par un lien plus puissant que celui des institutions sociales. . . .[56]

Only two Paris papers gave Ballanche the honor of a review, the *Journal de Paris* and the *Journal des Débats;* of these two, the former was by far the more understanding and judicious. The *Journal de Paris* dedicated three articles to the essay, the 27 germinal, and the 3 and 4 floréal an X. The anonymous editor did acknowledge in the second article that he had lost his notes, but he had read *Du Sentiment* closely enough to do it justice. In the main, his reaction was favorable:

> Les avis des différents lecteurs (et ce livre en mérite beaucoup) seront probablement partagés, il pourra même s'en trouver de diamétralement opposés; mais l'ouvrage n'en a pas moins des mérites sur lesquels tout le monde sera d'accord. On y reconnoîtra l'amour le plus sincère de la religion et des lettres; on y verra tout ce qui peut annoncer l'instruction, la méditation, le talent, j'oserais presque dire le génie. On le trouvera par-tout, à un peu trop d'emphase près, écrit avec autant d'élégance que de chaleur, et le seul vrai reproche qu'on pourra lui faire, sera de n'être point assez fait.[57]

The jibes at the classicists, the *romantisme avant la lettre,* failed to disturb the critic, but he did shy at the sentimental and poetic use of religion on the grounds that it might enfeeble the Church. All of Ballanche's talent, his pious artifices and ingenious arguments, though used to further the cause of Catholicism, seemed like gilding the lily: "[La religion] ne se donne point pour une muse, elle ne cherche point à faire des poëtes, mais des saints."[58]

With the second critic, Ballanche had an unfortunate encounter. The abbé de Féletz was making his début as a literary critic and was determined to do so brilliantly, even though it killed all the authors he treated. He seemed to agree with Sainte-Beuve that "chaque critique a son gibier favori sur lequel il tombe et qu'il dépèce de préférence."[59] In this case the victim was the citoyen Ballanche, for the abbé lost all sense of Christian charity in lampooning the young author's maiden effort. The erudition irritated him; he was shocked to find Marius and Saint Pélagie, Julius Caesar and Saint Theresa, Saint Vincent de Paul and Pythagorus thrust into the same paragraph. That the latter should be a favorite of Ballanche displeased him immensely.[60] He carefully pointed out all the errors in scholarship, gloating when Ballanche unhappily wrote of the circle of Proculus. "Je persiste . . . [smiled the critic] à croire qu'il fallait mettre le cercle de Popilius, et assurément s'il était aussi vaste que celui que le citoyen Ballanche a tracé autour de lui, Antiochus ne devait pas y être gêné."[61] De Féletz refused to find anything of value in the book, ridiculing Ballanche's advice to "respirer le genie dans les émissions balsamiques des végétaux."[62] He dismissed the young man's æsthetics with the greatest contempt:

> Il est évident que le citoyen Ballanche n'a fait que ramasser les différentes amplifications, les morceaux de déclamation qu'il avait composés étant écolier, et les réunir en un volume; nul ordre, nulle méthode, nul enchaînement; qu'on en supprime un ou plusieurs chapitres; qu'on les transpose, il n'y paraîtra pas.[63]

More than the *Journal de Paris,* the abbé seemed to mirror the contemporary attitude toward Ballanche's book. Though the year IX was favorable to the renaissance of Catholicism, *Du Sentiment* sold slowly, earned little glory, even after Beuchot, a Parisian friend, had sent La Harpe, the contemporary prince of critics, a copy inscribed with one of Beuchot's poems.[64] The moment for such a book would come, but Ballanche had missed it by a few months. He felt that he lacked talent, that de Féletz had been right, and he resigned himself to obscurity. In reality, the review in the *Débats* had cut so deeply that the timid young author preferred abandoning literature to facing another such attack.[65] As he wrote to Beuchot, "le métier d'auteur ne vaut pas le diable."[66]

CHAPTER II

Chateaubriand—Literary Life in Lyon

I

THE failure of *Du Sentiment* actually threw Ballanche into closer touch with contemporary literature. Hugues-Jean, worried by his son's dejection, tried to make him forget the ill-fated essay by employing him in the firm. In this new capacity Ballanche fell into the path of Chateaubriand, the man who published with the *Génie du Christianisme* the book Ballanche thought he had written.

The two had much in common, from a literary point of view. As early as the year X, the critic of the *Journal de Paris* had pointed out the marked resemblance between their books.

> On nous annonce depuis longtemps, et je crois même qu'on publie déjà un ouvrage plus considérable ayant, dit-on, pour titre: des Beautés *poétiques,* ou seulement des Beautés du Christianisme, et dont ce livre-ci (*Du Sentiment*) paroît avoir été l'avant-coureur; semblable à ces petits aérostats qu'on a coutume de faire partir avant les grands pour juger des courants de l'atmosphère.[1]

The same themes, the same likes and dislikes, and, in some cases, the same expressions, have led to the conclusion that, since *Du Sentiment* preceded the *Génie,* Chateaubriand had borrowed some of his material from Ballanche. The charge became serious with the discovery that Ballanche had even used the expression *génie du Christianisme* when writing of *Télémaque:* 'Ce beau livre est fondé tout entier sur une base mythologique; mais combien de choses, et ce sont les plus belles, qui n'ont pu être inspirées que par *le génie du Christianisme!*'[2]

Jean-Jacques Ampère seems to have started the claim shortly after Ballanche's death. Not only did he point out the strange similarity of the books, but he broached the matter of the title as well.[3] From then on, it was assumed that Chateaubriand "owed" much to Ballanche.[4] Partisans of each have gone to battle over questions of priority and influence, and, on superficial analysis, Ballanche does seem to have been the source of much of Chateaubriand's material, even furnishing phrases and images. While both books constitute free translations of the Concordat, Ballanche, shorter of breath than his contemporary, did publish his work before the *Génie*.

But did Chateaubriand copy from Ballanche?[5] The question is complicated by the fact that Ballanche quotes in his notes from *Des Beautés poétiques du Christianisme* by Chateaubriant *(sic.)*[6] At least two theories are possible: either both men reflected public opinion so closely that they arrived at similar conclusions, even similar expressions; or, through an intermediary, Chateaubriand caught glimpses of *Du Sentiment* before the *Génie* went to press and thus had opportunity to use some of it.

The question of the title furnishes a major point for debate. Although Ballanche used the phrase, Chateaubriand claimed this succinct and arresting expression to have come to him almost intuitively, even before he began to write. Unfortunately this is not so. In a letter to Fontanes, August 19, 1799, Chateaubriand called his book *De la Religion chrétienne par rapport à la Morale et aux Beaux-Arts.* By October 27 of that same year, he had changed it to *Des Beautés poétiques et morales de la religion chrétienne et de sa supériorité sur tous les autres cultes de la terre,* a more descriptive, yet more awkward title. By November 1800, Fontanes was referring to *le Génie du Christianisme,* and Chateaubriand, in his *Lettre au citoyen Fontanes* of that same year, signed himself *l'auteur du Génie du Christianisme.* Thus, it seems certain that Chateaubriand's book, though not christened at its inception, had received its name before the appearance of *Du Sentiment.* Both apparently arrived at the same expression independently, not a strange phenomenon considering that authors had been working toward such a book for a long time. They were merely attempting to satisfy a need of the times and stumbled on an apt descriptive phrase.

How, then, did Ballanche know the *Génie* by one of its earlier titles? The solution to this lies in the precise dating of the essay. The exact day of publication of *Du Sentiment* is not known, but first mention of it seems to occur in the *Journal typographique,* December 16, 1801. Ballanche himself states that "pendant l'impression de cet ouvrage, on a publié l'*Exposition* des principes fondamentaux de la philosophie transcendentale d'Emmanuel Kant. Je n'ai pas lu ce livre, mais j'avoue que j'ai été dérouté par tout ce qu'en ont dit les journaux."[7] This *Exposition* by Charles de Villers, was announced in the *Journal typographique* August 3, 1801. Since some of the notes to Ballanche's book were later added, probably in September, and the book was probably published in October, he could have read the *Lettre au citoyen Fontanes* before completing his book.

A variant to this solution is also possible. The passage on Bossuet which Ballanche quotes from Chateaubriand differs slightly from that in the *Lettre au citoyen Fontanes*. Then, either Ballanche misread the *Lettre,* or he had occasion to see some of the sheets of the unfinished London edition that were being circulated through literary circles in France. Granted Ballanche's usual care in handling all of the material he used, the latter appears the more probable explanation.

On the other hand, how could Chateaubriand have known of the essay unless an intermediary had notified him of its existence? No documents exist to prove such a contention, merely internal evidence to be found in the two books, but the theory seems possible when that intermediary could have been Fontanes.[8] Fontanes had lived in Lyon, had even married a Lyonnaise. He was a member of the Athénée, and, when he spoke before it in October, 1800, had stated that "Lyon est ma seconde patrie."[9] Thoroughly familiar with the city, acquainted with many of Ballanche's friends, he must have heard of the *Essai* that had been read in part to various groups of the city's writers. Furthermore, it seems unlikely that he failed to note a book in which there appeared an extraordinary political manifesto in favor of Bonaparte. The similarity of images and arguments strengthens this belief, as, for instance, when Chateaubriand in chapter IV, part III, follows very closely a section from Ballanche's chapter, *De la Mélancolie*. Since part III of the *Génie* had apparently not existed in the London edition, material for comparison may legitimately be drawn from it. In sifting the evidence, it becomes apparent that no indisputable proof of this contention can be offered; only enough data exist to infuriate the partisans of either author without settling the question of priority.

Yet the similarity is startling and leads easily to a strong suspicion that Ballanche's ideas earned more fame in the *Génie* than in *Du Sentiment*.

II

Ballanche and Chateaubriand, therefore, resembled each other sufficiently in ideology to make their initial meeting promise much. Ballanche immediately warmed to René and, in his own way, Chateaubriand came, in the course of events, to feel some friendship for the lonely little man. Their appreciation of each other actually developed despite their relationship, for the bare facts seem to belie any mutual appreciation. Much stood in their way. The lord and the tradesman, the successful author and the lampooned beginner, the extrovert and the introvert, faced each other from apparently opposite poles. Yet friendly they did become in the face of great odds, though most of the desire for sympathy and kindness came from Ballanche. In a way, he showed a marked hero-worship for Chateaubriand that helped him see beyond the unpleasant incidents that disturbed the first phase of their acquaintance. Ballanche wanted more than anything else to be treated as an equal by the author of the *Génie* and took pride in calling himself René's friend, though it may be doubted that Chateaubriand considered him such.

Ballanche first seems to have met Chateaubriand in the early days of 1802, when his father sent him on a business trip to prevent brooding over the failure of the *Essai*. A clever business man, Hugues-Jean had eyed the success of the *Génie* with considerable interest, and he packed his son off to Paris with a proposition for the successful author: Ballanche, père and fils, planned a new edition of the *Génie* and a French Bible with *discours*. Only the *discours* were to be by Chateaubriand, the text itself was to consist mostly of de Saci's translation, interspersed with the portions translated by Bossuet and other famous ecclesiastical writers.[10] Chateaubriand hesitated, then consented to begin a project he never finished. Ballanche may have suspected this lukewarm attitude, for, determined not to return empty-handed, he stopped at Corbeil to propose to the exiled La Harpe an expurgated edition of selections from Voltaire. The death of the critic ended the project before it had progressed beyond the initial arrangements.

Back in Lyon, father and son waited to see how the temperamental author of the *Génie* would treat their proposal.[11] They dreamed of making their publishing house a center of distribution, with the south of France their undisputed territory. Basing their calculations on the first success of the *Génie,* they hoped to fill the firm's cash box. With Migneret, they would cover France with irresistible prospectuses: "Il faut que le coup soit porté en même temps partout, et que la facilité de se procurer le livre soit telle que ce soit une espèce de tentation à laquelle on ne puisse résister!"[12]

But Chateaubriand apparently forgot the Bible and the new edition of the *Génie* in the enjoyment of his rôle as the latest literary lion of Paris. The 25 germinal an XI, Ballanche instructed Beuchot, the firm's representative, to continue arrangements with the reluctant author, refreshing his memory on the matter of the Bible. A new edition of Carrière's Bible had appeared and he feared a loss of market: "Il faudra qu'il songe sérieusement à notre affaire. Quand il aura bien médité son plan et son travail, on conviendra d'un prix, et il n'aura d'autre embarras que de recevoir son argent aux échéances convenues. Un auteur qui fait le commerce est une chose contre nature."[13] Ballanche also sent Beuchot advice on an article the latter was planning to write on the *Génie,* with a caution to beware of the author's pride yet, at the same time, to satisfy the priests and the pious. Only such an article would materially help business.

The wrangling over the amount to be paid for publication rights to the *Génie* continued until the Ballanches decided in desperation to buy the book: "Il valait mieux acheter que d'être toujours à rendre compte et à traiter avec un homme qui n'entend rien aux affaires."[14] In prairial, 1802, Ballanche optimistically informed Beuchot that negotiations were well advanced; an illustrated edition of the *Génie* was already in preparation.

However, in January, 1804, a penniless Chateaubriand upset their peace. He wrote Ballanche that he expected to pass through Lyon on his return from the Embassy at Rome, and proposed that the firm buy for the modest sum of five hundred louis the copper plates Migneret had used for his editions. But Ballanche had had his fingers burned too often in dealing with the great man, and he

suspected that the plates might be the property of Migneret. Consequently he sent Beuchot instructions to inquire into Chateaubriand's
affairs, whether he had been recalled or sent home, whether or not
he needed money badly. The publishers had no intention of paying
more than necessary, especially since Chateaubriand had for two years
kept them wondering about the state of the negotiations for the
Génie. Guessing that the financial distress of René might make him
more amenable, Ballanche asked Beuchot to visit him immediately:

> Chateaubriand sera arrivé à Paris lorsque tu recevras cette lettre.
> Il loge, comme tu sais, dans la rue Saint-Honoré, près de la rue de
> l'Echelle, au *Singe vert*. Il a emporté tous les manuscrits que tu m'avais
> envoyés relatifs au volume de supplément du *Génie* in-8°. Il s'occupera
> à le compléter de concert avec toi. Il fera même un petit travail qu'il
> m'épargnera, et qui sera toujours censé de moi. Je ferai mon travail
> sur les grandes critiques, telles que celles de Ginguené et de Boufflers.
> Chateaubriand fera pour notre édition un petit avertissement relatif à
> ce volume de supplément. Cet avertissement sera signé de moi. Arrivé
> à Paris, s'il trouve que les éditions sont bien avancées d'être vendues,
> il fera annoncer la nôtre dans le *Journal des Débats* par un article
> précurseur de l'édition. Il sera question, dans cet article, du volume du
> supplément fait par moi.[15]

At the end of the letter Ballanche asked wistfully if Beuchot would
ask Chateaubriand to make a kind reference to *Du Sentiment*.

Negotiations for the *Génie* dragged on, with much haggling on
both sides. Chateaubriand's asking price was so high that the
Ballanches refused to consider meeting it, even hinted that the
best solution to the problem would be the sale of their rights. Then,
to make matters worse, Pierre-Simon proposed further dealings with
the stubborn author. He informed Beuchot the 24 fructidor an XIII
that the firm had taken preliminary steps for the publication of
Chateaubriand's *Voyages,* a travel book on France that never appeared. When Chateaubriand made known his plans to journey to
the East, Ballanche kept a business eye on the possibility that some
choice manuscripts might return with René. For some time there was
even hope that he might go at least part way. Chateaubriand cava-
lierly left Pierre-Simon in the dark as to his status. He intended to
leave Paris July 13, 1806, but on June 28 Ballanche still did not
know whether or not to pack. Yet, although he complained to

Beuchot, he trembled lest a letter from Chateaubriand had been lost in the mail, leaving "le pauvre malheureux" to wait for him at Lausanne.

When the illustrious traveller returned to France, Ballanche waited for news, remembering the half-promises given before his departure. Chateaubriand was to return to Paris June 5, 1807, passing through Bordeaux, Blois, and Augerville, but on April 25, Ballanche still remained ignorant of his exact route. "Passera-t-il par Lyon? Qui achètera ses manuscrits? Ce voyage a singulièrement tourné les idées du côté de Chateaubriand. Voilà qui renouvelle absolument sa réputation. On attend tout de lui, et le premier ouvrage qu'il publiera sera enlevé." Prospects seemed so bright that Ballanche whispered to Beuchot that he and his father still hoped to buy the *Génie* outright.

As before, time brought bitter disillusionment. On March 29, 1808, Ballanche noted that the *Martyrs* had been finished, though he did not know whether Chateaubriand would consider bids from him. About a week later, he received an inkling of the fate of the *Martyrs* when Hugues-Jean informed him that the fantastic price of 100,000 francs had been set on the book, a figure they could scarcely hope to meet. Bertin, of the *Journal des Débats,* had offered 50,000 francs, but Ballanche doubted that Chateaubriand would accept the reduction, or that Bertin would increase the sum:

> J'ai peine à le croire, surtout après la conduite qu'il a tenue à l'égard du *Génie,* qui devenait une propriété nulle, si elle ne fût pas retombée toute entière entre nos mains . . . Je suis un peu étonné que M. de Chateaubriand ait ainsi caché son jeu avec nous. Je croyais que les *Martyrs* étaient bien loin d'être terminés, et la première nouvelle que j'en reçois est pour apprendre en même temps le marché commencé et peut-être consommé. M. de Chateaubriand a pu croire que nous n'étions pas assez riches pour nous élever à ses prétentions. Mais cela ne devait pas l'empêcher de nous en faire part. Ne suis-je pas son ami beaucoup plus que son libraire?[16]

Ballanche perforce had to relinquish all thought of the *Martyrs,* and the lack of good faith rankled him:

> M. de Chateaubriand est un excellent homme, mais tous les services qu'on peut lui rendre ne doivent pas faire penser qu'il puisse en tenir compte quand il s'agit d'affaires d'intérêts. Malheureusement, avec son

goût des choses honorables et son peu de fortune, il est obligé de penser beaucoup à l'argent. Nul n'apprécie mieux que moi son caractère et ses manières, mais il y a longtemps que j'ai pensé qu'avec lui la qualité de libraire exclut celle d'ami. Je crois donc désormais impossible de faire avec lui aucun marché de librairie. Comme je te l'ai dit, nous sommes marchands et obligés de songer à faire nos affaires le mieux possible comme marchands.[17]

After such treatment, Ballanche might have been excused for enjoying the abuse heaped on the *Martyrs* by the *Journal de Paris;* instead he leaped to the defense of his friend. Though recognizing that provincial opinion counted little in the controversy, he none the less planned to use the *Bulletin de Lyon* to swing the "honnêtes gens" to his point of view. Through Beuchot he notified Chateaubriand of the plan and was given a condescending permission to proceed that provoked a bitter observation: "Je crains qu'il n'y ait dans son acceptation que de l'obligeance et même de la complaisance, et qu'il se soucie fort peu d'une défense dont je sens en effet toute la difficulté." Perhaps it was for this reason that the brochure never was written, but, to keep his word, Ballanche inserted, from May 13 on, seven articles in defense of the *Martyrs,* all by his friend Deplace.

Characteristically, Chateaubriand forgot the services rendered. Neither Ballanche nor Deplace received any acknowledgment of his pains, nor was a copy of the *Itinéraire* sent to Ballanche. He complained to Beuchot that, since the defense of the *Martyrs* had cost him a lot of money, the least he expected was a letter of thanks. As for the *Itinéraire,* he felt Chateaubriand owed him a complimentary copy. Beuchot mentioned this slight to Chateaubriand, who immediately dispatched the *Itinéraire* and the *Martyrs* along with the news that he soon expected to visit Lyon, but the gift failed to soothe Ballanche. He cared little for the books but a great deal for the sentiment they would have represented:

Quant au voyage de M. Chateaubriand dans notre ville, je ne m'en soucie point. J'aurai sans doute beaucoup de plaisir à le voir; mais franchement, il me gêne un peu. Je ne suis pas assez grand seigneur pour lui. Il s'agit, d'ailleurs, de savoir s'il voit en moi un ami ou un libraire. Autant je serais flatté de son empressement si c'est comme ami, autant je serais incommodé si c'est comme libraire qu'il a envie de me voir. Je ne crois pas à son empressement sous le premier rapport; reste donc le second, dont je me soucie fort peu.[18]

Business negotiations with Chateaubriand evidently kept the Ballanches from a dull life. In May, 1813, the question of the *Génie* suddenly popped up again. Because Chateaubriand had been dealing with a society for the sale of his works, it became necessary for him to buy back the rights to the *Génie,* but, whereas once he had valued the work highly, he now seemed to consider it worthless. When Hugues-Jean asked thirty thousand francs for the contract, Chateaubriand countered with a lesser sum and asked more favorable terms. But Hugues-Jean bargained closely now that he held the whip-hand. He explained to René that the firm had reached the point of profiting from the edition and that the sale actually would represent a real loss. Pierre-Simon agreed with his father but convinced him that, for thirty thousand francs, they could overlook future profits, provided that Chateaubriand bought all copies held by them and Beuchot. Even then he doubted the wisdom of his own compromise:

Si M. de Chateaubriand était accoutumé aux affaires, nous ne devrions pas nous inquiéter de cela [the payment of the sums proposed]. Nous reposant entièrement sur sa loyauté, nous serions bien sûrs d'être payés aux termes convenus. Je crois bien qu'il se mettra en mesure pour remplir ses engagements, mais, encore une fois, il est possible que, malgré sa bonne volonté, il ne le puisse pas. Déjà, ce sera une peine infinie pour nous de lui voir emprunter de l'argent à 12 o/o pour payer 20 000 francs comptant. Il est certain qu'il ne convient pas à M. de Chateaubriand de racheter son livre.[19]

Ballanche's kindness went to waste. By September Chateaubriand had decided not to purchase the *Génie,* reducing Ballanche to a state of bewilderment. But so partial was he to the writer that he attempted to soothe the fury of his father. To Beuchot he explained unhappily that questions of money always made people act peculiarly, that Chateaubriand simply lacked business sense. He would have been happy to yield to the latter if he could, but the Ballanches lacked sufficient capital to give Chateaubriand a bargain. He must have succeeded in impressing his father, for the *Génie* was sold for the original price.

The fantastic story of strange business dealings continued as long as Ballanche maintained connection with the printing house. Pierre-Simon's overwhelming desire for friendship with Chateaubriand probably kept Hugues-Jean from writing off René as a bad risk. In

1814 the firm reprinted *De Buonaparte et des Bourbons,* which privilege cost fifty louis. Chateaubriand exacted his money on time, but showed extreme reluctance in meeting his own obligations. In July they were desperately trying to get payment for the *Génie* before the author left on a proposed trip to Sweden. Two years later, in 1816, Pierre-Simon confessed to Beuchot that he hated to nag, but he thought the debt should be cleared. The affair threatened to continue forever when Ballanche's father died and, in haste, Pierre-Simon sold the printing house, terminating a business relationship that had cost him as much in pride as in money.

The sale ended the first period of their friendship, leaving the honors to Ballanche. He had been a rare jewel among publishers, though Chateaubriand had failed to appreciate this. Sometimes justifiably impatient, he had aided René as much as possible, receiving in return the haughty treatment accorded the merchant by the grand seigneur. Perhaps he was also paying for having written *Du Sentiment,* an essay too close in theme and tenor to the *Génie* to make close friends of two sensitive people.

III

Except for the uncertainty of business affairs with Chateaubriand, Ballanche's life had flowed more smoothly during this period. As his father's associate, he had occasion to meet the literary great of the area, and to help edit the newspapers published by the firm. With the advent of the Consulate, Ballanche, père et fils, had assumed a semi-official character. From the 1er nivôse an X to the 29 ventôse an X, the concern issued the *Journal de Lyon et du Midi,* an official organ of the Franco-Italian Consulate. There followed the *Bulletin de Lyon*[20] and the *Petites Affiches,* two much-read bi-weeklies. The *Bulletin* carried lists of bibliography, and literary items such as prose or poetry by Béranger, Delandine, Dumas, or Beuchot.[21] To take care of any leisure, Ballanche also aided in the preparation of the annual *Almanach de Lyon.*

Once, as editor of the *Bulletin,* Pierre-Simon even had the dubious honor of running into the Consular police. Charles Fourier, an habitual collaborator, sent Ballanche an article entitled *Le Triumvirat continental et Paix perpétuelle sous trente ans.* The 25 frimaire an XII, the essay appeared in the paper, informing the good burghers of Lyon that the foreign policy of France should be the hegemony of the strong, and advocated the maintenance of order in Europe by force, if necessary.[22] The police considered the article too revealing and discreetly warned Hugues-Jean to restrict his son's penchant for printing advice to the government.

Meanwhile, Ballanche had also grown in literary stature. On the 24 messidor an X, the Academy of Lyon elected him to membership, a signal honor for a young man, considering the great reputation of the society.[23] The election had been the gracious response of the Academy to the gift of a copy of *Du Sentiment,* and the warm reception of the ill-fated book came in no small part from the fact that many of the academicians were old friends. Dumas, Delandine, Ampère, and Dugas-Montbel doubtless remembered *Amicitiae et litteris.*[24] Furthermore, at least one author of major status had taken flattering notice of Ballanche. In 1802, in the preface of *Les Tristes,* Charles Nodier had advised his readers: "Lisez les belles pages de Gleizès et de Ballanche, et ne dédaignez pas une ébauche de Michel-Ange parce que ce n'est qu'une *ébauche.*"[25]

His faith, too, became stronger with the dispersal of his family. Early in 1802 Aimée married Mᵉ Polingue, a notary of Givors. His mother, ailing for a year, died in October, 1803, and her death shook Ballanche hard. Ever since his youth in Grigny he had been close to her; it was she who had taken infinite pains to amuse him, to lessen the deadly boredom of a long convalescence. To Beuchot he simply wrote in penance: "Tu sais combien j'ai coûté de peines, de sollicitudes à ma pauvre mère."[26] With his grief pent up, he wished her back to life. Each morning she had entered his room to ask anxiously how he felt. And for two mornings after her death he heard her open his door, walk quietly to the bed, and ask how he had passed the night.[27]

The lonesomeness drove him out of his customary solitude. In search of sympathy and companionship, he helped found on February 24, 1804, the *Société chrétienne,* the members of which gathered to examine scientifically the philosophical bases of Catholicism. All participants boasted local fame, some, national reputations. André-Marie Ampère assumed the presidency, and Claude-Julien Bredin became secretary. Meetings were to be held every Friday at 4:30, each member playing host in turn. One March 8, 1804, the assembled members decided to limit discussion to eight questions, which can be reduced to three essential points:

1) For what reason has man been created?
2) Was there a revelation?
3) What influence has Christianity exercised on humanity?

Not all the debaters were firm Catholics. André-Marie Ampère, for instance, had lost his wife July 14, 1803, and with her his faith. After struggling for some time against Ballanche's attempts to re-convert him, he returned to his religion and, by late in the same year, felt zealous enough to help argue with another backslider, Claude-Julien Bredin. Bredin enjoyed the prestige of having fought in the siege. Though a veterinary in the regular army, he had slipped through the federal lines to fight alongside his compatriots. Captured, he was released only on the plea of his father and Hénon, a professor at the Ecole Vétérinaire, who realistically pointed out that the scarcity of veterinaries should influence the tribunal's judg-ment. It did, and Bredin was sent to the Armé des Alpes, from which he was recalled in 1795 to the Ecole Vétérinaire.[28] Events had so undermined his religion that by 1803 Ballanche found him a likely subject for lectures on the truth and value of Christianity. Another member, Roux-Bordier, also had to submit to Ballanche's proselyt-ing. A Genevan of long residence in Lyon, he had introduced Bredin to the new group in 1803. His fame rested on the theory he so volubly upheld, that the only race of consequence was the Scandi-navian. The French he considered effete and decadent, frivolous followers of a useless Catholicism. "O Français! nation celtique," he muttered in disdain. Ballanche he thought scatter-brained for bothering with schemes to share the wealth, for upholding the freedom of the press, or momentarily becoming a disciple of Joseph Lancaster.[29]

The fierce debates at the meetings of the club held the members together until December, 1804, when Ampère, its ruling spirit, left for the position of *répétiteur d'analyse* at the Ecole Polytechnique. Before dissolving, the group had had some memorable sessions, as when Roux pointed out the deficiencies of the French and proposed a religion of his own making. Bredin could be counted on to raise Ballanche and Ampère to heights of eloquence. To their arguments he quoted the Scriptures, shifting his metaphysical position with every new book read.[30] As Roux later wrote, Bredin passed rapidly from one stage to another: "Brissotin enragé, puis fougueux cavalier de Précy, bonapartiste fanatique; en religion déiste, épicurien, stoïcien, panthéiste, disciple de Pyathagore et de Zénon, chrétien catholique à l'époque de la *Société chrétienne.*"[31] Though good Catholics, Ballanche and Ampère enjoyed such a strong taste for metaphysics that they welcomed any opportunity to do intellectual battle. Ballanche was now studying Pascal seriously, searching to prove to Bredin and Roux the doctrine of immortality evident in the very misery of man.[32]

Out of this group, came a smaller, more intimate one composed of the four friends. This *Petite Académie* or *Société psychologique,* formed by the gravitation of the four men toward each other, held meetings in addition to those of the parent organization. During vacations, they repaired to Bredin's quarters at the Ecole Vétérinaire or visited Ampère at Poleymieux. When the *Société chrétienne* collapsed after the departure of Ampère, the *Petite Académie* continued to exist; the members exchanged letters and collaborated closely in their works.[33] Though of extremely different character, they remained fiercely friendly to each other, and later the total dispersion of the group left them keenly aware of a great loss, so much so that Roux, in 1822, wrote Bredin from Geneva a long, melancholy letter on their past happiness, sealed it, and quietly shot himself.[34]

In the midst of this literary activity, there occurred an event of such consequence to Lyon that it sent Ballanche scurrying for his pen. Pius VII crossed Lyon twice on his trip to Paris for the coronation of Napoleon. The first time, November 19, 1804, he remained only a day, but on his return, he stayed three days, April 17-19, 1805. In the heat of his faith, Ballanche set down in a pamphlet, *Lettres d'un jeune Lyonnais à un de ses amis,*[35] letters supposedly written to a friend not privileged to witness the ceremonies. Proceeds from the sale of the book were destined for charity.

The letters were restricted largely to description. The first one,

November 27, 1804, painted the parades and the unending recep-
tions. Of the latter, Ballanche especially noted that given by
Cardinal Fesch, even printing the Cardinal's name in capital letters,
a distinction otherwise accorded only to the Pope. The second letter,
of April 16, contained some biographical items that show how
excited the writer himself had been. When the Pope's carriage
neared the city, a band of young men, Ballanche among them,
formed a guard of honor for it. He almost burst with pride as he
strode beside the Pontiff watching the delirious people attempt to
kiss the seat on which Pius sat, or throwing themselves in front of
the horses to receive his blessing.[36] The good burghers of Lyon were
expressing what the Concordat meant to them, a feeling Ballanche
summarized at the end of his pamphlet: "cette colonne éternelle de
la Religion, que la Providence a mise à l'abri des ravages du temps,
des révolutions et des attentats de l'impiété."[37]

The *Lettres* said much of the Pope, little of the Emperor, and the
very omission of more than a passing mention of the latter formed
a declaration of Ballanche's revised political principles. He had
welcomed the Consulate, had even written a panegyric of Bonaparte
in *Du Sentiment,* but the official organization of religion settled a
chill on him. Catholicism had seemed more beautiful than when
covered by the pomp of the Empire; he would have preferred freedom for it rather than the restricting embrace of official sanction.
The death of the duc d'Enghien had completely divorced Ballanche
from the growing despotism which daily seemed to constrict him
more closely.

To overcome this political claustrophobia, Ballanche began to
travel on a small scale. When Chateaubriand and his wife passed
through Lyon in 1805, on their way to Geneva, he gladly accepted
an invitation to go along. For two weeks, in the fall of 1805, he
left behind oppression, visiting Geneva, seeing Mme de Staël,[38]
admiring Chamonix, and climbing to the Grande Chartreuse.

The walk to the Grande Chartreuse impressed Ballanche deeply.
On his return home, he set down a discussion he had held in the
courtyard with a mixed group of priests and naturalists; and this
conversation between strangers developed into what later became a
classic argument in the nineteenth century: the compatibility of

science and religion. The naturalists, moved by their surroundings, voiced the opinion that science and religion are not mutually exclusive. Though the priests applauded this, a young man, evidently Ballanche, argued that religion should despise science, maintaining that the visible world was a veil God had thrown over the real universe. *"Il a livré le monde à la dispute,* c'est-à-dire les plis ondoyants du voile à l'esprit de système, aux recherches interminables, aux études laborieuses *des enfants des hommes."*[39] The melancholy young man firmly believed that "nous rêvons un instant sur la terre. . . . C'est la plus petite partie de notre histoire; la tombe nous révèlera le reste."[40]

This mood led Ballanche to contemplate entering a monastery. When several of the younger members of the *Société chrétienne* took orders, Ballanche visited them and was especially struck by the attitude of one of them, Noël Jourdain. In envy he felt called to follow the latter's example, and, in July, 1805, he wrote to Ampère asking about Saint-Sulpice. In spite of Ampère's scoldings Ballanche persisted but, before deciding definitely, he prudently sought specific information:

> Sachez donc quelle vie on mène au séminaire de Paris, quel en est à peu près le régime intérieur, non pas pour le boire et le manger, car cela m'est égal, je voudrais seulement savoir quelle somme d'exercice de piété on exige dans la journée, quelle somme de temps on a pour être seul avec soi-même, quelles sont les études qu'on y suit, à part la théologie et la philosophie, etc? Je voudrais savoir encore si on ne peut pas mêler à tout cela quelque étude étrangère, comme par exemple, le grec et l'hébreu. Il me passe par la tête d'étudier les preuves de la religion dans les sources mêmes. Je ne puis le faire qu'en me livrant entièrement et exclusivement. Il faut donc que je quitte le monde et que j'embrasse l'état ecclésiastique.[41]

Why this sudden urge to enter Saint-Sulpice? Paradoxically, it was because Ballanche's faith was not quite so secure as he would have liked. Too frequent exposure to metaphysical debate had cracked his firmness. Therefore, he reasoned, why not dedicate himself to Catholicism and thus fortify his beliefs? God, he explained to Ampère, gave faith to the simple, but people like him had to fight for it with the expenditure of much intellectual strength and the devotion of all faculties. He could not continue in his present state of uncertainty; he was afraid, and his very fear made him even more afraid.

Ballanche never did more than consider the idea, for Chateaubriand accidentally intervened to help clear his mind. When René crossed Lyon, full of dreams of the Orient and Nathalie de Noailles, he decided to make use of his publisher. Madame de Chateaubriand liked the little printer and, if she could be dissuaded from accompanying him eastward, perhaps Ballanche could fetch her home from Italy. Dutifully Ballanche snatched time from his work, arriving in Venice August 3, 1806. He continued with Madame de Chateaubriand to Rome, then escorted her back to France.

Back home, the tempo of a busy life dragged him from his misery. The *Athénée* appointed him to the secretariat of the section of *Belles-lettres,* for which honor Ballanche had to edit the *compte-rendu* of 1807. Another literary circle, too, kept him from introspection. A direct descendant of *Amicitiae et litteris,* the *Cercle littéraire* was founded April 7, 1807, and held its first meeting July 9, 1807, at the home of a professor of literature, E. Molard.[42] Partly because of his reputation, and partly because of the space available in the printing house, Ballanche was asked to join in 1808 and, from then on, periodic meetings took place in his shop. This group constituted his favorite literary society. To it, on January 12, 1809, he read a prologue entitled *La Mort d'un platonicien, racontée par un de ses amis.*[43]

La Mort d'un platonicien, part of a proposed work called *La Foi promise aux Gentils,* relates the story of Timagène, a disciple of Plato. Back in his own country after much travel, Timagène calls together his friends at the approach of death. The Athenian dictatorship seemed to menace his beloved democracy, yet he gave his friends a message of hope:

> Nous touchons à une rénovation de siècles. Les systèmes religieux croulent de toutes parts; les philosophes, que avaient méprisé les doctrines mystérieuses, les interrogent avec une curiosité inquiète. N'entendez-vous pas une voix sourde qui court par tout l'univers, et qui réveille toutes les puissances de l'âme?[44]

Philoclès, an old man, relates the story to Polydore who is so impressed that he determines to seek the truth described by Timagène.

Here Ballanche ended his fragment, though he had originally intended to describe Polydore's travels, painting the entire world of the period immediately preceding the advent of Christianity. Polydore was to return to Athens, still confused, in time to hear Saint Paul's first sermon and be converted to Christianity. Ballanche was still working on his epic, and slowly revolving in his mind the themes of religion and revolution. By now they had almost become a fixation with him. They had marked his adolescence and were to remain in his mind for the rest of his life.

CHAPTER III

The Love Affair—Antigone

I

WHAT, however, had plucked Ballanche from the *mal du siècle* after the death of his mother was not literature, but love. Early in 1806, Ballanche met Mazade d'Avèze, a poverty-stricken nobleman then engaged in launching a "cure-all" patent medicine called Angostura. This suave and unintelligent aristocrat met Ballanche when writing for the *Bulletin* a series of letters published in the column *Promenades lyonnaises*. Addressed to a daughter in Montpellier, they described the sights and delights of the city in a manner calculated to attract tourists.

Somehow, Mazade d'Avèze induced Ballanche to believe in the magic properties of his medicinal bark, even convinced him of great promise for its financial supporters. On the strength of this wild faith, Ballanche gave Angostura a great deal of free publicity. He thus became more intimately acquainted with Mazade d'Avèze and, in May, 1806, met his daughter, Bertille-Honorine.[1]

Bertille-Honorine was younger than Ballanche. Ten years his junior, she had been born at the Château d'Avèze, in the southern Cévennes, where, during the Terror, she had known all the turmoil of revolution, the mad flight from the house, confiscation of family property, and a life which the tightening fingers of poverty daily made more dingy. Her mother had been forced to slave as a maid of all work. For herself, she crocheted gloves that her mother sold; and her father, after his return from the emigration, pursued sudden riches with the magic medicine while he wrote lyrically for the *Bulletin de Lyon*.

She came to Lyon that spring to see the sights her father had described in his column. Particularly she wanted to make the ascent of Mont Ceindre, where perched an abandoned hermitage. Since

Mazade d'Avèze disliked exertion, he asked his employer to act as her escort. Ballanche gallantly agreed and, on the trip, fell hopelessly in love with the girl. In some ways, the affair seemed natural, despite the great age difference. Both had the same taste for sadness, the same religious fervor, and the same grave conception of existence.[2] The walk so impressed her that later she wrote an account of the promenade. At the oratory, her first prayer was for her guide. When she asked Ballanche to scribble a sentiment on the wall of the abandoned hermitage, he wrote: "Cet hermitage rappelle assez bien les destinées humaines: resserré dans des bornes étroites, on y jouit d'une étendue immense."[3]

Ballanche thought he had found happiness in the girl despite the marked social gap between them. Although admitting his passion to Beuchot, he approached the Marquis more subtly. In return for favorable consideration of his suit, he would rescue Mazade d'Avèze from the ruin which speculation with Angostura threatened. He thought the matter over carefully, then sent d'Avèze to Paris to help Beuchot with publicity, not broaching his proposition until June, 1807, when the Marquis' creditors clamored more vociferously than usual. The Marquis accepted; Ballanche could have his daughter and his debts. What the girl thought is not known. Certainly, as a dutiful daughter, she accepted Ballanche, though probably she did not view the approaching marriage with as much enthusiasm as he. However, the Lyonnais printer offered a good match since his fortune more than compensated for personal defects. Caste differences bothered her little. Thus, a happy Ballanche could write to Beuchot, November 26, 1807:

> Tu sens bien, mon cher Beuchot, que nous ne prendrions pas sur nous les fardeaux et les risques de l'angostura, si les affaires de M. d'Avèze n'étaient à la veille de devenir les nôtres ou plutôt les miennes. . . . A présent, je te dirai que je te prie de m'éviter le voyage de Paris. Il me gênerait beaucoup en ce moment, à la veille d'un mariage qui me donnera et beaucoup d'occupations de différentes sortes et beaucoup de règlements d'affaires.[4]

But Ballanche's happiness smashed against the prejudices of Bertille's maternal aunt, Mme de Guilleminet, who housed and fed the d'Avèze family in Montpellier. She had gravitated into the dominant position in the family after the death of Bertille's mother, retaining all the class notions of the Ancien Régime. She refused to sanction such a mésalliance and since she was expected to furnish Bertille with a dowry of 100,000 francs, Mazade d'Avèze yielded to financial necessity. He did not care to break with his sister, especially after her kindness to his daughter, nor did he wish to condemn Bertille to what he considered an ignominious life with a bourgeois husband. For her part, Bertille was too pious and not enough in love to oppose her family. She herself went to Lyon with her refusal. He understood that the answer did not come from her, but the knowledge gave cold comfort and once again he dropped into black despair.[5]

The sharp disappointment soured Ballanche on marriage. Bertille, however, after having refused several offers, docilely accepted her aunt's candidate, Victor de Bonald, the youngest son of the apologist, whom she married April 23, 1812, six years after the pilgrimage to Mont Ceindre. She lived a quiet, uneventful life until her death, August 14, 1825. Ballanche long remained unaware of her death, yet, so deep was his love that when he discovered the news on March 31, 1830, he set down in one of his *Fragments* a tribute to the girl he had hoped to marry:

> Je n'ai été averti par aucun pressentiment; du moins, si une corde de ma lyre a rendu un son funèbre, le mouvement du monde m'a empêché de l'entendre; le 14 août une belle et noble créature qui m'était jadis apparue, et qui habitait loin des lieux où j'habitais moi-même, une belle et noble créature, jeune fille alors, jeune fille à qui j'avais demandé toutes les promesses d'un si riche avenir; en ce jour, cette femme est allée visiter, à mon insu, les régions de la vie réelle et immuable, après avoir refusé de parcourir avec moi celles de la vie des illusions et des changements. Hélas! je dis qu'elle avait refusé, mais il y a là un mystère de malheur, que je ne saurai jamais sur cette terre. Suis-je donc le seul dont toute la destinée se soit trouvée à jamais incomplète.[6]

For most of his friends it was the first intimation of an unsuccessful love affair. He kept his peace until later he encountered the Marquis. For many years Mazade d'Avèze had regretted his shabby treatment of Ballanche, especially in view of the latter's willing assumption of his debts. Mazade d'Avèze partially revealed the secret when he began to call Ballanche "mon fils," and muttered about the "réparation d'un passé irréparable."[7]

II

In his loneliness, Ballanche once again turned to literature. He felt need of fixing his thoughts on paper, where they would cease to torment him. As he wrote to Ampère on March 16, 1808, "Nous sommes deux misérables créatures à qui les inconséquences ne coûtent guère. Un brasier est dans votre coeur; le néant s'est logé dans le mien."[8] He began jotting down his thoughts, composing lyric effusions that were inserted in the *Bulletin de Lyon* between May 28, 1808 and October 25, 1809. They constituted at the same time a last desperate attempt to correspond with Bertille.[9] Two of the *Fragments,* I and VIII, recalled directly the tragedy of his love affair. The first told of his solitude before Bertille came to fill his days, hinted at her tears when she stammered out a refusal. The last spoke at length of the story of Hermann and Dorothea and summed up past events in a paragraph:

> Un jeune homme et une jeune fille s'aimaient. Le rang de leurs familles n'était pas la même, et leur fortune n'était pas égale . . . Comme ils étaient sans expérience, ils ignoraient que l'amour ne suffit pas pour assurer le bonheur . . . Lorsqu'ils connurent les obstacles qui s'opposaient à leur union, ils s'affligèrent et n'en murmurèrent pas.[10]

The other *Fragments,* however, repeated a theme from *Du Sentiment.* It was time, Ballanche wrote, for writers to return to religious ideas since they could not succeed without them. Here and there he scattered observations that later would serve as the fundamental thought of many a romantic poem: "quelle que soit la route que nous ayons choisie, nous sommes toujours déçus;"[11] "ils se sont donc évanouis pour jamais les rêves de la jeunesse."[12] Later, Sainte-Beuve was so struck by the similarity between the *Fragments* and *Les Méditations* that he remarked that if Ballanche had put his thoughts into poetry he would have stolen from Lamartine the honor of introducing lyrical philosophizing to the nineteenth century.[13] Both works contain the same literary and religious material; both spring from similar sources of melancholy inspiration; each is harmonious, lyrical, and elegiac. Time, for Lamartine and Ballanche, became a concrete reality, something inexorably fleeting, especially in moments of happiness. At the basis of their respective works lay a hint of bitterness and dissatisfaction with the continually unfulfilled promises of life. Ballanche's prose flowed easily and poetically, as suggestive as the *Méditations* in its ability to convey subtle shades of emotion. Writing of his own love affair, Pierre-Simon had attained the simple beauty of expression for which he had fumbled in *Du Sentiment.*

Though Ballanche continued working, worrying over Chateaubriand, and writing, sometimes he wished himself out of Lyon, away from the memories it held. In April, 1809, he planned to obtain through Fontanes and Chateaubriand a position as inspector general in the new university. Beuchot, however, objected so strenuously that Ballanche abandoned the project.[14] He continued working spasmodically at his epic, *La Foi promise aux Gentils,* a kind of preface to the *Martyrs* of Chateaubriand, and began a *Jeanne d'Arc.* He moved restlessly from one to the other but, for all this vacillation, he still determined to create the great French epic.

He found a more congenial subject, not in his own country, but in Portugal. From Camoëns he borrowed the story of Inès de Castro, satisfying simultaneously a desire to write of thwarted love and an urge to finish a successful epic. The allusion to Ballanche's past is transparent: Don Pedro, the son of Alphonso IV, king of Portugal, secretly marries Inès de Castro. Alphonso has her condemned to death during the absence of his son for daring to countenance a mésalliance with royalty. Don Pedro suffers in silence until the death of his father when, with macabre devotion, he has the skeleton of Inès crowned queen of Portugal.

The subject was not new, but it received a hearty welcome from the Academy of Lyon, to which Ballanche read his short story in 1811.[15] Camoëns, Ferreira, Houdart de la Motte, and Guiraud had already told the fate of Inès, but the Academicians, most of them friends of Ballanche, sympathetically paid more attention to the biographical allusions than to the manner in which Ballanche had handled a part of the third book of the *Lusiades.*[16] Delandine offered encouragement in the form of vellum for several copies. Twenty-five were to be printed for friends, but Ballanche demurred, remembering too vividly the critics' reception of *Du Sentiment.* The scheme was abandoned and the manuscript lost.[17]

For the most part, *Inès de Castro* verged on the sentimental, offering little of literary value. With some success, Ballanche had, curiously enough, imitated Chateaubriand's *Renè* and *Atala* in the handling of his material. Here and there, however, flashed glimpses of the philosophy later to be the basis of most of his works. Ballanche preached, not pessimism, but the concepts of trial and expiation; he was nearing a solution for the problem that tantalized him: original sin.[18] Likewise, through his discussion of mésalliances he moved toward a theory that social inequalities result from the constant struggles between the aristocracy and the people.[19] From a consideration of his own case, the thoughtful printer progressed to meditation on the problem of all inequality.

III

Somehow, the routine of daily existence dulled Ballanche's bitterness. He read as omnivorously as usual, investigating various branches of occult philosophy, dabbling in the *Neuf Livres* of Coëssin, or examining the theories of Fourier.[20] At other times he worked on the construction of the new press he hoped would revolutionize printing. He kept Ampère informed of his work, and the latter persistently urged him to move to Paris, where his talents would be better appreciated.[21] For companionship in Lyon he had the numerous literary societies to which he belonged.

More important than this, he had begun to work on the story of Antigone. Her tragic fate had caught Ballanche's fancy immediately. For a long time he had toyed with the notion of using the Œdipus legend for the Christian epic he stubbornly tried to create. As far back as *Du Sentiment* he had spoken admiringly of Antigone,[22] then, after the break with Bertille, he had locked up his old manuscripts and turned to the popular *Voyage du jeune Anacharsis*. When this spurred him to reread Sophocles' *Antigone,* he found Bertille again. In Hémon, passionate and stubborn, he saw the sharp image of himself, blinded by love to the point of suicide. For some time he merely rolled the plot around his mind, mentally enjoying his sorrow, until, during the year 1811-12, he ceased pitying himself and began to write.[23] Dugas and Bredin kept him at the task so rigorously that by July 9, 1812, he was able to read the beginning of the first *chant* to the *Société littéraire.*[24] The minutes of the meeting stated that

. . . le but de notre confrère a été de rassembler dans un cadre tout ce que les poètes et même les historiens nous apprennent des infortunes de cette femme célèbre et de celles de sa famille et d'en composer, s'il est permis de s'exprimer ainsi, une espèce de poème en prose qui retraçât avec une scrupuleuse fidélité les événements souvent merveilleux et invraisemblables de l'âge héroïque dans lequel vivaient Œdipe et ses enfants.[25]

The book evolved continually as he worked, but suddenly the whole story took on additional meaning when there occurred what was probably the most important single event in Ballanche's life: he met Madame Récamier. For having dared side with Madame de Staël against Napoleon, she had been ordered to remain at least forty leagues from Paris. In June, 1812, she came to Lyon to visit her husband's family and to see old friends. After Madame Récamier settled at the Hôtel d'Europe, near her friend, the eccentric Duchesse de Chevreuse, she summoned Camille Jordan, a friend of long standing, whom she expected to present her to the proper people.

Jordan undertook to keep Madame Récamier amused and, accordingly, he arranged for her and the Duchess a trip through the printing house of Ballanche which so delighted the latter that she honored the *Bulletin de Lyon* by composing part of a galley. Later he read her parts of the *Fragments,* explaining their significance. He spoke so enthusiastically of their shy author that Madame Récamier consented to receive him.

Their meeting has given literary history one of its strangest and most famous anecdotes. Ballanche arrived the very next day, resplendent in his best clothes, to talk with the woman noted as one of France's greatest beauties. On the way he had even paused to have his boots polished with the egg batter then fashionable. The room was warm, Ballanche quiet. Madame Récamier tried to put him at ease but soon fell silent as an obnoxious odor began to permeate the room. Finally she informed her guest that the smell had become intolerable and he, oblivious to all but the polished woman opposite him, suddenly realized that his shoes had been shined with rotten eggs. Without a word he walked out of the salon. His hostess expected that he had gone, but a moment later he padded back in stocking feet, ready now to converse. The shoes had been pushed into a corner of the hall. Madame Récamier sat stupefied for a moment, then proceeded to question him, interested in this eccentric printer, so ugly and so clumsy, who was sometimes silent to the point of embarrassment.[26] Yet, when Ballanche decided to leave, she gave him permission to call often, a favor of which he took full advantage.

Ballanche became so attached to Madame Récamier that soon his whole universe began to revolve around her. He haunted the Hôtel d'Europe, ran errands for her, and eagerly asked advice about *Antigone*. In her he saw a model for his heroine who surpassed even Bertille, now crowded into a corner of his mind. Evenings, after his departure, he would sometimes write notes to her, telling what his self-conscious tongue had refused to say in the salon:

> Oui, vous êtes bien l'Antigone que j'ai rêvée; oui, cette destinée à part, cette âme élevée, ce génie de dévouement, sont des traits de votre caractère. Vous auriez enfin inspiré l'hymne à la beauté qu'Antigone chantait parmi ses belles compagnes. Je commençais seulement à travailler à *Antigone,* lorsque vous m'êtes apparu à Lyon, et Dieu seul sait pour combien vous êtes dans la peinture de cet admirable personnage. L'antiquité est bien loin de m'en avoir fourni toutes les données, cet idéal m'a été révélé par vous. Souvenez-vous que c'est encore auprès de vous que j'ai écrit l'Ephithalème funèbre. J'expliquerai un jour toutes ces choses; je veux que dans l'avenir on sache qu'une créature si parfaite n'est pas tout entière de ma création.[27]

Madame Récamier finally left Lyon for Italy at the end of January, 1813, leaving behind a lonesome Ballanche. He helped her prepare for the trip, even chose her reading, putting in the carriage among other books the *Génie du Christianisme* and Michaud's *Histoire des Croisades*. No sooner had the carriage disappeared than he began to write. In February, 1813, he shyly announced that he intended to make Antigone as much like her as possible, in partial thanks for the many moments of happiness she had given him.

Madame Récamier reacted suitably to the compliment; she invited her new friend to come to Rome. Camille Jordan resented the invitation, hurt that his seniority of acquaintance had been overlooked. His pout, however, only lasted until a conciliatory letter arrived from Rome, in which Madame Récamier confessed that, next to Camille, Ballanche was the person with whom she best liked to travel, but only next to Camille. Jordan immediately withdrew his objections,[28] and Ballanche left Lyon in such excitement that he forgot his hat at a coach stop and did not miss it until his arrival.

Day and night he travelled. The last month had been a trying one and he hoped to straighten out his perplexities away from home. Money matters had brought many an embarrassing worry to trouble his peace. Ballanche had fallen in love with Madame Récamier, though he explained away his feelings as brotherly affection, complete and without reserve. He felt too shy, too unimportant to mention it to her. Besides, his affair with Bertille had taught him that, to assure a measure of happiness, he had better reserve his thoughts.

Ballanche had planned to stay a week in Rome, but a few days after arriving, word came from Hugues-Jean asking immediate return to Lyon. In the short moments allowed, he was escorted by Madame Récamier and Canova to the Coliseum and Saint Peter's. In return for this kindness, he consented to read at her salon the funeral scene from *Antigone*. The thought of leaving her saddened him, not only because it meant separation from Madame Récamier, but because he had found something in Rome for which he had long searched. The sight of the monuments, the old churches, tangible evidence of his faith, cured him of any wavering. He knew now that there could be something permanent amidst the change that had washed over Europe since 1789.

Before Ballanche left Rome, he paid his respects to the city in another fragment, *Adieux à Rome*. After expressing a debt to the many wondrous monuments, he wrote for Madame Récamier a paragraph containing thanks for her faith in him as a writer:

> Je le sens, il manque déjà des cordes à ma lyre. La poésie et les arts ne m'offrent plus que de faibles enchantements, et ont perdu tout pouvoir de me distraire et de m'exalter. Ma vie s'est comme réfugiée dans mes affections: elles seules peuvent me faire jouir et souffrir.[29]

No sooner had Ballanche passed the city limits on the way home than he began a letter to his friend. He felt he had grasped happiness, but had been unable to close his fingers tightly on it. Incoherent thoughts spilled onto the paper until, realizing that the sentiments were becoming exaggerated, that the sentences seemed to carry a simper, he closed by swearing eternal allegiance to her.

Back home he began scheming to leave Lyon. In September, 1813, he confided to Beuchot a need for escape from his environment. Business affairs with Chateaubriand had reduced him to helpless despair. The Angostura speculation still hung over the firm:

Il y a bien longtemps, mon cher ami, que je n'ai point reçu de tes nouvelles. Je te prie de répondre à cette lettre courrier par courrier; mais il y a des choses que je ne voudrais pas montrer à mon père; ainsi tu peux mettre dans ta lettre une autre lettre pour Mme R. . . . Je ne puis supporter de rester imprimeur. L'établissement que nous avons est trop minutieux et trop assujettissant pour moi. Voici trois ans et demi que je ne suis point allé à Paris. . . . Actuellement la responsabilité est trop grande pour que je puisse me permettre des absences. Mon père devient vieux; je vois avec peine qu'il est toujours à la chaîne. Nous sommes mal placés pour les spéculations de librairie. Je voudrais donc me défaire de mon établissement aux meilleures conditions possibles. Je me propose de ne pas me marier; le temps est passé; d'ailleurs, j'ai beaucoup de raisons pour m'en abstenir. Voici le genre de vie que je voudrais adopter. Je soignerais quelques spéculations isolées de librairie; je ferais quelques entreprises littéraires que je surveillerais, que je soignerais, et auxquelles je travaillerais moi-même. Cela améliorerait ma position de fortune, sans me gêner et sans contrarier mes goûts. . . . Je ferais quelques petits voyages: je me livrerais à quelques études. Je partagerais mon temps de vie sédentaire entre Lyon et Paris.[30]

To console himself Ballanche worked feverishly on *Antigone*. He hoped to finish it before Madame Récamier's return to Lyon, but, on her arrival in May, 1814, *Antigone* was still not published.[31] An edition actually went to press in 1814, but the collapse of the Empire prevented its completion.[32] Five books had been printed by July, but publication lagged, partly because Ballanche hesitated over fixing the number of copies to be issued. However, the announcement that the Duchess of Angoûlême planned a visit to the city made him hurry the printers. Her Royal Highness arrived August 6, 1814, and left August 9; during this time countless fêtes were organized, at one of which Ballanche acted as *commissaire*. Camille Jordan had access to the Princess, and knowing his friend's weakness for royalty, presented him to the Duchess. Burning with zeal for the restored monarchy, Ballanche gallantly offered *Antigone* to Her Highness and was permitted to dedicate the book to her.[33]

IV

But there was no politics in *Antigone*. Ballanche's version of the old story followed fairly closely that of Sophocles. At the court of Priam, shortly before the war of Troy, Tirésias retraces the history of Greece. He sings for Priam of Œdipus, king of Thebes and Corinth, and of his daughter, Antigone. The book opens with a description of Œdipus's presentiments at his investiture as ruler of Corinth. Plague strikes Thebes, and the royal family is swayed by undercurrents of jealousy and hate. To cheer himself, Œdipus reviews past triumphs, especially his divination of the enigma of the Sphinx. As the king dreams, Créon, his brother-in-law, plots to seize Corinth, while the two royal princes, Etéocle and Polynice, greedily covet their father's power. Créon and the two sons finally usurp the thrones of Œdipus, and the late ruler, blind now that he has plunged pins into his eyes to shut out terrible visions, walks into exile followed by his daughter. Antigone escorts her father on his wanderings until his death on a lonely mountain, then returns to Thebes. Here she discovers that Etéocle has ousted Polynice, and he refuses to hear her plea for the latter's right to the throne. Antigone has lost everything through her family's misfortunes; because of a promise made to her father, she cannot even admit her love for Hémon, the son of Créon. Her misery becomes even sharper when war flames between Thebes and Argos, the king of which is upholding the claim of Polynice. Armies surge over Thebes, giving Argos a Pyrrhic victory and leaving Etéocle and Polynice dead; Créon has won both thrones. When, in the sorrow of the city, the latter refuses Antigone permission to bury her dead, she creeps forth to perform the last rites over her brothers. Créon retaliates by condemning her to be buried alive. Hearing of this, the seriously wounded Hémon crawls to the cave and the lovers die gazing at each other.

When *Antigone* was first to be published, Ballanche had intended to preface it with a discussion of the limits of poetry and prose, the history of the epic and its true character. The philosophical implications of the tale he would indicate in a discourse on the concept of fatality in antiquity and an explanation of two symbols, the Sphinx and Nemesis, the first of which characterized the mystery surrounding human destiny, the second, the different concepts of destiny.[34] In lieu of this essay, he merely prefixed as an epigraph some verses of Virgil: "Il est des choses qui semblent contenir elles-mêmes des larmes, et les peintures de la condition mortelle peuvent seules toucher notre âme."[35]

Hitherto, Ballanche had concerned himself primarily with story. Here and there, as in *Inès de Castro,* had appeared a few indications of preoccupation with the problem of human misery. But, in *Antigone,* he became more conscious of what had driven him in the earlier essays. He saw in the story the history of man and his miseries, the infinite sadness of existence. Humanity stumbled blindly toward an unknown goal, helped only by religion. Œdipus symbolizes the trials demanded of man, his daughter, the expiation exacted of him. His hero, continuously persecuted by misfortune, personifies the peoples of the world succeeding each other ceaselessly, and, at the same time, sums up the entire progress of humanity.[36]

This view caused the author to introduce changes in the original story. The subject was ancient, but it had been plucked from its setting of old beliefs and put amidst modern, Christian beliefs. Ballanche had originally intended to write in imitation of the Bible, then changed his style. His thoughts filled the legend not with a vengeful fate, but with a Christian Providence.[37] Thus none of the events chronicled were whims of Nemesis, but steps motivated toward a definite end. Each sorrow had a compensation, each unfortunate a hope. The colors of the Bible mingled with those of Sophocles and Euripides to produce an original work.[38] To this end, certain changes became imperative. The Sphinx is not a monster to be exterminated, but a divine creature. Œdipus did not die; he disappeared from the summit of Mount Cytheron. Hémon, of course, could not commit suicide, nor could the long-suffering Antigone be submitted to the garrote. Since they symbolized expiation and sacrifice, Ballanche had to grant them some recompense.

The general public ignored Ballanche's message to read another into *Antigone.* The dedication misled it into considering the heroine no other than the Duchess of Angoulême. Most readers were sure of this when they reached Œdipus's consecration of Antigone to loneliness: "Ame sublime d'Antigone, que t'importe le bonheur ou le malheur? N'aura-tu pas toujours la paix de la conscience, les louanges des hommes et l'amour des Dieux?"[39] In reality these words had been meant for Madame Récamier, but the politically-minded citizens of the Restoration passed lightly over personal considerations in search of commitments to monarchy. Liberals complained that the moral of the book, that man must sacrifice, must submit to Province, hid a political trick, while the ultras purred at the compliments to Her Royal Highness. Few saw deeper, though one perspicacious friend told Ballanche: "Vous ne savez pas ce que vous avez fait? Un poëme martiniste."[40]

With an eye on the political barometer, the critics trod cautiously.[41] Malte-Brun, in the *Quotidienne,* December 9, 1815, and the critic of the *Constitutionnel,* on February 2, 1816, commented favorably, though the latter displayed some animosity in pointing out the banality of the subject.[42] Only the *Biographie des hommes vivants,* in September, 1816, considered the book a total loss, but this opinion was more than counterbalanced by the three articles Nodier consecrated to the work in the *Journal des Débats.* In the first article, Nodier merely discussed the history of the epic in France as a preface to the consideration of *Antigone;* the other two probed into the book itself. Nodier was unwilling to call *Antigone* an epic, but rather a religious story. Ballanche, he noted, had utilized a delicate style to create a prose poem of first rank. "Qu'il me suffise donc de recommander la lecture d'*Antigone* à ceux pour qui ce poëme est encore nouveau, et dont l'âme se complaît dans des pensées élevées et dans des sentiments tendres. Peu d'ouvrages modernes leur promettent des jouissances aussi vives et aussi pures."[43]

The book attained a small amount of success, not like that of the *Génie,* but enough to make the author sure of his talent. As a result, modest honors fell to him: the government named him *chevalier de l'ordre du lys,* and his business associates elected him *juge au tribunal de commerce.*[44] In a burst of pride, he sent *Antigone* to Chateaubriand, then in Constantinople, asking for his opinion:

Puisque vous avez bien voulu vous associer aux destinées de mon *Antigone,* permettez-moi de vous annoncer qu'elle a un certain succès, bien que toutes les idées soient tournées du côté des spéculations politiques. . . . Des universités allemandes se sont occupées de cet ouvrage;

il s'est fait, à l'Académie de Nîmes, un rapport plein de recherches qui m'obligera à entrer dans quelques discussions littéraires sur le génie de l'antiquité et sur l'esprit de certaines traditions poétiques.[45]

V

The Sphinx of *Antigone* seems to have given Ballanche the answer to his own problems. Henceforth, he would abandon individual feelings and lamentation over personal losses to concentrate on the development of institutions. He now had a philosophy ready for use in greater subjects. As his ideas grew, so did his desire to quit Lyon, to be near Madame Récamier in Paris. He began to formulate hopeful plans for taking his entire family to the capital.

Part of this fretting resulted from a knowledge that Madame Récamier considered him highly, even more highly than Benjamin Constant. This was sufficiently apparent to make the latter complain. Ballanche had travelled to Paris as much to see her as to talk with Beuchot of a new edition of Voltaire and, while there, had occasion to meet many of the celebrities who frequented her home. Some of them failed to impress him, a few seeming merely leaders of factions.[46] He remained silent and reserved, calculating the powers and talents of the people he met to discover whether he could expect happiness in such an environment. What he saw evidently did not kill his desire to move.

Back in Lyon, Ballanche attempted to live like a hermit. He saw his friends rarely, having lost all taste for the provinces. Literature had lost its delights; he began a work on poetry only to abandon it a short time later. News from Madame Récamier provided his only joy and he continually worried her for more and longer letters. His replies expressed a concern for the state of the nation that contrasted oddly with his first enthusiasm for the Restoration. The royalist reaction seemed to him no better than the Terror. France still needed more tolerance, a great many of his fellow citizens to the contrary. Ballanche therefore abstained from political argument, undecided as to which opinion suited him, but sadly disappointed in the hopes he had founded on the reigning house.[47] Nothing seemed right, he told Camille Jordan:

Depuis que j'ai quitté Paris, les circonstances ont pris une nouvelle
gravité et une gravité telle que les questions se répandront chez nous
et autour de nous. Je crois que les souverains prennent un mauvais
moyen pour parvenir à la solution du problème actuel. Nous sommes
à une époque où les armes ne décident rien. Les rois ne peuvent
vaincre qu'avec leurs peuples et déjà ce sont les peuples seuls sans les
souverains qui se sont affranchis du joug de Buonaparte. . . .

Le Voltaire-Touquet contrarie fort mes idées. Il eût été si sage et si
moral, puisqu'on faisait un Voltaire réduit à 15 volumes, d'en re-
trancher les infamies et les choses irreligieuses. La *Pucelle,* par exemple,
est autant un crime contre la nation et contre la morale du genre
humain que contre la religion. N'est-il pas vrai que l'homme le plus
cynique n'oserait pas à présent publier pour la première fois ce pré-
tendu poème? Pourquoi donc le publier dans une édition où l'on fait
un choix? Nous voulons mieux que cela. L'esprit de parti ne doit pas
porter à sanctionner l'usage du poison. Cette ironie de distribuer ce
Voltaire le dimanche, m'a paru surtout d'une grande indécence. Les
prêtres attirent à la religion d'affreux scandales, mais ceux que don-
nent ces scandales n'en méritent pas moins le blâme de tous les honnêtes gens. M. Kératry a bien mal fait à mon avis de laisser louer dans
le *Courrier* le Voltaire-Touquet. . . .

J'ai toujours compté demeurer trois mois à peu près à Lyon, mais
en vérité je ne sais comment me tirer d'ici. L'état de santé de ma
pauvre soeur est pour moi un grand sujet de tristesse et d'amertume.
Ma situation est beaucoup trop compliquée pour un être aussi simple
que moi. Mais j'ose à peine me plaindre, quand je vois Bredin.[48]

In his solitude he amused himself by telling Madame Récamier
of his little satisfactions and successes. Still full of *Antigone,* he made
rash statements about the book. "A présent, je ne doute point
qu'*Antigone,* dans l'état où elle est, ne soit intimement unie à la
langue française et ne dure autant qu'elle."[49] Sometimes he indulged
in literary criticism for her benefit. When, in 1816, the Vicomte
de Saint-Chamans published the *Anti-Romantique,* he refrained
from joining the pack that howled on the heels of the new school.
Though he admitted the vagueness of the romanticists in theoretical
discussion, his ideas stood too close to theirs for him to quarrel. As
he told Madame Récamier, in a letter reminiscent of Young:

Il y a deux sortes d'imitations: l'une puisée dans la nature, l'autre
puisée dans l'imitation des modèles. Je crois vous avoir expliqué, un
jour, ce que j'entendais par imiter la nature. C'est, à mon avis,
reproduire non pas la nature mais les impressions qu'elle fait naître.

La véritable imitation des anciens consiste à imiter la nature comme ils l'ont imitée et non point à les copier . . . Voyez comme Mme de Staël a fait entrer le climat de l'Italie dans sa *Corinne;* voyez comme M. de Chateaubriand a fait entrer dans ses livres les sites qu'il a vus! S'ils ont réussi à ce point, c'est parce qu'ils ont exprimé les impressions qu'ils reçevaient lorsqu'ils étaient sous le climat ou en présence des sites.[50]

On the matter of local color he backed Chateaubriand and Madame de Staël, but in the matter of poetry he dissented violently. Ballanche asked more radicalism than they were ready to support. According to him, Madame de Staël, Sismondi, and Schlegel placed too much emphasis on the form and not enough on the essence of poetry.

Once, in September, 1815, he had thought himself all prepared to leave for Paris. He had arranged to take along his widowed sister; everything appeared settled, even the transportation of his lares and penates. A buyer, M. Durand, had been found for the printing house. Nothing remained, Ballanche thought, but to close the inventory, check the books, do the thousand and one things that complicated the sale of a large and prosperous business. Paris and Madame Récamier came within view only to vanish when his sister, then Hugues-Jean, fell ill, necessitating cancellation of all arrangements.[51] When Madame Récamier asked why the moving took so long, he sadly told of his new difficulties.

Plagued by these worries, Ballanche deserted the many literary societies to which he belonged, limiting his activity solely to the Académie de Lyon. As the ranking member of the literary aristocracy of the community, he had been elected to the presidency for 1816, a tribute to his credit rating, his status as author, and the purity of his political principles. The president of the Academy pushed into the background his own theories when he made the annual report in 1816, limiting his remarks to the common ground he shared with all his colleagues, politics. After a careful catalogue of the accomplishments of the group, M. le Président announced that the next subject for the annual prize *discours* would be "Les moyens à employer, après une longue révolution, pour confondre tous les sentiments d'un peuple dans l'amour de la Patrie et du Roi."[52] The few remarks Ballanche permitted himself continued in a similar vein his praise of the Bourbons or expressed a heart-felt desire that France return to tradition.[53]

Time eventually solved most of Ballanche's problems. His father died after an illness of two months on October 19, 1816, leaving him saddened but with a knowledge that he was now almost free to live his own life. André-Marie Ampère carefully suggested a plan. Ballanche should come to Paris with his sister; with Ampère's sister she could busy herself with charitable works. Pierre-Simon could then devote himself to writing for the more sophisticated audience in the capital.[54]

The plan made sense to Ballanche, though he did not follow it completely. He sold the press to M. Durand, began to pack his bags, and arranged for his sister's comfort. At the last moment she refused to change homes, but Ballanche stood too near the fulfillment of his greatest desire to argue. She could stay in Lyon. In May, 1817, he bade goodbye to his friends and set off to be near Ampère, Dugas-Montbel, Lenoir, Camille Jordan—and Madame Récamier. Though forty years of age, he was starting a new life.

CHAPTER IV

Introduction to Paris—Essai sur les institutions sociales

I

IN PARIS, Ballanche immediately moved close to Madame Récamier as an accepted member of her entourage. She lived on the rue d'Anjou-Saint-Honoré, while he found a home on the rue Mont-Blanc. Now that her closest companions had left Paris, he could comfortably settle into her affections without rivals. Adrien de Montmorency was travelling in distant Spain, Constant in London. Life became fuller and more pleasant than ever.

At first the habitués of the salon eyed him askance. What did this provincial bourgeois possess that made Madame Récamier esteem him so highly? Certainly not an attractive appearance, for, at first sight, irregular features and a twisted cheek made him almost repulsive. He looked weak and feeble; his short legs carried him with difficulty.[1] His conversation confused listeners, for not only did a slight stutter garble his phrases, but continued distractions prevented his finishing many sentences. It could not be his reputation. Most of the others boasted greater ones. Few had heard of *Du Sentiment* and not many more had read *Antigone*. As far as Paris was concerned Ballanche still had to prove himself.

But, on closer acquaintance, his gaucheness and timidity slid into the background to reveal more attractive characteristics. A high forehead and magnificent eyes drew fascinated attention from his scars, and a gentle, diffident manner of presenting opinions compensated for physical faults. Once the assembled company grew accustomed to his manner of speaking, it realized that his conversation, when untangled, bespoke a depth of thought rarely encountered in a Paris salon.[2]

Some of the established writers of the time soon began to include him in their circle of friends. Constant, still jealous of an intimacy he coveted, nevertheless treated the ex-printer as an intellectual equal:

Remettez cette lettre à M. Ballanche. Je voudrais qu'il me jugeât bien, qu'il ne travaillât pas contre moi, qu'il ne m'empêchât de devenir par vous ce que la nature veut que je sois, et que la Providence m'a rendu la possibilité d'être, en faisant descendre sur la terre un de ses anges pour me diriger.[3]

Sometimes they quarreled, especially over the occult writers in whom Ballanche was interested, or over the true meaning of religious forms but both considered philosophical differences as less important than friendship.[4] Charles Nodier, of course, welcomed the opportunity to make Ballanche's acquaintance. Long before, he had confided to his friend, Weiss, that Ballanche's works, together with the Bible, Ossian, Werther, and Linnaeus would accompany him should he ever go into exile.[5] He and his friends had made a habit of reading *Du Sentiment* aloud and of using is as a guide for further topics for study. Later, in the prospectus signed by Nodier and placed at the head of the *Œuvres complètes* of Alexandre Dumas,[6] Nodier proudly enumerated the authors he had helped launch, first among whom he placed Ballanche.[7] Ballanche, on the other hand, seems to have led Nodier towards exoticism and anti-classic traditions in his rôle as a full-fledged precursor and teacher. Since both shared an enthusiasm for the work of Charles Bonnet,[8] it seemed only natural for Ballanche to become a frequent visitor at the Nodier home, so intimate with his fellow writer that when the latter fell into difficulties, he turned instinctively to Ballanche for help. Mme Menessier-Nodier relates that, on the occasion of the publication of *Les Exilés,* an anonymous writer crudely attacked her father. Nodier discovered the identity of his insulter, demanded a retraction, and, while waiting for an answer, began to put his affairs in order. Satisfaction was refused, and he stood on the eve of a duel when a special messenger delivered a complete apology. On finishing it, Nodier threw the note to the table with an exclamation:

Est-il sot, cet animal-là! Il est cause que j'ai écrit hier à Ballanche une épître qui devient tout à fait ridicule.

De quoi s'agit-il? interrogea Mme Nodier, qui ignorait tout;—et que pouvais-tu donc bien raconter à Ballanche?

Tu n'es pas au courant . . . mais tu vas comprendre tout de suite. Au cas où ce monsieur qui renonce à me tuer, à ce qu'il paraît, n'aurait rien changé à ses premières intentions, je priais Ballanche de se charger de toi et de Marie.[9]

In this new environment Ballanche blossomed. Here at last were men who could understand his ideas, prod him to greater intellectual effort. Now that he had more time for personal interests, he read many of the illuminists, Bœhme, for instance, brooded over Coëssin, or paged through his beloved Pythagorus.[10] In his baggage were several manuscripts to blacken with the countless changes and corrections continually inflicted on them. For a time he planned a prose poem on lost Atlantis. One of his characters would find the first people on Plato's island and, in the manner of the eighteenth century *philosophes,* would appraise the language, institutions, literature, and general traditions of these people, and through them the institutions of western civilization.[11] Later Ballanche dropped the subterfuge of Atlantis and began to work on an *Essai sur les institutions sociales* that he had brought from Lyon.

Paris, however, had changed many of Ballanche's ideas. The writers he daily encountered lacked much of the enthusiasm and depth of conviction he had left in the *Amicitiae et litteris* or the *Cercle littéraire.* On the other hand, they were more subtle, more keenly alive to nuances, so sensitive to contemporary thought that they could read meaning into apparently harmless and disparate facts. Since the fall of the Empire had released writers from the threat of imperial displeasure, they could once more indulge in the expression of their own ideas. Ballanche happily escaped the fog of sterility that had reduced a large part of French literature to pomposity. He had not known censorship so strict that it forced Sieyès to answer "je ne pense pas," when a friend asked him his thoughts. Now that the Empire had ceased making history, France could well ask what that history was.[12]

In the keen, new air of this invigorating intellectual climate, Ballanche suddenly discovered more profundity in his own thoughts. He now saw in *Antigone* the secret of the revolution that had aroused all Europe. Bonaparte was the Œdipus whose dramatic adventures he had chronicled. The destinies of the ancient king and the modern emperor held much in common. The infanticide of Œdipus imposed on his parents by the oracle of Apollo symbolized the past fighting vainly to strangle the future. Œdipus, murderer of his own father, Laius, along the crooked road to Delphi, was the lusty future shoving aside a decrepit past. Œdipus, king, stood for Bonaparte the

hero and the legislator who discovered the enigma of the Sphinx
of the Revolution. Œdipus, exiled and blind, meant Napolean
conquered, relegated to Saint Helena because he had lost touch
with the destiny of France. These new ideas impelled him to sketch
his picture on a larger canvas. The feeling of an impending catastrophe prompted him to note the signs of the immediate future. He
remembered, now, that the sight of Roman monuments had struck
him as revealing the successive appearance of empires, and had
given the sensation of seeing in one moment the sequence of crises
that produced the modern world.[13] He had completed the *Essai sur
les institutions sociales* in 1816, but what he saw led him to revise his
first pages and to publish them in 1818.[14]

II

The furious and bitter struggle between the ultras and the liberals
disheartened Ballanche. Each side believed itself the sole possessor
of the truth and claimed the backing of all men of good will.
Ballanche decided that, independently of the passions and personalities involved, the debate could be reduced to a fundamental
antagonism of ideas regarding the origin of power and, consequently,
the theory of language.[15] De Maistre and Rousseau, de Bonald and
Condorcet had to be set face to face. Was thought anterior or
posterior to language? In other words, was society man-made or
God-given? The ultras regarded society as divinely instituted, upheld
the thesis that language had been revealed to man, and that
authority originated in tradition, whereas the liberals presupposed a
society formed by contract, a language invented by man himself, and
firmly maintained that the future promised an evolution towards
a classless society. On examining the rival contentions, Ballanche
found neither to his taste; both shared some truth; both were
partly wrong. Instead of siding with either, he tried to explain
wherein each side erred.[16] To the former he granted the past; to the
latter, the future. But he considered it worthwhile to demonstrate
the existence of a middle ground, the acceptance of which would end
the perpetual civil war that flamed through France.[17]

Between these warring factions Ballanche stepped, holding an
olive bough. To the liberals he carefully explained that the sole

fault of the ultras consisted in remaining faithful to the traditions on which French society rested; the ultras he scolded for their confusion of liberalism with anarchy.[18] What both failed to grasp was that the rôle of society and language had changed, that language once had a mission that was now accomplished. Though they seemed unaware of it, all reason for antagonism had ceased.

Ballanche's theory of the origins of language and society was directed primarily at the liberals, since he considered the latter the potential winners in the contemporary struggle and, as such, in need of moderation.[19] In a passage that contains the germs of many a romantic poem, especially the *Méditations* of Lamartine, Ballanche began to explain his position:

> Dieu ne cesse de parler à l'homme parce qu'il ne cesse de veiller sur lui. Les cieux *racontent* la gloire de leur auteur: tous les êtres *disent* qu'ils sont l'ouvrage d'une main toute-puissante. La création tout entière est une manifestation de la parole divine, la pensée de Dieu écrite.
>
> Une émanation de la parole divine a été communiquée à l'homme. Au commencement, Dieu voulut enseigner la parole à l'homme pour lui parler au moyen même de cette parole. Dieu apprit donc à l'homme le nom de chaque chose, de chaque être, et de toutes les idées premières. Dieu revêtit d'un nom tous les sentiments de l'homme et le lui enseigna. Dieu se donna à lui-même un nom pour que l'homme connût le nom de Dieu.[20]

He refused to consider the possibility of the human creation of language. This view could only lead to another, more repulsive, one, that man had evolved from an oyster. Evolution might offer a suitable topic for salon conversation, but Ballanche rejected it as a matter for serious consideration.[21] Rather, language forms a general revelation which is transmitted from generation to generation. Hence all societies, the living and the dead, form a collectivity joined to God through language. In the mind, affections, and intelligence of each man there exists a connection between the past, present, and future, the finite and the infinite, time and eternity:[22]

> On aura beau faire, il faut absolument choisir entre deux opinions: ou l'homme a reçu le pouvoir de créer les langues, ou cette faculté lui a été refusée. Dans le premier cas, l'invention du langage serait un résultat nécessaire de la forme même, si l'on peut parler ainsi, de notre

intelligence: les langues seraient alors comme un ensemble de signes convenus, devenu graduellemnet plus ou moins complet, graduellement perfectionné, à mesure que de nouveaux besoins se seraient fait sentir. Dans le second cas, l'homme aurait reçu sa langue d'une tradition obscure et mystérieuse, qui remonte d'anneau en anneau jusqu'au berceau du monde, mais dont la société a toujours été dépositaire. Ceux qui attribuent à l'homme le pouvoir de se faire sa langue ne disent autre chose sinon que la pensée naît d'abord en lui, et qu'ensuite il choisit, pour l'exprimer, un signe qu'il adopte ou qu'il trouve déjà convenu. Ceux, au contraire, qui refusent à l'homme la faculté de se faire sa langue ne disent autre chose sinon que, par l'habitude de l'éducation, ou par une loi primitive qu'ils ne connaissent pas, ils ne peuvent penser sans le secours de la parole. En un mot, la parole est nécessaire à l'homme pour penser, et alors l'homme n'a pu inventer la parole; car on ne peut supposer un temps où il ait été sans penser, et on ne peut expliquer comment il aurait pu créer la parole, sans laquelle il ne pouvait penser; ou la parole n'est pas nécessaire à l'homme pour penser, et alors il a pu graduellement inventer la parole.[23]

Language, of course, has evolved considerably, for in the beginning, words contained a power presently unknown. Once they furnished not only signs for objects and ideas, but, in some manner, the very essence of objects and ideas. As the manifestation of God himself, they reigned throughout the world.[24] Thus it became necessary for the early priesthoods to conserve the empire of language as the source of power and, consequently, reserved for the patrician in the form of sacred languages and secret doctrines.[25] Gradually meanings were embalmed in writing as a method of protecting and maintaining them, but, for a time, the written and the traditional, or spoken, word existed simultaneously, the former endowing the latter with vestiges of its primordial energy and meaning. The first writing, hieroglyphics, had maintained the elasticity and clarity of the traditional word, but progressively the use of writing dulled its inner meaning and the advent of printing completed its perversion, even changing the manner of human thought.[26] By the nineteenth century, written laws were used to govern society without the intervention of the traditional word: the letter replaced the spirit.

The new era, Ballanche warned the liberals, was not that of liberty, nor even that of equality before the law or the admission to all types of work. Rather it was the age of the independence of thought, of the separation of religious and social institutions. The concept of social welfare had now spread to all classes under the aegis of minds grown adult and capable of responsible decisions.[27] In this respect, Ballanche's conception of the desirable society of the future was remarkably close to that Guizot would make into a watchword:[28]

> Le bien-être social descendra graduellement à toutes les classes de la société; car il y aura toujours des classes, et l'on ne peut concevoir la société sans cela; mais les individus de toutes les classes pouvant s'avancer sans obstacle dans la hiérarchie, elles se recruteront les unes dans les autres, jusque dans les classes inférieures, qui elles-mêmes rempliront leurs cadres par le simple effet de la population. Tous les hommes marcheront à la fois, mais chacun à son rang, sous peine de ne pouvoir marcher. Tous ne peuvent être rois, tous ne peuvent pas être appelés dans les conseils des rois.[29]

Proportionately, therefore, as civilization was thus advancing, the human mind was freeing itself of dependency on language, less earth-bound and more adventurous.[30]

Ballanche's theory, then, presupposed progress. For him, man groped along a dark road, unable to retrogress, never stationary. Nations might degenerate, but the mind stumbled to maturity through recurrent crises.[31] Behind any given generation lay countless others, all creating pressures on the living; every destiny is, in a sense, predetermined by those preceding it.[32]

Only Providence, declared Ballanche, set the limits of human action, circumscribing man within the boundaries of language and society.[33] To protect humanity from wasting its energies, Providence bound men to institutions which themselves evolve toward perfection.[34] Sometimes perversity led man toward dubious goals and, then, Ballanche predicated, like de Maistre, the *fléau de Dieu* appeared to scourge the people and disappeared, like Napoleon, into the limbo of the forgotten.[35] Man must not forget the law, Christianity, and any action not founded in Christianity was lawless.[36] By law, Ballanche referred to the "constitution" of humanity, a state of mind originating in the revelation of language, a general conscience that had gradually evolved along with language.[37]

Slow accretion and gentle evolution, that was the doctrine

Ballanche preached to the liberals and to the ultras. Above all, no savage repressions in the name of tradition, nor sudden, catastrophic revolutions.[38] Man was a social being doomed to the inequalities of rank and personal talent. His destiny called for the completion of progress in another world; in this he had to accept some unpleasantness.[39] He could not question the social state too rigorously. Jean-Jacques to the contrary, society and language had been imposed on man, and he must fit his pace to the gradual development decreed by a benign Providence. A compromise should be effected. The ultras should accept the concept of change, the liberals cease discrediting tradition and religion, thus providing a doctrine all might embrace.

With these statements, however, Ballanche himself ceased compromising. Although the business man in him had trembled with rage at what happened to property rights in time of revolution, the writer defied the defender of commerce and led him into literary heresies of the first order. The thesis of change convinced him that the nineteenth century represented an age in which society would rid itself of superannuated taboos in favor of the new and the brave. Since social institutions had to change with human progress, it followed logically that the arts, too, must evolve. Therefore, France needed a change; her writers had mouthed too long the same precepts.[40] What had been written at the time of Louis XIV now verged on the archeological and the ancient, shot through with the same dry rot that had weakened the ancient regime. Contemporary criticism, also, could use fresh views. France had had a surfeit of critics who saw the paint instead of the painting, became lost in superstitious comparisons of models, the kind of second-rate criticism at which La Harpe excelled. The modern world demanded rather an appreciation of the essence, and not the form, of all human creations. Words had to be brushed aside in search for the thought. For the same reasons, Ballanche appeared willing to discard the study of Latin and Greek, languages wrung dry by countless generations. To replace them, he offered the Oriental tongues, thus becoming one of the first in his century to see in the East the successor to classical antiquity in the formation of new literary traditions.[41]

Ballanche, however, did not intend to limit himself to destructive criticism. Long before most of his contemporaries, he had taken sides in the struggle between romanticism and classicism:

> Nous appelons littérature classique celle qui est fondée sur l'étude et les traditions des langues anciennes, celle qui a puisé ses règles dans l'analyse des chefs-d'oevre de ces mêmes langues, celle enfin qui s'astreint à l'imitation de ces chefs-d'oeuvre, et qui prend ses sujets à la même source. Par opposition à la littérature classique, on a nommé littérature romantique celle où l'on professe une plus grande indépendance des règles, où l'on se permet de nouvelles alliances de mots, et sur-tout de nouvelles inventions de style; où l'on secoue les lois de l'analogie, où l'imitation étend son domaine, où la pensée fait effort contre la parole fixée, la parole écrite; où les sujets sont tirés des traditions modernes. Nous luttons, en ce moment-ci, de toutes nos forces, contre l'invasion de la littérature romantique; mais les efforts mêmes que nous faisons prouvent toute la puissance de cette littérature. Bientôt peut-être . . . la littérature classique ne sera plus que de l'archéologie.[42]

In much the same terms that Stendhal would later use in *Racine et Shakespeare* to distinguish between the two literary doctrines, Ballanche considered classicism the cadaver of an unburied age. Not that France should cease honoring her dead, but it should be understood that the nineteenth century was molding its own classicism, "classique dans l'ordre des choses qui va naître."[43]

The positive side of Ballanche's thesis contained many an idea that later would be blared forth in the *Préface de Cromwell*. A few points were additions to Ballanche's aesthetics, but most harked back to the days of *Du Sentiment*. In the matter of imitation, he disdained the copying of mannerisms, of form and style, or the burlesque of systems of composition. Instead Ballanche asked the painting of nature and the human mind, the fixing of impressions received. The less he copied, the nearer an artist would approach the greatness of antiquity. The servile aping of old mythologies irritated Ballanche to the point of rage. The mind, he maintained, must contemplate more than a collection of dryads and nymphs; it should reach into the magnificent cosmogony of Moses and the metaphysics of the Indian gymnosophists.[44] Following the dictates of the modern world, poetry must consecrate itself to celebrating the attributes of God or to discussing the moral liberty of man.

Nemesis yielded to Providence. Equality was about to be infused
into literature with the consequence that human feelings would
attain their true literary evaluation.[45]

Furthermore, like Mme de Staël, Ballanche saw a new field of
poetic endeavor in the history, not of France, but of the human
race. History really belonged to the poet since he alone had consistently told the story of his fellows, and the sooner he returned
to it, the sooner a gap would be filled in the national literature:

> Nous nous sommes dépouillés nous-mêmes de notre propre héritage
> . . . Les antiquités juives, les antiquités chrétiennes, nos temps héroï-
> ques modernes, c'est-à-dire ceux de la chevalerie, les sombres et sauvages
> traditions de nos aïeux les Gaulois ou les Francs, nous avons tout
> abandonné pour les riantes créations de la Grèce. L'architecture nous
> a donné le style gothique; mais les terribles inondations des Sarrasins
> et des hommes du Nord, mais les croisades n'ont pu féconder notre
> imagination. La voix de nos troubadours et de nos trouvères a été
> étouffée, par les chants de l'Ionie. Ce jour religieux qui éclairait nos
> vieilles basiliques ne nous a point inspiré des hymnes solennels. Nous
> avons refusé d'interroger nos âges fabuleux, et les tombeaux de nos
> ancêtres ne nous ont rien appris.[46]

Ballanche leaned heavily to the side of the poet in the argument
of prose versus poetry, a preference which led him into a theory
even his romantic friends would find too radical. His concept of
the function of poetry, added to his theories of the evolution of
language, presented him with an elementary theory of symbolism.
"La poésie," he claimed, . . . "fut à l'origine l'expression de la
parole traditionnelle; la prose . . . fut seulement l'expression de
la parole écrite."[47] Since the function of poetry is to transport the
reader into an ideal world, where human limits disappear, into an
order where the purity of forms and expressions had escaped
tampering hands, it seemed to him that the poet must therefore
attempt a return to the origin of things, stripping down the word
to its evocative power.[48]

> De chaque chose, de chaque état de choses, il sort une révélation. Le
> spectacle de la nature est une immense machine pour les pensées de
> l'homme. Les propriétés des êtres, les instincts des animaux, le spec-
> tacle de l'univers, tout est voile à soulever, tout est symbole à deviner,
> tout contient des vérités à entrevoir, car la claire vue n'est pas de ce
> monde. Ce grand luxe de la création, cet appareil de corps célestes

semés dans l'espace comme une éclatante poussière, tout cela n'est pas trop pour l'homme, parce que l'homme est un être libre et intelligent, parce que l'homme est un être immortel.[49]

Poetry, then, must search for the expression of a universal thought, and the poet should fill his epoch with meaning. He alone embraces in a single point of view all human generalizations or grasps the true meaning of Providence, speaking to God or superior intelligences, encompassing past, present, future, and infinity.[50]

Thus Ballanche helped father the romantic theory of the Messiah. Long before Hugo, Lamartine, or Victor Cousin, he advocated the opinion that the few lead the many, and that the function and right of the artist is to be among the elect. As he understood it, the ideas of these chosen seeped downward through the people, creating conceptions which in their turn bred new ideas. They act as guides to progress, give humanity a continuity of action. Like Vigny's Moïse, they marched ahead of others, not creators, but cursed with the ability to know the future.[51]

These were the main contributions of Ballanche to the stream of ideas into which the romanticists could dip, but, occasionally, other ideas and opinions sparked off from his main theses. Here, for instance, is a remark that platonism served as a precursor to Christianity, an idea not new with Ballanche, but one Lamartine used for the *Mort de Socrate*.[52] Again, in turn with the dislike for flaring violence that marked most of the great romanticists, Ballanche spoke out against the futility of war, or assailed capital punishment as the mark of the barbarian. His zeal for the reform of his contemporaries even carried him to doubt the surge of nationalism that was sweeping France. He saw beyond frontiers, even into the Provisional Government's stand for the emancipation of colonies and the abolition of slavery.[53]

III

The *Essai* represented a long step forward from Ballanche's first book. As in *Du Sentiment,* the composition of the book could scarcely withstand the probe of the purist. There was the same uncontrolled erudition lavishly applied in learned references. Ballanche advanced in circles and digressions, embarrassed at hav-

ing to choose, stuttering with the effort of trying to say everything
at once, or to explain co-existing thoughts separately and articu-
lately.[54] And yet there appeared a greater mastery of his tools and
a surer use of the intuitive approach to great philosophic problems.

Ballanche had also advanced ideologically; he left the *Essai* a
liberal Catholic. Didactically poetic, he had united traditionalism
with progress. The theory of the divine origin of language had been
popularized by Bonald and utilized by Ballanche, but the idea of
its emancipation was his own. To escape the charge of contradiction and in the hope of pleasing every one, he made the two
successive. But a deeper meaning lay in his words, a warning. He
had, in his own way, assayed contemporary society and found that
the Bourbons had learned too little in exile. When Ballanche spoke
of legitimacy in the *Essai,* he did not mean divine right as commonly understood by those seeking an excuse for social liability,
but a historic legitimacy tested by time. A restored dynasty was a
tree that sent its roots back into the soil, sucking strength from its
support. This seemed common sense. Yet he feared that the Bourbons would imitate not the tree, but a buried piece of wood. The
Essai subtly explained that the reigning house should, and must,
identify itself with the nation, become the political and civil
expression of a liberal and enlightened Christianity.

Literally, Ballanche had moved away from the classicists nearer
the position of a full-fledged romanticist, with almost all the
attributes later to be found in the authors more commonly associated with that movement. Years before the *Préface de Cromwell,*
while young Hugo was still composing verses in imitation of the
classicists and neoclassicists, before Lamartine had finished his first
lyrical effusions, Ballanche published an essay that contained in
germ much of later romanticism.

He was pre-eminently fitted for such a task, for even his life
story displayed romantic overtones. The sick child, ugly and bed-
ridden, had successfully overcome great handicaps. Almost the
living model for Hugo's theory of contrasts, with his scarred face
and gentle character, he had educated himself passionately, using
literature for solace in monotonous loneliness. Though deprived of
action, he none the less preferred a solitude in which to dream brave

dreams. Sometimes visions haunted the dreary hours, but visions on a grand scale, in which the mind communicated with the supernatural. There had even been a mad love affair, frustrated, of course, when a class-conscious aunt separated the young couple. Following this, the despairing philosopher had become enamoured of a woman he could not hope to win, one of France's most noted beauties. For her he had willingly abandoned family, fortune, and friends, content only with her presence and the promise of the quick smile that greeted his appearance.

In his book, *Du Sentiment,* he had displayed many of the characteristics usually associated with a certain element of romanticism, with what may be called extrinsic romanticism. Nature appealed little to him personally, but his first work counselled melancholy and praised the sentimental. The *Fragments* contained some of the disillusion and despair of a Werther, while *Du Sentiment* emphasized the chiaroscuro. And certainly the abbé de Féletz had not failed to notice the weakness of his architectonics, the formlessness of his literary structure. Ballanche's style betrayed a penchant for the descriptive words dear to the romanticist; the list of topics he had drawn up for fellow authors included the usual mixture of tears and love, the ubiquitous weeping willow and the gnarled oak. He even advised meditation in a cemetery over the tomb of a beloved one, with a consequent emphasis on introversion and the subjective, and the apparent proposal of the romantic cult of death. The frail little philosopher had failed to follow the path of the classicists, though treating them with all honor as fleshless skeletons. His heresy even carried him to the point where he advised forsaking Latin and Greek for the Oriental languages and literatures. Ballanche did not hesitate to wander into the mysterious and the infinite, displaying a marked preference for Christianity as a source of the supernatural.

Yet these themes fail to encompass by any means the scope of romanticism, that of Ballanche or any of the later group. Most of these subjects had wandered into the nineteenth century from the eighteenth century as the legacy of a neo-classicism busy devouring its own father. For this reason, the apparent romanticism of *Du Sentiment* had not unduly shocked its critics, though its lack of form irritated them considerably. They recognized the themes for what they were, mostly commonplaces of an earlier age.

But in the *Essai,* Ballanche had deserted these superficialities to take a position closer to the actual core of romanticism; his attitude and thought became those of one who seemed to sense the coming changes of social values with their corresponding reversals in all fields of thought. First, and most important of all, his concern with institutions denoted a recognition of the wide gap between man's actual and potential position in the universe. Consequently he inquired closely into the past and drew from it the ideas expressed in the *Essai.* As Hugo, Balzac, and Vigny later, he became acutely aware of the presence of evil. Each of the romanticists would solve this problem in his own way, but Ballanche remained content with the explanation furnished by Catholicism. Though this social and sociological point of view imbued his work with an aura of idealism, it also forced him to the study of history, one of romanticism's great conquests, and it enabled him to propose a compromise between the liberal's demand for personal freedom and the conservative's desire for a strong social order. Like Lamartine, he conceived of man as a part of a great collectivity, not the empire of the classicist, but the universe, able to live as he wished, yet constrained ultimately to choose the good of society. As a pre-romanticist, Ballanche adopted a humanitarian point of view that brought him to the kind of pacifism later exemplified in the *Marseillaise de la paix,* and this same respect for his fellow man would not allow him to sanction capital punishment. Though not completely original, nor scientific enough for the modern linguist, his study of language none the less contributed no small bit to the growing interest in the origin of words, out of which was to come the science of philology, another of romanticism's contributions.

For all his fondness for the theory of divine right, Ballanche forsook the classic camp with the recognition of time as an ever-present factor in human affairs. In the *Essai,* his concern with progress and change naturally tinged his theory of language, but, more important still, it denoted a suspicion that history is a process which absorbs all institutions, even religious ones.[55] In this respect, Ballanche differed radically from de Maistre and de Bonald, as he did in his belief in the reality of time. With others, he established the concept of fluid time, time the healer and time the killer and the thief. On this idea, too, he would base most of his own works.

The reception accorded the *Essai* was that to be expected by the volunteer peacemaker. The nineteenth century sensed in Ballanche a social surgeon. The conservatives felt toward him the same antipathy that would greet Lamennais, for whom he had opened the way with his attempted conciliation of democracy and Christianity.[56] Besides, he had related all too clearly a series of unpleasant truths. His announcement of the credo of the coming literature pleased few, although he had by no means inextricably attached himself to the new ideas. Even the liberals viewed with horrified distaste parts of his æsthetics, little realizing that the ugly bourgeois from Lyon had outdone them in radicalism. They might approve of his recognition of the new history or the formation of a new mythology, but they recoiled from establishing Christianity as the principal source of lyric poetry. Ballanche, however, had once again seen more clearly than his adversaries.

It was no surprise, therefore, to Ballanche's friends when they found that he had successfully antagonized those whom he had hoped to reconcile. Joseph de Maistre answered for the traditionalists in a letter of thanks for a complimentary copy of the *Essai:*

Votre livre, Monsieur, est excellent en détail: en gros, c'est autre chose. L'esprit révolutionnaire, en pénétrant un esprit très bien fait et un coeur excellent, a produit un ouvrage hybride, qui ne saurait contenter en général les hommes décidés d'un parti ou de l'autre. J'ai profondément souri en voyant votre colère contre les châteaux et contre les couvents, que vous voulez convertir en prisons, et contre la langue catholique que vous prétendez abolir, par la jolie raison que les Latins n'ont plus rien à nous apprendre. C'est encore une chose excessivement curieuse que l'illusion que vous a faite cet esprit que je nommais tout à l'heure, au point de vous faire prendre l'agonie pour une phase de la santé; car c'est ce qui signifie au fond votre théorie de *l'émancipation de la pensée etc.* Si vous trouviez quelque chose de malsonnant dans l'expression *esprit révolutionnaire,* vous seriez dans une grande erreur; car nous en tenons tous: il y a du plus, il y a du moins sans doute; mais il y a bien peu d'esprits que l'influence n'ait pas atteints d'une manière ou d'une autre; et moi-même qui vous prêche, je me suis souvent demandé si je n'en tenais point. . . .

Tout ce que vous avez dit sur les langues et tout ce qui en dépend
est excellent. Enfin, Monsieur, je ne saurais trop vous exhorter à
continuer vos études et vos travaux. Je ne crois pas, comme je vous
l'ai dit franchement, que vous soyez tout à fait dans la bonne voie,
mais vous y tenez un pied, et vous marcherez gauchement jusqu'à ce
qu'ils y soient tous les deux. . . . Le sans-culotte vous attend dans son
camp; moi, je vous attend dans le mien; nous verrons qui aura deviné.
Si je vis encore cinq ou six ans, je ne doute pas d'avoir le plaisir de
rire avec vous de l'*émancipation de la pensée*.[57]

Quite to the contrary, the *sans-culottes* did not await the adher-
ence of Ballanche. Lemontey, a compatriot and editor of the anti-
Catholic *Journal de commerce,* paid Ballanche the compliment of
an article, but defined him as a hybrid, *le libéral à son insu, et le
classique malgré lui.*[58] Lemontey preferred to see the *Essai* as a
sign of the defeat of the ultras. On November 26, 1818, he told
his readers that "ce livre a été écrit dans un camp ennemi des
idées libérales, mais il peint avec tant de vérité la confusion qui y
règne et il fait à la raison humaine des concessions si décisives, qu'on
peut le regarder comme un projet de capitulation."

CHAPTER V

Le Vieillard et le Jeune Homme—the Abbaye— l'Homme sans nom

I

THE *Essai* received its meed of praise only in the inner circle of Ballanche's friends, but he was satisfied. As long as Madame Récamier considered the book worthwhile, he felt himself a success. Ampère gave high praise, unaware of the carping appraisals made by professional critics:

> Ballanche [he wrote to Bredin on May 18, 1818] est beau de senti-
> ments, de pensées, de style; ne voyant presque personne, je ne sais
> pas l'impression qu'il fait à d'autres; ceux avec lesquels j'ai voulu
> causer de son oeuvre n'en savaient pas l'existence. J'en veux à tout
> le monde de ce qu'il en soit si peu question.[1]

Ballanche kept his thoughts to himself, worried now that Madame Récamier had left Paris. In 1818 she had gone for the season to Aix-la-Chapelle, where she met an old lover, Prince Augustus of Prussia. Ballanche, waiting in solitude for the mail, fussed at the thought of a rival. He filled page after page with advice and scoldings as he transferred his loneliness to the bits of paper he sent her:

> Moi qui voulais tant vous voir partir, je ne savais donc pas ce que
> c'était! Ce que je vous écris-là ce soir, tout seul, ne sera vu par vous
> que dans cinq jours. Ce que vous m'apprendrez de vous sera changé
> lorsque je le lirai. . . . Songez bien que je suis ici en sentinelle, qu'au
> moindre signe de vous, je partirai ou pour vous porter quelque
> adoucissement à vos tristesses ou pour vous ramener. . . . J'achèterais
> de ma vie un des cheveux de votre tête.[2]

While waiting impatiently for the center of his existence to return to Paris, Ballanche continued his studies. He worked sporadically at the *Fragments,* which he sent to Bredin for criticism in

December, 1818. Bredin was one of the members of the unofficial committee to which Ballanche submitted each of his manuscripts and one of the few persons with whom he could exchange information on occult philosophy. An omnivorous reader, Bredin had recently stumbled on Bœhme and, in his enthusiasm for the new doctrines, sent excerpts to Ballanche, wakening the latter's interest in his find.[3]

Madame Récamier returned, momentarily making Ballanche happy, but, in 1818, an old acquaintance snatched this bit of comfort from him. Chateaubriand reëntered Ballanche's life by becoming a successful suitor for Madame Récamier's affections. The senior members of her court resented the intrusion of the great egoist, but Ballanche felt the rivalry more keenly than the others, partly because he sensed his inferiority to Chateaubriand, partly because he recalled past treatment all too vividly. His only hope lay in the fact that he had lost the taint of business. Perhaps he and Chateaubriand could meet as colleagues who shared largely the same ideas. The hope was soon to die, for always in their relations would continue patronage and amused contempt on the one hand, admiration, envy, and resentment on the other. Chateaubriand seems to have been one of the few men capable of arousing Ballanche to strong emotion.

Foreseeing the disappointments in store for Madame Récamier, Ballanche sought to protect her. He even went so far as to speak openly of the danger of any relations with Chateaubriand, fighting desperately for his place in the sun. Once he even considered leaving Paris as he told her in a note written after a slight quarrel, though he quickly reconsidered this rash offer.[4]

Instead, Ballanche proposed a diversion that would give him a full share of her time. On February 11, 1819, he proposed that she occupy herself with literature. She had met so many authors, had so many ideas, that writing should come easy to her. Style could come later. Her candid impressions of people and literature would suffice for a start, providing she worked seriously.[5]

One by one he overcame scruples and protests, until she consented to write. They bravely began a translation of Petrarch when she complained of an inability to express herself freely. Each afternoon, they gave an hour to music, then three to literature or reading. But the translation dragged. She felt discouraged, restless, and her meeting with Chateaubriand left her sadly distressed. The mood infected Ballanche, increasing a natural tendency toward spleen. To combat it, he sought refuge in mysticism, even attempting to win her over to it. When this met indifference, he countered with the proposition that she collaborate on a book about Coppet and Mme de Staël. He sketched the outline of the book and sent it to her, explaining that

> . . . Coppet, dans cette donnée, serait le berceau de la société nouvelle. Cette frontière des idées allemandes et des idées françaises, des sentiments allemands et des sentiments français serait aussi la frontière des idées anciennes et des idées nouvelles, des sentiments anciens et des sentiments nouveaux. . . . C'est là aussi que l'on trouvera la fin du règne classique et le commencement du règne romantique. Le personnage de Mme de Staël aura alors toute son importance historique. Nous finirions par avoir une peinture assez complète et vraie des temps singuliers où nous vivons. Nous serons ensuite bien étonnés d'avoir fait de si belles choses. Ce sera de l'histoire et de la poésie: une telle alliance, au reste, est tout à fait dans notre génie.[6]

Like the translations of Petrarch, the book on Coppet soon died of Madame Récamier's boredom. Only a few pages survived, and these had been written by Ballanche. Noteworthy among the fragments are two portraits, one of Napoleon, the other of Mme de Staël. Since 1801, Ballanche's enthusiasm had steadily declined into a dislike that grew proportionately with the rise of the Napoleonic legend. He remembered the emperor primarily as a great tyrant:

> Il comptait sur ses armées pour jeter un trône dans la poussière; mais il ne pouvait compter que sur l'asservissement général de la pensée pour affermir son étrange pouvoir. Toute exaltation de l'âme l'épouvantait comme un présage de sa chute. Tout sentiment noble et élevé, dont il ne pouvait à l'instant même étouffer l'expression, lui inspirait mille terreurs. . . . Il essayait de flétrir les idées et les sentiments qu'il ne pouvait parvenir à attendre dans l'âme, à arracher du coeur.[7]

Madame de Staël, by contrast, reflected the best of the nineteenth century. Ballanche's estimate of her is perhaps enthusiastic, yet it states what later generations have for the most part come to believe.

> Mme de Staël avait reçu de la nature des facultés immenses et cette prodigieuse activité qui les fait toutes valoir. Son esprit vaste embrassait tout le domaine de l'intelligence et son âme ardente était faite pour en reculer toutes les limites. Elle était douée de cet ascendant qui

rallie les pensées des autres autour de sa propre pensée; et elle avait
en outre cette grande puissance qui remue les esprits tranquilles, qui
donne un aliment aux esprits inquiets, qui déplace les bornes du
convenu. Elle pouvait s'associer à la fois et à la fermentation des
idées de l'infini qui travaillait les têtes allemandes et à ce quelque
chose de positif qui voulait s'établir en France. Elle portait dans sa
pensée tout l'avenir de l'Europe. Ses idées étaient de veritables créa-
tions; ses rêveries même, lorsqu'elles s'appliquaient à la littérature
ou à la politique, étaient les essais d'une grande et forte imagination. . . . Une poésie toute nouvelle sortira sans doute des profondeurs
de la pensée; les premiers accents de cette poésie ont été entendus
par Mme de Staël.[8]

II

Madame Récamier may have lost her desire for literary immortality, but Ballanche continued to exorcise political demons
from France with his pen. A bout of illness, one of the many that
plagued him, slowed his progress, though not for long. Alarmed,
Madame Récamier packed him off to the Vallée-aux-Loups, Chateaubriand's small estate at Aulnay, near Sceaux, to recover and to work
on his numerous manuscripts. In August, 1819, he informed
Beuchot that convalescence was proceeding apace.[9] A month later
he sent Bredin the manuscript of his latest work, *le Vieillard et le
Jeune Homme,* and was rewarded with an enthusiastic letter of
thanks. What Bredin had just read, he said, lifted him from the
doldrums of personal worry. Ballanche had better publish quickly.
People had need of doctrines that would enable them to weave
patterns into contemporary chaos.[10]

The *Vieillard* continued the study of political and social problems
begun in the *Essai,* but, whereas the latter had been prepared for
savants, the new book was for the masses. For this reason he had
omitted the long arguments of the *Essai,* instead emphasizing their
consequences. His enthusiasm for the Bourbons and, above all, for
the *Charte,* his esteem for the liberal ministry of Decazes soon pushed
him into another adventure in pre-sociology to fix for a moment
his changing politics and the doctrine of liberal traditionalism. Like
others of the time, Sismondi, Fourier, Louis Blanc, and Proudhon,
Ballanche believed a new social dynamism could overcome the harm
done at the end of the Ancien Régime. Yet he ever remained a poet,

his social philosophy having only vague contours, specific primarily
in its insistence that society is governed, not by contract, but by
natural laws.[11]

The *Vieillard* contained the seven dialogues of an old man to a
young friend. The *vieillard* is unquestionably Ballanche; the *jeune
homme,* Jean-Jacques Ampère, the son of André-Marie. During the
period 1817-1818, the precocious son of the great scientist had succumbed to the *mal du siècle* that ushered adolescent romanticism
into the century. His letters to friends, Jules Bastide, Frank and
Albert Stapfer, Adrien and Alexis de Jussieu, show the despair and
aspirations common to the generation that came of age after the
Empire. Because of his profound affection for André-Marie Ampère,
Ballanche used Jean-Jacques for the recipient of his lectures in an
attempt to whip into him an appreciation of the potentialities at
hand. He lectured the young romantic like a father, but reversed
the usual rôles given to the young and the old. Ballanche preached
the doctrine of progress and the great hope of the new-born age,
combatting the state of mind that cringed from society to see ruins
everywhere, to love ruins for themselves. Once again Ballanche
stepped forward to do battle for his cause, this time against the
somber cult of conquered ideas and the stoic abjuration of the
future.[12]

The first *entretien* recorded the state of mind then prevalent in
a large section of French youth. The old man scolded his friend for
having abandoned life before living, for clutching to himself the
fragments of pitifully few memories. He had frequented only books
and because of them he forgot to close his fingers on reality. Youth
had grown prematurely austere from its effort to embrace mentally
the whole of human destiny without sharing in it:

> Tous les peuples deviennent ses amis, tous les hommes sont ses frères,
> les opprimés de tous les pays et de tous les temps ont droit à sa pro-
> fonde commisération. Le sentiment égaré de l'amour erre dans l'univers
> entier pour chercher quelque aliment à sa flamme dévorante. Ces plus
> hautes conceptions des sages, qui pour y parvenir ont eu besoin de
> vivre de longs jours, sont devenues le lait des enfants.[13]

To cure this malady, Ballanche offered an abundance of advice.
He warned the youth to stop worrying about society; what the

nineteenth century heard was only the death rattle of a former age, not the knell of Europe.[14] Society had withstood the Revolution and would endure to the end of time. What mattered was the recognition of the new era sprung from ruins.

The second *entretien* began an attack on some of the ideas to which youth held. Chief among them, and one that spelled anathema to Ballanche, was the concept of a primitive contract. Nonsense, he told the boy, that way led to another Napoleon. Ballanche could see no sense in universal suffrage and equality.[15] There must be a chief, even though he reigned with the tacit consent of the people. Man is born into society and only enjoys whatever liberty society grants. Nothing has been relinquished; instead all has been gained.[16]

Youth's aimlessness came from a lack of roots, yet the young attacked what few institutions could give them these roots. They failed to realize that property had to be the basis of the new order until society could find one more acceptable.[17] It took time for the new faith in humanity to spread, to seep out from select circles, beyond the walls of cities, over frontiers. Sometime a different kind of patriotism would arise, but the feeling of a united mankind had just begun to grow. New traditions had to be knitted together, especially in the realm of literature, where imitation had made a mockery of the arts.[18]

In the meantime, only religion could hold society together during its period of transition. All changed but Christianity, which, as the perfect religious institution, cemented the cracked seams of the social order. On this point Ballanche delivered a terrible indictment of the nineteenth century that included with rare perspicacity a host of later writers. It foreshadowed the aspirations and intellectual searching of Vigny, Lamartine, Hugo, and all like them who, in their religiosity, tried to anchor change in stability:

> Vous n'avez point de croyance fixe et positive; votre sentiment religieux, très intime et très profond, n'a point d'expression extérieure; en un mot, vous n'êtes pas sans religion, mais vous êtes sans culte. Vous voudriez être affranchi de vos doutes; ne trouvant pas la certitude en vous, vous voudriez la trouver dans la société; vous voudriez enfin que la société vous imposât une croyance ferme et dogmatique. Quelquefois néanmoins il vous semble que vous êtes tout près d'entrevoir la vérité; et alors la religion de vos pères vous apparaît, non plus

comme une foi vive et pure qui vous donne du repos, mais comme une
foi qui vous accuse; quelquefois aussi elle devient une superstition
aveugle et irrationnelle que vous saisit et s'empare de toutes vos
facultés pour leur infliger de cruels supplices. C'est un grand malheur,
mon fils, de ne point trouver d'appui autour de soi.[19]

Despite well-meant intentions, Ballanche discovered once again
that the way of the peacemaker leads most often to war. His kindness merely collected a reward of jeers and insults. Even among his
close friends, *le Vieillard et le Jeune Homme* created a scandal that
widened the breach between Ballanche and the ultras. The latter
saw no ncessity for reconciling the king and the Charte; the sooner
legitimacy divorced the principles of the Revolution, they thought,
the better for France. Some of them pointed out how he had to
strain his metaphysics to justify the electoral law of the Restoration.[20] The ferocity with which the two parties hammered at the
Vieillard earned Ballanche the dubious fame of being parodied. Yet
he remained unperturbed, his skin thicker now from frequent exposure to uncontrolled criticism. With even more than the usual
amount of Christian charity, he ignored even the sneers of M. le
comte Edouard de la Grange in the *Défenseur:*

J'ai lu, avec je ne sais quel sentiment de tristesse, le dialogue de M.
Ballanche, intitulé: *le Vieillard et le Jeune Homme* . . . C'est au
nom de ce qu'il y a de plus saint et de plus sacré parmi les hommes, que
M. Ballanche nous conduit à des résultats funestes. Tout ce que l'on
aurait éprouvé de charme à s'associer à la pensée intime et aux sentiments de l'auteur se tourne en dépit contre les séductions de son style
et les couleurs brillantes de son imagination, qui, en adoucissant le
poison, nous cachent le danger des conséquences où l'amour d'une
perfection idéale a pu seul entraîner M. Ballanche.[21]

III

Ballanche's own troubles vanished when disaster threatened
Madame Récamier. After Monsieur Récamier, that most unobtrusive
of husbands, lost his money speculating, Madame optimistically
turned over to him her own fortune. By 1819, Monsieur had succeeded in scattering this, too, and Madame was forced to economize.
Accordingly, she moved to the third floor of a convent in the
quartier de la Croix-Rouge, rue de Sèvres, where she could live
within her means. The Abbaye-au-Bois still housed some nuns, but

the group was diminishing rapidly and indigent ladies of good character and the proper religious attitude were allowed to room in the upper floors. Madame Récamier's apartment lay just under the roof, three flights up, though later she changed to the floor below. When she moved, Ballanche followed, to 23, rue du Cherche-Midi, five minutes' walk from the Abbaye.[22]

Under the skilled hand of Madame Récamier, the salon of the Abbaye-au-Bois became famous. Guests mounted the wide stairway to the salon on the second floor, and crossed two tiny dark rooms before penetrating to the salon. The latter seemed to exude an atmosphere of religion and mystery as though in subtle preparation for the conversation to be heard. At one end of the room hung Girard's dominating portrait of *Corinne au Cap Misène.* Opposite it, on the mantel, in front of the mirror, there stood amidst the girandoles and the Greek vases the famous *branche toujours verte.* Of the other walls, one held two windows that opened onto the closed garden, the other was covered with book shelves. Heavy blue curtains permitted the entrance of just enough light to make Madame Récamier appear like a white phantom. Everywhere there floated the vague odor of carnations or *poudre à la maréchale.* The floor, almost without covering, reflected light from its polished surface onto the Louis XV screen. On a table lay the sketch of a bas-relief of Eudore and Cymodocée. A tidy mind had scattered the twelve chairs and the twenty-six bergères at intervals along the walls and in front of the fireplace. On important days, these chairs, ornamented with the head of the sphinx, were arranged in five or six circles for the benefit of the ladies. The gentlemen circulated from one group to another, carrying with them the threads of the conversation of the adjacent circle. On days when some author read from his latest manuscript, the chairs formed a single circle, the center of which was reserved for the lion of the moment. Madame Récamier sometimes passed among her guests, but more often she stretched out languidly on the chaise longue or curled up in a big armchair near the fireplace.[23]

Chateaubriand became increasingly the center of the small, select, self-sufficient universe enclosed in the Abbaye. Habit led him to the convent every day at 2:30, to spend an hour with Madame Récamier chatting over tea or simply resting in companionable quiet. About an hour later, the steps of the first guest echoed in the hall. Ballanche, or one of the inner circle, was coming for his daily visit. While Madame Récamier sat in the corner embroidering, Chateaubriand silently eyed the newcomers from his vantage point under the portrait of Corinne. Ballanche sat in another armchair with the assured air of one at home.

The program for the salon was carefully planned for the entertainment of Chateaubriand. Each day Madame Récamier racked her brains to keep the great man interested.[24] She labored mightily to attract the great men of Paris and to force them to worship at the shrine of René without, at the same time, frightening the newcomers. Mostly she succeeded, except with a Stendhal, too observant and malicious to be taken in, who promptly left calling Chateaubriand *le grand Lama*. To maintain an atmosphere soothing to a poet's nerves, she inflexibly enforced a set of rules subtly passed on to guests: no sudden movements or loud talk, but conversations carried on in voices as veiled as the light that flickered onto the portrait. Any infractions were punished by the hostess with a movement of surprise, or a sharp word.

Occasionally some iconoclast revolted. The younger generation preferred tempered admiration to blind worship. Sosthène de la Rochefoucauld, for instance, had written a pen-portrait of Rachel which he wanted to read to the guests at the Abbaye. When he politely asked permission of Madame Récamier she replied, "Je vais le demander à M. de Chateaubriand." The great man, however, thought that the reading would bore him, at which Sosthène bowed, saying, "Puisque vous désirez entendre cette lecture, je commence," and calmly read his sketch in the teeth of the master's cold fury.[25]

Usually the evening gatherings were more serious, however. France was passing through a period in which people were experiencing a strange avidity for knowledge. People crowded the Athénée, or attended the Société des Bonnes Lettres. The heaviest of theologies was applauded in the courses of Daunou; Latin poetry drew throngs to hear Tissot. Animated with a cold passion, Guizot praised individual energy and the human will at the Sorbonne. The youth of France, precociously mature, following in the steps of its respected elders, displayed a fondness for large and serious books; persiflage had gone out of fashion. The death of Byron at Missolonghi had exalted imaginations, and the slightest political allusion in either play or book was eagerly seized. Europe heaved with a spirit of nationalism that inevitably found its counterpart in France. All subjects, but particularly history, government and religion, were of interest. Here in the Abbaye, the young and the old met to produce a new style and a new taste. What particularly moved the age was a series of scenes or tableaux. The Greeks and the Romans had given way to troubadours or helmeted soldiers. Color and movement replaced the dry cataloguing of ideas. Madame Récamier's salon served as a clearing house for the young who came to listen to the old, to find ideas they could modify, or to meet writers who had opened the way for their own talents. They listened to readings of the works of these masters and were given the opportunity to try their own wings, to benefit from the keen criticism of their listeners or from the information they could obtain from the audience.

For the most part Ballanche sat quietly in his corner, answering in disconnected phrases the questions put to him. When guests became too serious, he tossed a jest at them or fashioned a pun.[26] Sometimes he startled the assembly with profound observations. Regarding this aspect of Ballanche, Barante coined an epigram that quickly ran through Paris, "Il vivait dans un nuage, mais le nuage s'entr'ouvrait quelque-fois."[27]

Sometimes, indeed, the cloud opened to release a thunderstorm. One evening, after a good dinner at the home of the Duchess of Devonshire, Ampère and Ballanche returned about ten o'clock to Madame Récamier's, where were gathered some of the inner circle. In the course of the conversation, a guest quoted Bossuet. Ballanche, deserting his customary silence, opened a bitter attack on the bishop, became increasingly more excited, and finally cried:

> Non! qu'on ne me parle plus des vertus et des talents de Bossuet, d'un homme qui a osé dire que Dieu n'a pas révélé le dogme de l'immortalité de l'âme aux Juifs parce qu'ils n'étaient pas dignes de recevoir cette vérité! Par ces mots, il mérite le feu et les cinquante mille bûches de l'Inquisition ne suffiraient pas pour le rôtir. . . . Il y aurait cinquante mille fenêtres que je m'en précipiterais d'un coup en témoignage de ce que j'avance![28]

A burst of laughter brought him back to his senses. He had been marching back and forth the length of the salon, not only breaking all accepted rules, but, red with indignation, he had been emphasizing points by slapping on the shoulder all within reach.

Ballanche suffered from having been relegated to a secondary position by the arrival of Chateaubriand, but he kept his peace, distrust leaking through his words only when Madame Récamier became agitated over some turn of Chateaubriand's affairs. As he put it politely, yet clearly, he could understand M. de Chateaubriand's agitations, but thought that if René could learn to take matters more simply, he would take a great step towards tranquillity.[29] What Ballanche could not forgive was the bitterness Chateaubriand injected into *la Monarchie selon la Charte*. Chateaubriand revelled, too, in more conservatism than Ballanche thought necessary. Liberal ideas, he was certain, would triumph throughout Europe in spite of determined opposition. A great writer only harmed himself when he undertook to speak for a whole nation.[30] For this reason he felt sorry to see Chateaubriand leave for Berlin as a member of the French delegation, fearing that the sovereigns, with an eye to consolidating their own positions, would thrust on Europe a set of out-worn institutions, thereby separating themselves from their peoples.[31]

Jealousy and admiration, dislike and a sincere desire to be liked, underlay in a complicated fashion all Ballanche's later dealing with his successful rival. Chateaubriand could not forget that Ballanche had been tainted by trade; he could ask services, even money, from him and repay with haughty acknowledgment. Not one of Madame Récamier's lesser triumphs was her ability to maintain a truce between the two men. They grew old near her, each conscious of the other's presence and rivalry. But Ballanche so loved Madame Récamier that he scrupulously maintained a correct attitude toward the man who had won the place he coveted. Anything to be near her, even if it mean running errands, planning trips, or writing to hotels for her. Chateaubriand he learned to accept as one of the trials of life. Thus René became important insofar as he affected Madame Récamier's disposition. Therefore, Ballanche's letters to her often deal at length with Chateaubriand, sometimes even over-

flow with advice that seems misdirected. But Ballanche was trying to
explain the great man so that she could learn to take him more
calmly, thereby making his own life more bearable. There was a
chance, too, that she could actually make Chateaubriand see the
sense of his observations. Once in a while, this secondary position
wrenched from him a wistful remark. On December 28, 1822,
Chateaubriand was named ambassador to London. That same
month de Montmorency had left the ministry, leaving Madame
Récamier happy for one, sad for the other. The day after Chateaubriand's nomination, Ballanche begged, "Aimez-moi, quoique je ne
sois ni détrôné ni exalté contre notre gré."[32] For his part, Chateaubriand adhered as carefully as possible to Madame Récamier's un-
spoken rules. Occasionally, when he remembered, he made a real
effort to minimize potential friction with Ballanche, then faithfully
reported to her. "Ballanche a dîné chez moi hier. J'ai eu soin
d'écarter toute conversation politique. Cela m'a fait grand plaisir
de voir chez moi le vieil ami."[33] Normally, however, Chateaubriand
was a cross Ballanche had to bear all his life.

IV

Despite his personal problems, Ballanche had not neglected his
writing. Since coming to Paris he had been planning *l'Homme sans
nom*, a book on the Revolution.[34] He had communicated its essential arguments to Madame Récamier, who encouraged him, and to
Chateaubriand, who jeered in disapproval. In the face of this
opposition, Ballanche kept the manuscript in his trunk until
February 13, 1820, when Louvel assassinated the duc de Berry, the
son of the comte d'Artois.

Ballanche's first reaction to the murder appeared in an *Elégie* in
prose,[35] a short lyrical outburst of compassion and horror. Written
like the chant of a Greek tragedy, it was not a *récit* or a tableau, but
a message of commiseration for the Bourbons, in which all
Ballanche's terror of violence lent undertones that bring the *Elégie*
to the front rank of French prose. Like the Egyptians of old he
cried: "nous avons perdu l'un de nous; c'est notre premier-né que
le glaive de la mort a dévoré!"[36]

Yet, at the same time, Ballanche remembered to cry halt to the ultras and the liberals, now preparing for an even more vicious battle for power. The *Elégie* intended to paint the general uneasiness of the age, the birth of one epoch as another dies. Ballanche sensed that order was rising from the aftermath of the Revolution and he had no wish to see rival factions cut a skein so laboriously woven. For that reason he argued that the assassin had been the blind instrument of "cette triste volonté du mal. . . . Ce n'est pas seulement le sang humain qui peut la satisfaire, il lui faut le sang des rois, le sang d'une dynastie de rois."[37]

Sympathetic and gentle, Ballanche still felt the Bourbons needed to draw a lesson from the assassination. He warned that social forms aged, then perished. The dynasty had lost touch with the nation; Louvel had been the harbinger of impending disaster for the reigning house:

> Imprudents, apprenez donc. Apprenez qu'une dynastie est établie par Dieu pour diriger la société, mais la société telle que Dieu la lui a confiée, et non point la société telle que vous la faites dans vos rêves d'autrefois, telle que vous la concevez dans vos théories frappées de désuétude! Ecoutez cette vérité inexorable qui dit: Sitôt qu'une dynastie cesse de représenter la société . . . alors sa mission est finie. Vous m'avez forcé de sortir de mon silence, et que ce ne soit pas en vain. N'avons-nous pas assez gémi, assez pleuré.[38]

When the *Elégie* failed to stir the lethargic Bourbons, Ballanche watched carefully, for the assassination seemed to awaken in France a revolutionary fervor which had once led to regicide. He thought back to the death of Louis XVI, to the Empire and the return from Elba, and there grew in him the feeling that a Nemesis prowled through the world. As Ballanche had stated in the *Elégie,* the new principle of democracy was sometimes prematurely incarnated in certain individuals, nagging them into crime. He saw in them the Louvels of history, Œdipi inadvertently guilty, automata who sinned almost against their will, themselves victims.[39] Uneasy at this thought, Ballanche published in 1820 *l'Homme sans nom,*[40] another attempt to evaluate the political events of the day.

The edition was small; a mere hundred copies came from the presses, for Ballanche meant his book only for the king, his ministers, and the chiefs of the major parties. Admitting the public to the privacy of his opinions, he felt, would necessitate sketching in a great deal of background and explaining much of his philosophy. He would be forced to retrace the history of an age when political passions flamed hot. Rather than do this, he decided to appeal to the few who theoretically controlled public opinion. Yet, even with these few in mind, he later admitted that he had not reached all the readers he desired.

The theme of the regicide, victim of a prematurely expressed political philosophy, filled the book with ghosts from a not-too-distant bloody past. Ballanche told the story with himself as one of the characters. In August, 1814, while on the way to Italy, he was forced by an accident to pause near the Alps. To escape boredom, he wandered through the neighborhood, finally coming upon a seemingly abandoned village, peculiar in that all the houses but one huddled together in protective sympathy. A passing child informed Ballanche that the house belonged to a man known only as the Regicide. Interested, he walked to this house, where, after some difficulty, he persuaded the occupant to recount the events leading to a long, voluntary exile. The Regicide haltingly, then passionately fluent, recalled that once he had belonged to the Convention, happy and idealistic until the trial of the king.

His story concerned a trick the presence of the mob had played on his mind. He had not intended to vote for death. While waiting for his turn he had muttered repeated defiance of the crowd. He, at least, would keep faith with his principles. Then he climbed the long steps to the rostrum, opened his mouth, and inexplicably voted for death. He stepped down a broken man. Conscience nagged him out of Paris into the provinces, where he settled near the Alps. He wanted no humans near lest he infect them, and with his own hands he dug a grave, then settled back with a Bible to wait for death. He felt himself a symbol of the French nation, blindly led into a great crime. All this he poured out until, exhausted, the Regicide sat silently, reliving in anguish those few terrible moments. Ballanche tip-toed out of the cottage, not to see the old man for three years. On his return from Italy, he stopped there again to find that the Regicide had died, though not before two priests had reconverted him to Catholicism.

L'Homme sans nom contained in its clearest form to date the philosophy previously expressed in the *Essai:* "Epreuves, expiations, liberté: voilà toute la destinée humaine; voilà tout le problème de nos grandeurs et de nos abaissements."[41] He preached an interior and exterior morality, the former a meditation over, and repentance for, individual sin, the latter a political doctrine of slow, measured progress guided by enlightened Catholicism. From the story of the Regicide came the double thesis of the punishment of a nation, and the punishment of the killer. France had suffered for turning her back on fourteen centuries of civilization, but her expiation was finished. The prophets of the past had no further reason to demand more blood to close a paid account.[42]

Strangely enough, though Ballanche had created the story from whole cloth, there lay in it a frightening basis of truth which he did not discover until later. Another regicide, Lecointe-Puyraveau des Deux-Sèvres could have told the same story. Like the nameless man, Lecointe-Puyraveau had been present at the trial. He had shifted nervously on his bench and, when the crowd cheered each vote for death, had shown disapproval. When he spoke, threats greeted his opening words and, under the menaces, his words formed sentences that denied his thoughts. Bewildered, he stumbled to his seat after casting for death.[43]

Yet the ring of actuality could not save Ballanche's book. Lacking great talent for dialogue, he had turned his story into a series of long monologues. Sometimes the use of time-worn techniques made the tale trite. The Regicide, for instance, leaves behind letters designed to prove that Louis XVI actually had not been out of step with his people. The historical characters involved, too, act in a manner strangely unreal. Marie Antoinette became "cette vierge de lis,"[44] Louis, a savior unrecognized. Even the Regicide sometimes talked sentimentally of an age he helped destroy. Furthermore, Ballanche's manner of symbolizing an idea in a man succeeded better with ancient kings than with contemporaries subject to the ills of the average man.

Once again Ballanche beat the empty air. Later the romanticists would imitate his stand against the death penalty, but his contemporaries were blind to all but political implications. The ultras promptly used the assassination to seize power. The Abbaye divided sharply, those by birth closer to the Ancien Régime joining the new government. Two of them, Chateaubriand and de Montmorency, received portfolios, while Ballanche and Camille Jordan remained faithful to more democratic ideas.

Ballanche, nevertheless, paid for close association with Madame Récamier and Chateaubriand by being bracketed with the conservatives despite all he wrote. In 1821, a group of liberals published a *Biographie nouvelle des contemporains* in which Ballanche found a place as whipping-boy:

> BALLANCHE (Pierre-Simon), imprimeur-libraire, a récemment publié des ouvrages, où quelque esprit d'indépendance se trouve mêlé à la défense des vieux préjugés, et à une exaltation singulière d'idées religieuses. Né à Lyon le 4 août 1776, il fut longtemps éditeur et propriétaire du *Bulletin de Lyon,* journal où il insérait divers articles. On a de lui: *Du Sentiment, considéré dans ses rapports avec la littérature et les arts,* 1802, in-8°; *Antigone,* 1815, in-8°, espèce de poëme en prose, ou plutôt roman en prose poétique. Quelque riche qu'il soit en fictions, un ouvrage ne peut prendre le titre de poëme si elles ne sont revêtues du charme de la versification. M. Ballanche a aussi publié quelques romans politiques, qui peuvent être fort poétiques car ils offrent peu de pages écrites pour les amis de la vérité.[45]

V

L'Homme sans nom, however, was destined to reach fame indirectly when a greater writer reproduced much the same story.[46] In *les Misérables,* Victor Hugo painted a picture of a regicide *conventionnel* which so strikingly resembles the *Homme sans nom* that the question of borrowing inevitably arises.

Although *les Misérables* appeared many years later, the episode of the bishop and the regicide seems to have been a literary souvenir from earlier years. Emond Biré recalls that the prologue of the book originally was entitled *le Manuscrit de l'Evêque,* and that it once was to be published by Renduel. When, in 1861, Hugo was arranging with Lacroix, Verboeckhoven et Cie. for the publication at Brussels of a two-volume edition of the *Manuscrit de l'Evêque,* he stipulated that the company deal with Renduel, its proprietor. Accordingly, Lacroix purchased all rights from Renduel for eight thousand francs. From this it seems, then, that the *Manuscrit* had been

finished prior to 1848, the date when Renduel ceased publishing.[47]
Biré suspects further that it was written even earlier, at a time when
Hugo sympathized with Catholicism, and was revised after 1852, dur-
ing the years of exile, to reflect Hugo's new opinions.[48]

There is little question that Hugo knew well Ballanche's works,
for the latter's reputation, growing steadily from 1818, attained
major proportions between 1830 and 1847. His numerous studies of
the Revolution were known to all, like Hugo, who were fascinated by
such an event. Before succumbing to the Messianic fever, Hugo had
docilely plodded in the wake of Chateaubriand, and, knowing René,
he could not have failed to meet Ballanche, especially since the
latter played an important part in Hugo's election to the Académie
Française. Furthermore, Hugo's good friend, Sainte-Beuve, frequented the Abbaye salon, from which only illness could keep Ballanche. And, finally, by some strange quirk, the title *l'Homme sans
nom* entered the common coinage of popular language, thanks
probably to parodies. To such a point did the phrase become hack-
neyed that Gustave Planche, beginning his career in 1831 as critic
for *l'Artiste,* satisfied the curiosity of his readers by giving his autobiography the title, *l'Homme sans nom.*

Hugo, however, chose from the rich material Ballanche offered
with the sure hand of the master. Conflicting artistic and political
views differentiated the two pictures. Whereas Ballanche's regicide
reflected his creator's suspicion of mobs, his terror of the Revolution, and his deep faith, Hugo's *conventionnel,* fitted to the political
ideas of 1860, presented a sharp contrast. Ballanche had his hermit
kneel at the feet of the two priests who came to confess him, while
Hugo set his bishop at the feet of the old man. This divergence
springs almost solely from Hugo's selection of material. Ballanche's
conventionnel changes under the stare of the crowd, pushed by fear
of the many hostile eyes from feeble admiration of Louis XVI to a
declaration in favor of the lusty revolution. But, since Hugo felt no
interest in a study of fear, he retained only the idea of the regicide's
confession, disregarding Ballanche's psychological curiosity.

Hugo's setting reveals immediately its relationship to that of Ballanche. The hermit's dwelling stands apart from the town, Ballanche's in a "hameau perdu au milieu d'une nature affreuse, enterré

au milieu des fondrières et des ravins," Hugo's, a short distance from
Digne, "loin de tout hameau, loin de tout chemin," tucked into "on
ne sait quel repli perdu d'un vallon très sauvage."[49] Enveloped in an
aura of frightfulness, both men scared women of the neighborhood
into crossing themselves when passing their cottages.

The two men even resemble each other physically. *L'Homme sans
nom* was tall, noble-looking,, white-haired; his eyes sparkled, and
his whole bearing showed dignity and the assurance of intelligence.
Hugo's hero "était un de ces grands octogénaires qui font l'étonnement du physiologiste. . . . Si près de la fin il avait conservé tous
les gestes de la santé. Il y avait dans son coup d'œil clair, dans son
accent ferme, dans son robuste mouvement d'épaules, de quoi
déconcerter la mort."[50]

Their deaths differ according to the political ideas of their creators. Whereas Ballanche talked to his regicide inside the miserable
hut, Hugo placed his hero in a chair outside, gazing into a setting
sun. Both men were consciously drawn as symbols, the man without
a name dying in remorseful shame, expiating a crime unwittingly
committed, whereas G. sat erect in the dusk, proud, still convinced
of the righteousness of his act, protesting against the century that
felt ashamed of him. He had helped establish equality; his kind had
been the first to do more than murmur at rank abuse.[51]

Though details distinguish the two sketches, in the final analysis
there seems to be little doubt that Ballanche's nameless one was
Hugo's model. The latter's hero recognized that his mission meant
the death of a king and the repudiation of an age, but he foresaw
a better France. He acted in magnificent anger as a citizen full of
the republican zeal of the newly freed:

> J'avais soixante ans quand mon pays m'a appelé. . . . Il y avait des
> abus. Je les ai combattus; il y avait des tyrannies, je les ai détruites.
> . . . la France était menacée, j'ai offert ma poitrine. . . . J'ai déchiré
> la nappe de l'autel, c'est vrai; mais c'était pour panser les blessures
> de la patrie. J'ai toujours soutenu la marche en avant du genre humain
> vers la lumière, et j'ai résisté quelquefois au progrès sans pitié.[52]

The more delicate thesis of Ballanche fell to pieces under the bold
translation of Hugo. Ballanche's criminal, on the other hand, medi-
tates, studies, and worries. He went to the Convention with a

philosophy entirely different from that of his more republican copy. The Revolution meant a crisis in the nation's affairs. His subsequent repentance for his vote springs from a fear that he had misunderstood events. Through him and his concern over evil, Ballanche tried to reconcile adversaries of the past and present, regarding the problem from as objective a point of view as he could manage. These different preoccupations color the two portraits, but, essentially, Hugo's story reflects Ballanche's in characters and plot, if not in style and philosophy. In other words, Ballanche stole into history in another man's pages.

CHAPTER VI

Italy—Essais de palingénésie sociale—Orphée

I

ABOUT 1821, Ballanche began to set on paper his admiration for Madame Récamier. It seemed obvious that he could not hope to rival Chateaubriand, who had progressively replaced all her older friends. Now would Ballanche dream of declaring the amazing love that kept him close to her, however miserable he might feel. His timidity relegated him to the rôle of silent companion, yet he could confide in a piece of paper. Characteristically betraying his real feelings, he began a portrait of Madame Récamier supposedly for the *Galerie des contemporains*. At first a sketch intended to accompany a lithograph of her, his manuscript lengthened as he worked. He came to love his creation so much that he refused to relinquish it. On lonely days he could take it out and write eloquently thoughts which an awkward tongue feared to shape. By 1823 the pen portrait had grown to twenty-seven chapters of sheer devotion bound in violet morocco. Not until 1824-25 was it finished, at which time he added a table of contents and a long *avis*. Despite this, he returned at times to the manuscript, polishing, or adding, the last revision coming about the beginning of 1834.

He wrote like a priest praying to a beloved goddess. The first words warned that readers were being introduced into the presence of a superior being:

> Voici une célébrité d'un genre complètement nouveau, quoique, sous certains rapports, elle réalise, si l'on peut parler ainsi, la partie la plus éclatante de la destinée d'une femme. Cette célébrité, au reste, qui ne devait ressembler à nulle autre, a toujours été protégée par un caractère trop parfaitement inoffensif et par de trop nobles qualités, pour que le monde eût à s'en garantir ou à la contester.[1]

Several of Madame Récamier's letters were incorporated in the portrait; some were *inédites,* the property of the Duchess de Broglie, who watched them with a jealous eye. From these and his own memories, Ballanche constructed an *Evangile de la Madone* that brings smiles to the cynical.[2] He maintained this attitude until the moment came to write of Chateaubriand and then he faltered. The subject had now lost its interest. Here the manuscript contains only a few lines, vague references to an unpleasant incident. The affair so irked him that he refused to continue beyond the solemn reading of the *Abencérage* in Madame Récamier's salon in July, 1814.

In 1823, hope flared momentarily for the timid lover. Madame Récamier left a second time for Italy, taking with her Ballanche and Jean-Jacques Ampère. Rumor had it that she traveled on a political mission but, in reality, Chateaubriand was the reason for her departure. A philanderer of experience, Chateaubriand had allowed his fancies to wander after solemnly assuring Madame Récamier that he had reformed. She refused to share her entourage with anyone, especially when all Paris tittered over her predicament. Sainte-Beuve noted later that "il y eut . . . pour motif à ce départ de Mme Récamier, en 1823, une petite pointe de jalousie au sujet d'une fort jolie et très spirituelle dame, Mme de C. . . . , qui était alors très fêtée au ministère des affaires étrangéres."[3] Proportionately as Chateaubriand's stock fell, Ballanche's rose. Wisely he held his tongue, allowing René to protest too much. When Madame Récamier decided to avoid a repetition of the storm by forsaking Paris, Ballanche assumed his customary rôle of major-domo. He wrote ahead to hotels, saw that bags were packed and at hand, and provided suitable reading material for her moods, in this case books on religion and art. The small party crossed the Alps in November and though Chateaubriand showered Madame Récamier with conciliatory letters, she curtly told her entourage "Le *Monsieur* m'a glacée."[4]

They travelled slowly and regally, enjoying each step of the trip. With Ballanche and Ampère, Madame Récamier explored all the museums, churches, libraries, and monuments of interest. Ballanche and Ampère whiled away dull hours discussing history and philosophy. Not until December 15 did the cortège wind its way into Rome on a cold, grey day. Since Ballanche had fallen ill during the last stages of the trip, the travellers paid more attention to him than to the approaches of the city.

In Rome the salon of the Abbaye-au-Bois quickly reformed. Madame Récamier found there the duc de Laval and the Duchess of Devonshire, friends of long standing. The little colony established itself in the foreign quarter, on the via del Babuino, n° 65, near the foot of the stairs leading from the place d'Espagne, facing the Greek church.[5] Ballanche lived with Madame Récamier and her niece, Mlle Cyvoct, while Jean-Jacques rushed back and forth on restless travels, making the salon the center of his wanderings. Little by little the Abbaye reappeared when old habitués from Paris turned up in Italy, Dugas-Montbel, the abbé Canova and Delécluze.

Evenings, the faithful gathered to exchange witticisms, or to parry arguments in search of the grand prize, an admiring exclamation from the ladies. The duc de Laval animated the group with his lordly airs, his grace and aristocratic cynicism; Ballanche stayed in a corner wrapped in plans for a new book. Usually he listened silently or retreated into the security of his mind when the conversation turned to social doings, aroused from his contentment only by some alluring contradiction. He rubbed elbows casually with those noted for polish and charm, a fact which amused some of the retinue Madame Récamier had left in Paris.[6] Politics and literature furnished most of the tidbits for the conversation, with the assemblage split between liberalism and conservatism. Most of the guests leaned towards a conservatism that frowned on novelty. Despite formidable opposition, Ballanche stoutly held to his faith in romanticism. As he wrote to Jean-Jacques Ampère after the latter had returned to Paris:

> Il paraît que le parterre de Paris est toujours très-exclusif, qu'il aime mieux se passer de tragédies nouvelles que de courir des risques d'avoir du romantique; toutefois on ne doit pas prendre cela pour un arrêt irrévocable. Je vous ai souvent dit qu'il fallait se faire son public: c'est toujours ainsi dans les temps analogues à celui-ci.[7]

In Rome Ballanche worked industriously on his many projects. He and Ampère enthusiastically planned a *Guide du voyageur* which proposed to satisfy every curiosity a traveller might have. Needless to say, it was eventually consigned to the limbo of good intentions, but in seeking facts for it, Ballanche discovered material for many of his later books. His sense of change and a conviction of the ultimate reality of time, a sense that distinguished him from the apostles of the past, became more pronounced as he saw modern edifices casting shadows on the ancient. Here he drew up plans for the *Palingénésie* and the three books that were to compose it: *Orphée,* a kind of prehistoric epic, the *Formule générale,* an epic at once historic and symbolic,, and the *Ville des expiations,* including the *Vision d'Hébal,* a prophetic epic.[8]

Sometimes he managed to tear himself away from the salon to venture into other cities. On January 22, 1824, Dugas-Montbel enticed him into leaving for Naples. It was perhaps the worst possible season, but he felt eager to search for confirmation of his historical theories. For this reason he stopped at Pompeii. From here he posted nostalgic letters full of questions, advice and philosophy. Does uncontrolled industry give the proletariat of a democracy too much power? How should the Chamber of Peers be constituted? The two friends had planned to continue to Greece, but each found a reason for not going, Dugas-Montbel because of urgent business in Paris, Ballanche because he was homesick for Madame Récamier. This was a sacrifice; he had hoped to extract from Greece a great deal of historical material. As he had written to her from Naples, January 26, 1824:

> La Grande-Grèce est la patrie primitive de cette philosophie primitive dont je crois être appelé à renouveler dans le monde le sentiment éteint. Il me semble à présent que j'ai une destinée à accomplir. Cette destinée, je l'avais déjà entrevue plusieurs fois en France. Depuis que je suis en Italie, elle m'apparaît d'une manière un peu moins confuse. La vieille Europe a besoin de quelques apôtres comme moi. Peut-être serai-je seul, comme ce juif dont parle Cazotte; mais dussé-je être seul, il faut que j'exprime ce que Dieu a mis en moi.[9]

The countryside, the people, the sea, and the sky were witnesses of a past he wanted to question. He had seen trees, ruins, and houses before, but in these lay the reasons for progress. In case Madame Récamier should be confused by a seemingly loose use of the word history, he defined a historian as one who used the past to predict the future. Thus Ballanche, before Quinet, Michelet, and the other romantic historians, sought from yesterday the security to enable him to live in tomorrow. He pursued, as they would, the magic synthesis of events that would explain so much instability.[10]

Ballanche hastened back to Rome with plans for meditating on his trip in comfortable proximity to Madame Récamier. Unfortunately for his sedentary habits, she had decided to visit Naples and accordingly left for that city towards the end of June, 1824, arriving July 1 with her niece, the ubiquitous Jean-Jacques Ampère, and Ballanche. The trip was made in a strange manner. A guard of eighty Austrian soldiers formed their escort, and they travelled at night to escape the punishing heat. Each stopping place brought new expectations and the small adventures of daily existence. Jean-Jacques revelled in the constant movement, while Ballanche placidly found his contentment in that of Madame Récamier. Everywhere they met expansive hospitality, especially in Naples, where the Lefebvre family offered a luxurious welcome. Ballanche should have lived in utter bliss, but he noticed that Madame Récamier seemed distracted. *Les Martyrs* suddenly became her favorite book, and she worried quietly at the news that Villèle had "regretted" to be forced by royal decree to "replace" Chateaubriand in the ministry.

Just when Ballanche's existence had become fixed, the shadow of Chateaubriand fell on him again. On March 4, 1825, Ballanche received word from Mlle Amélie Cyvoct that René had renewed his correspondence with her aunt. Knowing that Madame Récamier's veneer of contentment hid a violent dissatisfaction with her separation from Chateaubriand, Ballanche bravely sent a letter of congratulations although well aware that his monopoly of her affections had ended.[11] Since there was little doubt what Madame Récamier would do when René beckoned, it did not surprise Ballanche when, in May, 1825, she began packing for home.

For his part, Ballanche felt sorry to leave Rome, a city where he really felt himself a citizen. Its ruins and air of permanency had at first puzzled him, as had the Revolution, but now he knew the answer to both riddles. Life was a constant struggle between two opposing principles, plebeianism and aristocracy. Without hesitation he had chosen sides. He had suffered too much from aristocrats to feel any obligation to them. Chateaubriand, the duc de Laval, Mathieu de Montmorency,, what could they offer to a progressive world? They represented, in fact, the backward elements that constantly impede the upsurge of liberty. Rome was a microcosm in which all this seemed evident to the curious; here humanity had developed Christian equality, the fundamental reason for the existence of the holy city.[12] He was now returning to Paris with a wealth of manuscripts and an enlarged store of experience with feminine logic.

Slowly Ballanche again became accustomed to a secondary place in Madame Récamier's life, though bitterness swirled through his mind. The Abbaye salon had become even more brilliant, graced by all the great names of France. Cousin, Dubois, founder of the *Globe,* Saint-Marc Girardin, Sophie Gay, all passed into the murky darkness of the great room to kneel for a moment at the shrine of Chateaubriand, some seriously, some mockingly, most of them out of curiosity. Ballanche watched silently from a chair near the fire. His health, never strong, often kept him confined to his room. There a ferocious but devoted maid, nicknamed *Dragonneau* by awed visitors, bullied him and his guests in determined concern for his health. In 1827, he fell ill enough to provoke a flurry of concern among his friends, who anxiously sought from each other bulletins on his condition. By February, however, he had rallied sufficiently for Jean-Jacques to express relief to Madame Récamier.[13]

His illness, however, ,did not prevent him from publishing again, this time the *Essais de palingénésie sociale.*[14] Only a few copies were printed, the edition being, as Ballanche termed it, *provisoire,* and meant only for a few close friends. The public could have the big edition of *l'Homme sans nom* which he had decided to release for general circulation.[15] The original work had grown in length and profundity until,, in 1827, it was launched under the patronage of "celle qui a été vue comme une apparition de Béatrix,"[16] in memory of the trip to Italy, 1823-25, during which time he conceived and polished a large part of the philosophy of the *Essais.*[17]

II

The *Palingénésie,* or as he sometimes called it, *la Théodicée de l'historie,* constitutes Ballanche's greatest effort to give France a new philosophy in the picture of the human odyssey. Divided into three parts, it consists of a series of prolegomena for books either written or projected. The *Elégie* he had published, but new names appeared, unknown even to faithful readers: *Orphée, la Formule générale de l'histoire de tous les peuples, appliquée à l'histoire du peuple romain,* and *la Ville des Expiations.* Of these, only *Orphée* would appear in complete form; the others were issued piecemeal.

Ballanche pretended no false modesty in the preface; he proudly stated that the book was addressed to all Europe, so important did he feel his new theories to be. The *Palingénésie,* he pointed out, stemmed from the *Essai sur les institutions sociales;* the latter, in fact, should be considered only an introduction to the present volume. For the earlier work he had relied more on logic than he now intended. Without subterfuge, Ballanche admitted his complete trust in a feeling for the truth of what he had to say about antiquity, a method justified by the fact that much of the *Palingénésie* concerned pre-history:

> Je veux exprimer la grande pensée de mon siècle. Cette pensée dominante, profondément sympathique et religieuse, qui a reçu de Dieu même la mission auguste d'organiser le nouveau monde social, je veux la chercher dans toutes les sphères des diverses facultés humaines, dans tous les ordres de sentiments et d'idées: je veux, si je puis, en signaler toutes les métamorphoses successives. J'en suivrai la trace . . . au travers des traditions et des évènements . . . Il faudra donc dire tantôt nos regrets, tantôt peut-être nos dédains, pour le passé; nos efforts . . . pour le présent; nos espérances . . . pour l'avenir . . .
>
> Le présent, le passé, l'avenir, relativement à la société en général, peuvent donc, à toutes les époques, et surtout aux époques de fin et de renouvellement, offrir le sujet de trois épopées réunies par une pensée unique, ancienne dans un ordre de chose et d'idées, nouvelle dans un autre ordre, et néanmoins toujours identique et toujours homogène; et ces trois épopées ainsi réunies ne formeraient qu'une seule et vaste trilogie.[18]

Ballanche audaciously imitated the plan of Dante. He, too, wanted to visit the mysterious regions where human destiny was determined, though without benefit of the frightening invocations of the Middle Ages. Because he was essentially gentle, his inspiration came instead from the concepts of emancipation and grace. Life, for him, passed, not under the fear of hell fire, but in the promise of complete civil liberty.

The entire philosophy of the *Palingénésie,* as Ballanche admitted, rested on the assumptions of Charles Bonnet, the Geneval naturalist and philosopher. Sixty years previous, Bonnet had concluded after a lifetime of research that there existed "un parallélisme parfait entre le système astronomique et le système organique; entre les divers états de la terre, considérée cômme planète ou comme monde, et les divers états des êtres qui devaient peupler ce monde."[19] He then proceeded to prove by analogy what he considered a new metaphysics: that the various forms of life may be arranged in a hierarchy, beginning with the most infinitesimal matter and progressing through the universe to those pure intelligences said to surround God.

The philosophy which Ballanche inherited from Bonnet boasted a long and hoary history. The notion of a graduated chain of beings seems first to have appeared when later generations fused two unrelated hypotheses of Plato and Aristotle which, when juxtaposed, produced the concept of world-soul in a form that was to exercise tremendous influence for centuries to come. From Plato, Plotinus borrowed the theory that the universe contained all the possible forms a perfect God could produce, adding to this an interpretation of Aristotle's law of continuity. Since Aristotle had maintained that "things are said to be continuous whenever there is one and the same limit of both wherein they overlap and which they possess in common," Plotinus assumed that things alike in quantity constitute a similar series.[20] The universe thus arranged itself in a sequence of forms stretching from the least possible existent to that intelligence nearest God.

In the Middle Ages, Augustine and the pseudo-Dionysius conceded the probability of the Neoplatonic cosmology and willed it to their successors in the Renaissance. Here, under the influence of the geographical and astronomical discoveries of Columbus, Kepler, and Tycho Brahé, this explanation underwent a modification in the hands of men like Giordano Bruno.[21] Though it led him to the stake, Bruno, as an ardent admirer of Copernicus, flung the limits of the chain of beings into the infinite, lengthening the ladder of life through space, one end lowered into unplumbed depths, the other raised to a God beyond the planets.

The eighteenth century picked up the philosophy from the Renaissance after it had lain more or less dormant for a century in the face of belligerent Catholicism. Leibniz and Spinoza eyed it favorably, though Voltaire attacked the chain of being with all the skill of his vituperative pen. Prior to the second half of the eighteenth century, adherents to the idea had accepted the concept of an unchanging continuum of living forms. However, under the attacks of the rationalists, its followers, among them Herder and Bonnet, adjusted their principles to meet the opposition by infusing motion into a hitherto motionless creation.

Four implications had stood out in the earlier form of the philosophy: 1) Each link of the chain existed, not to complete the fullness of the world, but for its own sake. Though unequal in dignity, all existents shared an equal claim to life. Their importance depended upon their respective relation to the whole, since the universe was created for the manifestation of all possible forms.[22] 2) Man occupied the middle link of the chain, not numerically, since more forms were believed to lie above than below him, but as the transition from the sentient to the intellectual.[23] 3) Thus, mankind differed infinitesimally from the nearest non-human series. 4) And, because of this, man possessed a dual nature that forced him to live in constant discord with himself. Since somewhere in the scale there must be a species in which the senses begin to yield to the intellect, man was elected to that dubious honor.

Various uses were made of this philosophy. Some deduced from it an ethics of "prudent mediocrity." Because every rung of the ladder must be filled, man's duty required him to keep his place; he sinned if he coveted advance or sank below his level. Others, more gloomy, found in it a potent weapon against popular discontent and equalitarian movements. The limitations of the masses, their low position in the scale, prevented attainment of a high degree of political enlightenment. Consequently, any hope of improvement in the social status of the average citizen flew in the face of reality. The universe was the best of possible universes, for God had engendered infinite variety only through inequality. These "optimists" pointed out that the divine will considered as essential the subordination of taxpayers, though, theoretically, a subordination without subservience.

Subtlety led these eighteenth-century scholastics into pitfalls. As Voltaire noted sharply, their argument stole from most men any hope for happiness in this world or the next.[24] Since the universal good necessitated the presence of evil, none could disappear. Had God created evil? All links must be filled, therefore no one could advance or fall without detriment to another. Of what use was virtue then? Had a just God condemned his creatures to slavery? He was answered in a manner which acknowledged the truth of the observation yet nullified his criticism. The proponents of "optimism" evaded the charges by placing the universe on a time basis as ever-developing. Although an existent occupied each link of the chain, they replied, nature constantly prepared new ones for individuals moving up or down. The destiny of man, therefore, changed from inaction and long-suffering to progressive self-transcendence.

Bonnet's contribution to the stream of ideas consisted in opposing Voltaire and the rationalists by offering proof for this conception of the universe. With less imagination, but far more scientific information, he accepted the pattern of life at which *Candide* jeered:

Un même Dessein général embrasse toutes les Parties de la Création. Un Globule de lumière, une Molécule de terre, un Grain de sel, une Moisissure, un Polype, un Coquillage, un Oiseau, un Quadrupède, l'Homme ne sont que différents traits de ce Dessein, qui représente toujours les Modifications possibles de la Matière de notre Globe. Mon expression est trop au-dessous de la réalité: ces Productions diverses ne sont pas différents Traits du même Dessein; elles ne sont que différents points d'un Trait unique, qui par ses circonvolutions infiniment variées, trace aux yeux du CHÉRUBIN étonné, les formes, les proportions et l'enchaînement de tous les Mondes, le CHÉRUBIN lui-même n'en est qu'un point, et la MAIN ADORABLE qui traça ce Trait, possède seule la manière de la décrire.[25]

His *Palingénésie philosophique* reproduced a familiar portrait of a progression of souls in which every possible form of life existed. The eighteen or twenty thousand varieties of plants known to Bonnet he classified as sections of a ladder of life which led to the animal world and to the planets.[26] At the head of the visible world stood man, himself divided into *échelons* ranging from *l'homme brut* to *l'homme pensant*. Thus Bonnet arrived at a second infinity, for which man served as the starting point. The sequence spiraled upward from one planet to another into the realm of pure intelligences. As the individual left earth, he entered a land where the sight of God rewarded the virtuous:

LÀ, comme des ASTRES resplendissants, brillent les HIÉRARCHIES CÉLESTES.

LA rayonnent de toutes parts les ANGES, les ARCHANGES, les SÉRAPHINS, les CHÉRUBINS, les TRÔNES, les VERTUS, les PRINCIPAUTÉS, les DOMINATIONS, les PUISSANCES.

Au centre de ces AUGUSTES SPHÈRES, éclate le SOLEIL DE JUSTICE, l'ORIENT d'EN HAUT, dont tous les autres ASTRES empruntent leur lumière et leur splendeur.[27]

III

Ballanche knew well the works of his predecessor, had, in fact, so much confidence in him that he borrowed outright the title *Palingénésie* as best fitting his own thought. More than that, the preface of the *Palingénésies sociales* announced a closer bond than that of intellectual offspring: "Ce que Charles Bonnet a essayé pour l'homme individuel, je l'ai tenté pour l'homme collectif: l'ouvrage que j'imprime aujourd'hui a été écrit tout entier dans cette vue."[28] The three sections of the book, therefore, were dominated by the same thought, the metamorphoses man had undergone in a divinely inspired society. He scarcely hoped to be as successful as Bonnet in unveiling the plan of Providence, though he did expect to demonstrate that such a design did exist.

Ballanche's primary concern lay in portraying only that portion of the chain occupied by humanity. According to him, man followed a destiny bound to, yet distinct from, the rest of the creation. He hoped to present for the first time an exact tableau of society from its inception to its highest development. His intention demanded a synthesis of history that would permit foreseeing the future. The other aspects of the metaphysical problem he left to Bonnet.

According to the *Palingénésie,* the presence of man on earth itself implies a punishment, since, according to all religions, he must undergo a lifetime of trials. Man is held to conquer first his own dignity, then the grandeur of a destiny.[29] Taken from eternity, humanity has been circumscribed by time, made successive and susceptible to perfection. No human escapes this law; the individual and the collectivity are subjected to the same conditions of existence.[30]

Immediately after the creation, man spread out to populate the earth, judiciously guided by Providence. Each tribe carried with it some of the traditions common to mankind. Instinct prompted these groups to raise in the wilderness cities in the primitive mentality, cast almost in the form of hieroglyphics, plastic myths of social institutions. In the following age came colonization, the mixture of races, and the modification of the original traditions and institutions.[31] In these pre-historic traditions Ballanche believed could be found the law of the universe:

> Les données de l'histoire servent à compléter l'histoire: ainsi, en appliquant à l'avenir le principe de la loi qui a réglé le passé, nous parvenons à concevoir l'avenir. Mais lorsqu'en reculant jusqu'à la région du dogme et du mythe, et qu'ensuite nous portons nos regards dans l'avenir, il faut que l'analogie nous offre encore le dogme et le mythe.[32]

Ballanche first perceived a fact which he believed inflexible: After his downfall, man had accepted responsibility for his own actions, thus acquiring a capacity for good and evil. In creating the universe, God made this fundamental, though he reserved the right to interfere in human affairs. This arrangement of semi-responsibility presented Ballanche with a neat manner of solving the problem of evil. God could not be blamed for it; if evil resulted from excess liberty, the fault lay with humanity. Only conscience controls man, albeit a conscience progressively more capable of overcoming the obstacles God raises.[33] Eventually the social solidarity that fused men together would yield to the more desirable spirit of charity as individuals grew more cognizant of the meaning of life.[34] Evolution slowly carried society to this far-distant existence, though Ballanche thought his contemporaries insufficiently detached from the pantheistic whole to appreciate the fact. And he uttered advice to be followed by many in the romantic school along the lines he was himself tracing: "nous devons toujours travailler à deviner la grande énigme de nous-mêmes, qui est l'énigme de l'univers."[35]

Following Bonnet, Ballanche supposed that individual evolution continued in a super-life. As soon as man reached the limit of terrestrial evolution, he entered the world of pure intelligences. Providing the individual considered life a means and heeded the precepts of religion, he qualified for the next world. If not, he passed into another body, losing all memory of former life.[36]

Once free of the earth, the soul entered the new realm with the degree of perfection previously attained. Former acts and thoughts perished with the body, and man gained new faculties for a new environment. Here the climb began again, from one stage to another, even from one sphere to another. But, whereas Bonnet had confidently guessed at the metampsychoses to be undergone, Ballanche could not. Man was an *être palingénésique* but no one knew when his transformations would end.[37] Each world, perhaps, had its superior creature and a goal to be reached.

These views on the super-life seem to have been inherited not only from Bonnet, but also from Alexandrian Fathers, whose works had long furnished Ballanche with reading materials. A traditional belief in hellfire seemed to the sensitive Lyonnais equivalent to accusing God of creating evil. Hence he applied to Catholicism his views on progress. By reiterating the formula which Philonian exegesis had suggested to the Alexandrians, *littera occidit, spiritus vivificat,* he prophesied that Catholicism would abandon the doctrine of eternal damnation for his own theory of final pardon. This theological thesis of forgiveness, consequently, carried him outside the pale as far as most of his contemporaries were concerned.[38]

Ballanche's philosophy also departed from that of Bonnet in that it ignored the orders below man. Whereas Bonnet had treated chiefly of the lower chain, Ballanche considered these links important only as they affected humanity. The animals, to be sure, share in the original curse, since they were named in Genesis, thus partaking to a limited extent in social solidarity. Yet they were doomed, as Ballanche mystically believed, somehow to be absorbed by man.[39]

IV

Within the structure of this metaphysics lay the core of Ballanche's thought. Not only was he concerned with the evolution of life in general, he more especially meditated on the development of social structure. This occurred simultaneously with the rise of the individual up the chain, since man also formed part of a collectivity which existed in its own right. Actually, the prolegomena were more concerned with explaining the violent clash of nineteenth-century social forces than with the mechanics of the universe.

As Ballanche well understood, one of the sharpest divisions of contemporary opinion originated from a conflict over property and the power implicit in ownership. As few of his friends, he sensed that his age was preparing *Das Kapital*. He had little sympathy for contemporary socialism or its attempts to adjust the distribution of wealth. This verged on the sacrilegious for, as an erstwhile pillar of the Lyon commercial world, he considered the right to hold property of divine origin. Mine and thine formed an institution as necessary to society as the family, Rousseau notwithstanding. Property, language and society were insolubly wedded.[40]

However sacred the concept of property, Ballanche recognized it as the principal source of social discontent, historically and actually. In Rome, the monuments had revealed that new institutions developed from the friction between two groups, the patricians and the plebeians. In the *Palingénésie* the terms appear frequently, but with esoteric meanings personal to Ballanche:

> Le patriciat sera la spontanéité, le plébéianisme sera la force évolutive; l'Orient et l'Occident, l'infini et le fini, la permanence et la progression, l'initiation et la faculté de recevoir l'initiation; l'humanité envelopée et se développant, en puissance et en acte, diverse et la même, multiple et identique.[41]

And for all his conservatism, Ballanche leaned heavily in favor of the people, perhaps in recognition of his own origins and his efforts to gain a hearing in aristocratic Paris.

Ballanche's sociological theories stemmed directly from his metaphysics. After the Fall, the patrician was the first to understand the nature of existence. Before others, he appreciated the necessity for developing his faculties and hence could realize his potentialities. This knowledge held so much power that the few possessing it jealously prevented others from sharing in what they considered a perpetual and incommunicable right. The plebeian, on the other hand, was the primitive who had failed to comprehend the utility of a social structure and thus learned too late of the function of property. After the first division of wealth, or as Ballanche called it, *la première loi agraire,* the plebeian was forced to accept conditions imposed by the patrician in order to share in social benefits. The first laws, then, decidedly favored the aristocracy. The patrician identified himself with the ownership of the soil, protecting his position with laws calculated to uphold the prerogatives of a small group. Only he had ancestors, because he alone could marry; only he owned property because no other could have children entitled to inherit. He restricted to himself the privilege of tombs in order to destroy in the plebs any concept of family continuity. And to avoid protest against these actions, the primitive aristocrat preached the divine origin of property and the doctrine of property limitation. Through religion the *status quo* became fixed and the plebeian could only accept conditions forced on him. Thus he aided the patrician in the first struggle against the elements, uprooted forests, sowed crops and built houses. His task was to wrench order from chaos, but for his master to enjoy.[42]

After the subjugation of the elements, however, the plebeian could measure his own position. The work had been his, the labor and the pain; he was the productive source of social good. Inevitably reacting to the prodding of Providence, he rebelled against enslaving institutions, and a new phase of the social struggle began when the plebeian obtained a right to the soil.

According to Ballanche, progress demanded a continual reversal of rôles. The patrician of one epoch had been the plebeian of its predecessor. During the three ages he considered, historic, heroic, and cosmogonic, the plebeian and the patrician successively displaced each other. Thus, up to the time of the patriarchs of the Bible, the plebs had established three fundamental social principles:

> La première loi agraire fut la propriété personnelle et la limitation des ordres; elle établit les rapports respectifs de patron et de client. Le plébéien cesse d'être *pecunia*.
> La seconde loi agraire primitive fut la dignité humaine, manifestée par le mariage. Le plébéien entre dans l'humanité; il devient susceptible d'acquérir par la propriété une famille et des tombeaux.
> La troisième loi agraire fut la propriété transmissible, et le mariage produisant des effets civils. Le plébéien fait partie de la cité; il devient apte aux magistratures.[43]

When the inevitable subject of religion arose in connection with social evolution, Ballanche reiterated his former stand: that Catholicism offered the perfect form of religious institution. He even went farther. Christianity not only was the aim of mankind, but even prior to Christ its mysteries had impregnated all traditions and primitive religions. Christianity, or better still, Catholicism, had been expected for centuries. Explained in its general sense, as the core of human spiritual values, it was the only true plebeian religion. Because this seemed obvious, Ballanche predicted that the emancipation of man would come from the abolition of the difference between the religion of the people and that of the intellectuals.[44] Meanwhile the moment had come for governments to make professions of faith that included all social liberties by recognizing progress as synonymous with Christianity and Christianity as the law of human emancipation.[45]

The nineteenth century seemed to offer to Ballanche great promise of long strides toward this ideal. Tired of the mournful heritage of the eighteenth century, it stirred restlessly to disengage itself from all-enveloping incredulity. The only salvation for the proponents of Voltairianism of the past was to reject a deism that warped their political outlook. One of the greatest tasks facing the nineteenth century was the necessity of conquering its predecessor. There was reason to hope. Had not war been outlawed by civilization? Ballanche's pacifism convinced him that even the most important social questions would henceforth be settled amicably.

Ballanche saw further justification for optimism in the state of contemporary literature. His colleagues had finally realized that all artistic production centered in the people.[46] The prophets of gloom ranted that poetry had shrivelled in the hot breath of the new age, but this Ballanche stoutly denied. "N'avons-nous pas à notre disposition tous les évènements anciens éclairés par un jour nouveau?"[47] History could pump new blood into the muses by binding art to the age that produced it, the only true unity for art.

Progressively the poets of the nineteenth century were realizing the literary potentialities of the concept of a chain of beings. Soon, perhaps, they would recognize the symbolism implicit in all forms of matter and begin to construct their works on new premises. Ballanche stated these premises and, in so doing, he not only traced a theory to be accepted by the philosophically minded of the romantic age, a Lamartine, for instance, but he also added to the precepts uttered in former works to produce an elementary form of the æsthetics to be proposed many years later by the Symbolists:

> Tout est symbole, et ceci explique l'immortalité, la vie future. Notre vie est symbolique. La poésie et les arts, comme la vie, sont symboliques; et c'est à ce caractère symbolique, qui est leur essence, qu'est due l'immortalité de leurs oeuvres.[48]

The function of the artist, then, was to strip the veneer from reality to uncover the essence of the idea of things.

In further anticipation of later writers, like Vigny in *la Bouteille à la mer,* Ballanche also developed a new conception of the epic with his insistence that "l'histoire du genre humain dans les divers âges de la société" was the only subject of epic breadth. "Le représentant des idées d'un siècle, le législateur d'un peuple, le fondateur d'un empire: voilà le héros de l'épopée."[49] With this phrase Ballanche renewed completely this type of literature. He had forged an epic cycle that widened the horizon of philosophically minded poets, to break the restrictions that the *Martyrs* seemed to have set on modern epic poetry.[50] Under this definition can be placed Lamartine's *Visions,* some of which probably spring from Ballanche,[51] Vigny's *Poèmes antiques et modernes,* and, finally, Hugo's *Légende des siècles.*[52]

V

Ballanche trod firmly in the steps of his century when he undertook to publish the *Palingénésie.* In 1826, Jouffroy had offered the public a course on the philosophy of history; the next year Quinet published a three-volume translation of Herder, while Michelet followed suit with Vico's *Scienza nuova.* The nineteenth century had made so much history in such a short time that it began to reflect on other ages. It sought roots and more than one puzzled thinker found himself, like Ballanche, scurrying back into the past for explanations. More than ever before, France had become conscious of the future.

Ballanche cannot claim to be the first to have presented a ready-made philosophy of history to the nineteenth century, but he ranks among the leaders. Three years before the publication of the *Palingénésie,* while in Rome, he had discovered the Italian philosopher. On his return he brought a hearty respect for the *Scienza nuova,* which he immediately recommended to Bredin.[53]

The *Scienza nuova,* encountered early in the formation of Ballanche's philosophy, exercised a limited influence over the *Palin-*

génésie in that it strengthened ideas already possessed by the Lyon printer. Both men assumed that history unfolded in accordance with a divinely conceived plan, the pattern of which could be found in prehistoric myths and ancient traditions. They agreed, too, that progress depended largely on the whim of a watchful Providence. Long before Ballanche, Vico had found history divided into three ages: theocratic, heroic, and civilized. From this he deduced that the friction between the people and the aristocrats motivated progress by propelling society from theocracy to aristocracy, thence to democracy. Since Vico considered this last form of government degenerate, he noted with pleasure that popular government normally floundered until repeated errors forced a revival of monarchy. In the last instance, Vico proposed a social change that Ballanche could not accept. Vico maintained that progress might be described graphically as a spiral, the loops of which widen with every added circle. Each new government contributed to the advance, though monarchy most of all. Ballanche, however, refused to proceed beyond the democratization of society, for no other form of government seemed better adapted for the furtherance of what he considered the good life. Moreover, he saw no mathematical curve to progress. So much human effort went into sheer muddling that the most he could say was that society eventually developed for the better.

Ballanche knew that many of his contemporaries would notice the resemblance between his work and that of Vico, especially those intimates who knew he was occupied on a translation of Vico's treatise: *De antiqua Italorum sapientia, ex linguae latinae originibus eruenda.* Consequently, in the edition of 1830, he carefully explained that he had read the Italian jurisconsult, had even considered the advisability of translating him for the benefit of France when he learned that several philosopher-historians were already busy with such a project. He pointed out, too, that the book he had meant to write would have included a refutation of much of Vico, principally because of the latter's insistence on the degeneracy of humanity immediately after the Flood, and his contention that only the Jews shared in the primitive traditions.[54] Nor did he find palatable the theory that the religions of antiquity had been founded on a fear of thunder, an intriguing if ridiculous notion.[55] This he noted for possible detractors, with a bow in the direction of Michelet, the young man who had published the works of Vico while the first edition of the *Palingénésie* was still on the presses.

VI

Some similarity of views likewise evokes the suspicion that Ballanche felt the influence of another noted foreigner, this time Herder, a suspicion that grows with added knowledge of each of Ballanche's early works.[56] Certainly Pierre-Simon had ample opportunity to read the German philosopher's theories for, even prior to *Du Sentiment,* Herder's dissertation had seemed sufficiently important to warrant a French translation. That Ballanche had carefully considered some of Herder also seems likely since his first book included a note calling attention to Hemsterhuis's translation. Later Ballanche certainly read Quinet's translation of the *Idées.*

Definite similarities of ideas seem to indicate Ballanche as a prospective disciple for the German philosopher. In Herder he could find optimistic confirmation of his theory of sorrow, and of expiation as the condition of progress. Both showed man in constant struggle with nature; both indicated humanity's need to return to the lessons of experience. For each the faculty of speech ruled the mind, controlling and uniting all other faculties.

But the principal likeness lies in Ballanche's use of the concept of Nemesis. In the chapter "De la Mélancolie," along with other allegories of a moral aim, Ballanche mentions "le beau symbole de Némésis, fille de la Nécessité, veillant à ce que l'homme n'ait pas le temps de s'enorgueiller de la constance de la fortune." To emphasize this point, the author recalls the fate of Polycrates and Paul Emile, both victims of suddenly shifting fortune. And the *Notes* expressly mention the excellent dissertation of Herder, even quoting several bits "précieux par leur antiquité et par la beauté de leurs idées."

In *Antigone,* this symbol so dear to Herder reappeared, but in a more prominent position. At the beginning, when Tirésias set down his lyre to avoid saddening the audience, his daughter Daphne sang an invocation to Nemesis as an antidote to her father's tale. Ballanche had by then attached to Nemesis some of his own theory of individual sorrow and had promoted the goddess to the rank of Providence's chosen instrument of execution. It was as such that she would visit upon the nameless man punishment for his fault.

And yet, for all the apparent resemblances, and despite Ballanche's preoccupation with myths and language, it is seriously to be doubted that the Lyon philosopher experienced any great influence from his German contemporary. True, Ballanche had adapted for his philosophy of history a concept important to Herder's thought but, beyond this, serious differences separated the two men. Whereas Herder, for instance, considered death a benefit in itself, Ballanche ignored it as but a momentary break between existences. Likewise, Ballanche's theory of *épreuve* and *expiation* sharply differentiated the Frenchman from the German.

It is not exact to state that Ballanche copied anyone; rather it should be noted that he and Herder were of the same intellectual caliber, two idealistic dreamers, prophets who opposed art for art's sake, so comparable in many ways that the *Mercure de France au XIXᵉ siècle* could aptly remark that Germany had a greater admiration than France for "ce Ballanche aux vues immenses." With some slight inspiration from Herder, Ballanche developed a theory of mythology to aid the *idée palingénésique,* although most of his ideas were original. The delicate sense of tradition with which he tried to complete Bonnet he found in himself, perhaps in reaction against the eighteenth century. Even his taste for myths was personal. From antiquity he asked not what Herder sought, but a legend to envelop the thoughts stirring within him, or he went back into the past with philology as a new tool for prying into old symbols. The theory of the rise of the plebs grew from a resistance to the more conservative de Maistre and to the doctrine of predestination. Neither Vico nor Herder can claim credit for that portion of his work. Ballanche probably even remained ignorant of Herder's application of the theory of a historical Nemesis. For his part, he adopted the notion principally as a weapon against the social contract and as a mechanism for explaining events disturbing to a proponent of progress and divine goodness.

With the *Palingénésie,* Ballanche turned his back forever on the apostles of the past and the conservative elements of the royalist faction. Not only did his doctrines imply a determined step in the direction of the people, but Ballanche removed all doubt as to his position by incorporating into the third part of the book a eulogy of the recently deceased de Maistre:

> L'homme des doctrines anciennes, le prophète du passé, vient de mourir. . . . Paix à la cendre de ce grand homme de bien! Gloire immortelle à ce beau génie! Maintenant qu'il voit la vérité face à face, sans doute, il reconnaît que ses rêves furent ceux d'une évocation brillante, mais stérile et sans puissance. Il voulut courber notre tête sous le joug d'un destin fini.[57]

It was Ballanche's answer to the letter de Maistre had written him after the publication of the *Essai.*

VII

Now in the maturity of his talent, Ballanche plunged ahead with the many books he had planned, simultaneously reviewing and enlarging some already published. He worked restlessly, unable to let harden the form of his thought. Revisions were constantly made or new notes added. The *Palingénésie* had no sooner appeared in a restricted edition than it became swollen with supplementary material. Likewise, in 1828, Ballanche decided to publish a second ediion of *l'Homme sans nom* with the *Palingénésie,* although he admitted the latter "n'était pas encore destinée au public."[58] The next year, 1829, he had printed the text of Vico's *De antiqua Italorum.* He had intended to prepare a translation, but, learning of Michelet's plans for a French edition of Vico, he abandoned all right to the work, at the same time sending to Michelet an unedited text of Vico of 1701, *Sur la conjuration de Naples.*[59] More important, however, than the *De antiqua* was the limited edition of *Orphée*[60] for which it served as part of the preface. Here again, Ballanche had succumbed to a fear of criticism by restricting to friends a book which he suspected might evoke violent reaction.[61]

Like the *Palingénésie, Orphée* had been long in the making. Since the time of *Du Sentiment,* Ballanche had been fascinated by the myth of the great singer of antiquity; the fourth book of Virgil's *Georgics* had always been one of his favorites. In the *Vieillard et le Jeune Homme,* he had spoken of a work in which Orphée would interpret dogmas that, according to him, formed the basis of human associations.[62] A plan of it must then have existed, for he mentioned the *Essai* as a bridge between the *Entretiens* and *Orphée*. The latter itself was to form the preface of another, more ambitious book, the *Formule générale*. The *Formule* never was completed, but indications suggest a series of discussions calling for four interlocutors: a poet, a philosopher, a historian, and a jurisconsult. From their conversations, much like those of the *Soirées de Saint-Pétersbourg*, would come Ballanche's philosophy.[63]

Orphée, however, had existed in manuscript form when Ballanche published the *Vieillard*. On October 16, 1817, Bredin wrote thanking Ballanche for the promise of the speedy arrival of several sections of the manuscript and the plan for the rest of the book.[64] The next year Bredin received the finished work for the criticism his friend had come to expect from him. As the date indicates, then, Ballanche stands as a precursor in much of what he said, but his literary bashfulness held back the book until long beyond the moment ripe for publication. Realizing this, Bredin began a lengthy correspondence urging Ballanche to relinquish his stories.[65] In April, 1820, he questioned the need for further delay since Ampère reported that parts of *Orphée* had already become conversational fare in the salons.[66] In 1823 he still wailed: "Hâte-toi donc d'imprimer, le temps presse. Hâte-toi de te délivrer," all to no avail.[67] Not until six years later could Bredin finally write the great news: "Cher ami, hier j'ai reçu les douze exemplaires de ce cher Orphée tant attendu; reçois-en mes remercîments."[68]

Orphée is another attempt on the part of Ballanche to write the great French epic along the lines laid down in the *Palingénésie*. As he conceived it, the fable formed part of a cycle when placed alongside his own *Antigone*, the *Iliad*, the *Odyssey* and the *Æneid*. In form, *Orphée* is a humanitarian epic, but considering only its content, it may better be classified as a philosophy of history, for Ballanche's principal aim was to show the general continuity of human thought. The story synthesizes the first fifteen centuries of the history of man in an effort to indicate how Egyptian traditions become Greek, then Roman. It departs from the classic tale in that Eurydice does not die of snakebite escaping from Aristée, but because she dared love Orpheus. The latter's descent into Hell receives only cursory mention, and the poet is not killed by Menades, but dies a natural death. Also, for no given reason, Tirésias is blind, like Homer. Sober use is made of the marvelous, though it is to be noticed that the death of Erigone follows closely that of Velléda in the *Martyrs*.[69]

From the Latin fable, of a more cosmogonic character than the Greek version, Ballanche hoped to penetrate the symbolism of the myth itself. His story was constructed to make the reader feel rather than see the growth of civilization. Man is portrayed as detaching himself from the pantheistic whole, beginning a slow evolution to a state wherein an evolving Christianity would abolish class distinctions and property restrictions.[70] And yet, for all its ancient flavor, *Orphée* was really a poem, Alexandrian in form, which proffered the nineteenth century what Ballanche had been preaching for the past ten years.

Orpheus, therefore, was not treated as an historical, nor even as a mythological, personage. For literary purposes he acts as a contemporary of Hercules, but since he symbolizes a tradition, the question of his actual existence vanishes. This manner of envisaging the epic hero may have seemed a novelty, but it resulted from Ballanche's attempt to deal primarily with ideas. Orpheus represents the birth of society and the first trials submitted by the people. He is plebeian, a teacher, one of the Messiahs of whom the *Palingénésie* had treated. His function was to introduce a manner of life that would lead civilization to Christianity. As such, he might well have come from the aristocracy, but Ballanche believed that his poet had to come from the people. "La vérité est que les sympathies d'humanité générale ne peuvent naître dans la classe patricienne, mais dans la classe plébéienne."[71] His attitude originated perhaps from overlong contact with Chateaubriand.

Imitating the style of the ancients, Ballanche has the story of Orpheus, civilizer of Thrace, told by blind Thamyris to the pastor king of Latium, on the slope of a hill later known as the Aventine. Humanity had just discovered its conscience. The Titans, the Cyclops, and the Centaurs had disappeared; and the motionless Orient sat patiently while the West stirred restlessly. The Roman patriciat would soon rise, followed by an ambitious plebs, and the struggles of these two would emancipate humanity. Orpheus would promote this portentous change in fulfilling a destiny that required him to end the era of the ancient traditions of which Egypt had been depository. The lyre of Orpheus served Ballanche as the thunder had Vico. To the strains of his music, barbarism disappeared, the forests fell, animals were domesticated, property was born, marriage was instituted, and society reformed.[72]

The tremendous achievements of Orpheus cover nine books. Thamyris, a follower of Orpheus, and Evandre discuss his career (Book I). To satisfy Evandre's curiosity, Thamyris tells how Talaon, the last of the Titans, welcomed a stranger to his shores and, in recognition of Orpheus's mission, gave him his daughter Eurydice (Book II), how the poet civilized the Pélasges on a mission that brought death to Eurydice (Book III). Thamyris sang of the voyage to Samothrace (Book IV), and of Erigone's unhappy love for Orpheus (Book V). He followed Orpheus to Egypt, hoping to be initiated into the mysteries of the wise men (Books VI-VIII), but failing to satisfy them, he was sent to locate Orpheus. He found him, only to have the poet disappear into the clouds, not, however, before singing a last song about the approach of democracy and Christianity.

Orpheus's teachings in a large measure rested on a modified version of the chain of being. While in Egypt, Orpheus had a vision that explained to him the workings of the universe. Curiously enough, the vision parallels strikingly that which Lamartine maintained he saw on January 10, 1821, while on a walk near Naples. The date suggests precedence over Ballanche, but Lamartine did not reveal his experience until after Ballanche's death, when he was compiling the *Cours familier*.[73] Like Lamartine,[74] Orpheus first dropped into a trance:

> Je fus alors saisi d'une sorte de vertige, je m'échappai de la prison de mes organes, mon âme plana sur le monde. Il me sembla que, dans une illusion ravissante, ma pensée assistait au commencement des choses. . . .
>
> Les éléments sortaient du chaos avec leurs lois primitives et leurs propriétés, et ces lois gouvernent les atomes et les sphères célestes; et les sphères célestes agissent les unes sur les autres comme les atomes s'attirent et se repoussent.

La création fut pour moi l'acte d'un magisme divin; et cet acte, je sentais intuitivement qu'il était un acte continu, éternel.

Je vis la terre d'abord peuplée d'êtres, et cependant solitaire, à l'époque où aucun des êtres qui l'habitaient ne levait les yeux vers le ciel, ne savait contempler la lumière et l'ombre; et l'homme vint pour apprécier et connaître, pour prendre possession des solitudes inutilement enchantées de la terre, pour prendre possession de lui-même. . . .

Je devins cet homme par la puissance de sympathie, par la réalisation d'une synthèse primitive; je devins cet homme à qui la création tout entière apparut, une première fois, comme au sein d'un rêve magique. Je prophétisais donc, et je donnai un nom à toutes choses, et ce nom était l'essence de chaque chose.

Je fus quelques instants cet homme dont les facultés existaient, mais endormies, puis se réveillèrent, puis participèrent à la création.

Je fus cet homme universel qui, ayant saisi la responsabilité de ses pensées et ses actes, pécha et fut condamné.

Et le décret qui le condamna fut en même temps un décret de condescendance, puisqu'il était le moyen de reconquérir l'être perdu.

Je devins, après un malheur qui me paraissait irréparable, cet homme universel dispersé par la génération; je me sentis successif, de stable et de permanent que j'aurais dû être; et je compris comment Prométhée a été dit avoir fait l'homme; mais je compris en même temps qu'il n'avait résolu qu'une moitié du problème, celle de la responsabilité. . . .

Je compris ainsi la raison des épreuves de l'humanité, épreuves dont les mystères d'Isis offrent une image.

Et je connus les grandes harmonies du monde, les harmonies entre les éléments, les corps célestes, les individus des trois règnes de la nature, et l'homme.

J'appris que l'homme est un abrégé de l'univers, qu'à lui aboutissaient les influences des astres, aussi bien que celles des minéraux, des plantes, des espèces variées des êtres. . . .[75]

More clearly than in the *Palingénésie*, Ballanche sketched the classic portrait of the chain of being. Before Orpheus-Ballanche, as before Lamartine, streamed the sequence of form. As Hugo would write in *Ce que dit la bouche d'ombre*, life flowed from the bowels of the earth to the highest intelligence. What gaps occurred in the vision, Ballanche later had filled in by the priests from whom Thamyris sought instruction. To him they gave the doctrine of motion within the great structure, showed how merit determined the form of each essence.[76] This time, however, Ballanche laid more emphasis on the reason for the pattern of the vision. The scholars stressed to Thamyris that life existed only because man had been cursed. Precisely why, they could not say despite all their study. They admitted the unhappy coincidence of evil in a world created by a God who knew no evil, but could suggest nothing other than acceptance and prayer. Man, according to them, had to undergo rehabilitation through ordeal; he had to fight his way back to the infinite. Here, Ballanche seems to imply that evil resulted from the existence of time and would disappear progressively as mankind approached its original state.

More than ever, he was convinced that ultimate salvation lay in the people. For him they constituted the source of everything potentially good and beautiful. Thus, the function of Orpheus is to give the common man the tools with which to fashion a life for himself by his own intelligence, to build a consciousness of God and a sympathy for his fellows. Through music, the teacher would found various institutions commonly associated with a civilized state: the family, marriage, burial, and property. He would point out the continuous flux of life within the eternal unity of existence. In this respect, Ballanche formulated an elementary theory of evolution that echoed strangely from the mouth of Orpheus:

> Le globe que nous habitons, en sortant du chaos par la vertu insondable de la parole ordonnatrice, était doué d'une vie universelle; et cette vie universelle, sans cesser d'être la grande vie de tout ce qui a vie, va formant toujours, par un développement continu, des vies individuelles, qui elles-mêmes deviennent des sortes de vies universelles produisant à leur tour des races, des familles.[77]

A great part of *Orphée* merely reproduced arguments from the *Palingénésie,* but some of these yielded more far-reaching conclusions. He repeated his warning to the socialists concerning the divine origin of property, stressed the ultimate outlawing of war in future civilizations. With the reiteration of his views on the symbolism of the universe, he enlarged his first remarks to formulate specific doctrines later to be used by men like Rimbaud.[78]

Like Baudelaire and a great many poets after him,[79] Ballanche saw beyond the material into another world. Ultimate reality lay not on earth, but in the supernatural to which humanity aspired. For this reason, the priests of Egypt promised to teach Thamyris "qu'il y a une génération intellectuelle, dont la génération des êtres est une image imparfaite."[80] Thamyris himself, though gifted above his contemporaries, could not describe this other world. Words shrank or spilled over the boundaries of their meanings, giving only an impression of things seen:

> Trop souvent mon intelligence est restée au-dessous des choses dont j'étais témoin, des discours que j'entendais: les sphères des diverses facultés humaines, celles des différents degrés de civilisation, ayant entre elles et avec les sphères célestes de mystérieuses analogies; l'univers idéal et l'univers plastique correspondent l'un à l'autre; la pensée heurtant par-tout contre un centre universel d'-où rayonne incessament une circonférence infinie: mille notions confuses que j'ai peine à saisir moi-même.[81]

The function of the poet, then, was to seek the essence of meaning. Ballanche's advice apparently echoed the feeling of other writers, for soon many would be turning to Creuzer's great work for inspiration and guidance. More specifically, Rimbaud would meditate the following lines to the eternal profit of French literature:

> Mais ce qui étonne le plus, c'est que tout est symbolique, et qu'on a de suite un sentiment indéfinissable de ces créations symboliques. . . . La langue présente a un sens mystérieux et un sens littéral, un sens caché et un sens découvert, un sens profond et un sens superficiel. . . . Le apparences voilent toujours des réalités.[82]

With only worn-out words at his command, the poet must suggest to the mind and to the ear the existence of the parent world. He must also cultivate the capacities of a *voyant,* the better to recount things glimpsed. In Egypt, Thamyris is admonished by the priests to seek visions, the visions that surpass fantasy and material objectivity, venturing over the horizons of fact into the past, present, or, preferably, the future.[83]

Few could accomplish this. Ballanche, therefore, returned to the theory of the leader to point out that the great man of the future would seize the empire of poetry. By the time *Orphée* appeared, similar concepts had become commonplace. Almost all the romantics had felt the mantle of the Messiah slip onto their shoulders. Nevertheless, conscious of priority, Ballanche repeated that the new poetry had to show man's relationship to God and nature if it hoped for survival. A writer need only study man to create simultaneously the epic and the *drame*.[84] Ballanche expected that the young writers around him would at last found a strong school of philosophical poetry in the lyric form they cherished. For them, he placed nine strings in Orpheus's lyre, seven of them for ordinary music, but two of which "enseignaient la dignité humaine, fondée sur la conviction d'une essence unique."[85] And to clinch the argument, he added example to precept:

> Genèse obscure:
> Le chaos
> Genèse lumineuse:
> Le monde,
> l'être. . . .
>
> Les âmes humaines
> Lorsqu'elles descendent la première fois
> Sur la terre,
> Viennent de Sphaïros.[86]

VIII

The same faults that marred Ballanche's other books appeared in *Orphée,* though here the author's hand was somewhat surer. Obviously, the book was intended only for those already initiated into the writer's thought; no attempt was made to make the prose-poem palatable to the public. But even a limited audience did not save Ballanche from his usual state of embarrassment. No thread of logic connected the sections; used to seeking subtleties, the Lyon philosopher often employed hidden analogies that seem digressions. Demands are made of the reader to collaborate continually in unifying the book. Ballanche had so much to say that he stuttered. He used intuition to such an extent that the reader sometimes loses the meanderings of his mind.

Yet, on the other hand, Ballanche had meditated so long over his philosophy by the time of the publication of *Orphée* that it lost some of the vagueness evident in the *Palingénésie.* Orpheus told what was in Ballanche's mind as clearly as these thoughts ever were to be expressed by him. *Orphée* is not the reconstruction of a past era. Only in a general way did Ballanche pretend to establish a fitting background for his characters. He insisted primarily on conveying an attitude and a frame of mind which he considered necessary for the completion of the task facing his century.

In the fulfillment of this task, Ballanche had so closely attuned himself to the various attitudes and opinions of his contemporaries as to drop tentatively over the edge of accepted theology into the occult. Most of his illuministic reminiscences appear in the chapters dealing with Thamyris's stay in Egypt, where the priests discuss the mysteries of the universe. The name Egypt simply symbolizes the wisdom of the age Ballanche was discussing, though often the priests seem to speak from out of the nineteenth century.

It is difficult to associate Ballanche with any specific illuminists. He had read so much occult literature that a multitude of sources might be cited, but this does not establish a definite influence. There may have been contact with the *martinistes* and the Freemasons of Lyon, but of this there can be no certainty. It is apparent only that Ballanche trod close to illuminism in *Orphée,* whatever the origin of his ideas, thereby associating with many distinguished figures.

Certainly, illuminism throve in the nineteenth century atmosphere of curiosity. Plain mysticism or a desire to replace Catholicism had led many into strange fields. Not only did one hear the old familiar names, Pico de la Mirandola, Saint-Martin, or Fabre d'Olivet, but there were countless others, the marquis de Puységur, the duchesse de Bourbon, and the abbé Faria. Swedenborgism grew when Moët translated during the Empire the in-folios of the master, and the disciples like Captain Bernard searched France for prospective converts. Edouard Richer formed a mystic cénacle at Paris to which came all interested in the new theology. Œgger found it so entrancing that he abandoned the post of grand-vicar of Notre-Dame to consort with Le Boys des Guays and Richer. Each had his own doctrine, sometimes a hodge-podge of borrowings, rarely with a few original ideas. In general, they all supposed that the universe had emanated from, and returned to, God. Many professed a fondness for a variation of the chain of being, and almost all talked vaguely of the "harmony" of the universe, albeit a harmony inextricably interwoven with somnambulism, Free-Masonry, miraculous cures, and the Pythagorean theory of numbers. The age, full of the credible desperately in search of grand beliefs, was the Utopia of the occult philosopher. It is not strange that Ballanche brushed close to them; no curious man could have avoided their doctrines.

CHAPTER VII

1830—Friends and Disciples

I

*O*rphée brought Ballanche a measure of success, but the energy he used up dragging out his ideas for publication so worried Madame Récamier that, in 1829, when she went to visit Dieppe for a much needed rest from salon life, she bundled Ballanche off with her. By now the Lyon philosopher had become indispensable for her comfort on trips. Of the entire group, the hazy-minded Ballanche seemed the only person capable of concern with the prosaic detail of Madame Récamier's well-being. He had demonstrated remarkable ability for satisfying the numerous travellers who usually accompanied her on periodic trips, carefully planning the itinerary, procuring reading for every taste, fussing over the baggage, even selecting the day of departure. All this he performed with the equanimity of a born philosopher, for Ballanche well knew that some whim of the highly individualistic entourage might momentarily force a complete reorganization of arrangements.

Once in Dieppe, Madame Récamier installed Ballanche in a tower where he could work in peace during the time allotted for literary labors. He worked feverishly at revising the *Palingénésie,* added to *Orphée,* and dreamt of a *Zénobie,* an epic of the first days of Christianity. When bored with these pursuits, he jotted down notes for his *Ville des Expiations* or the *Vision d'Hébal.*[1] Madame Récamier, however, made certain that he rested sufficiently. A large part of the day was spent reading or talking to her. This he enjoyed immensely, now that Chateaubriand and other annoying rivals stayed in distant Paris. It was extremely pleasant to be alone with her, explaining the subtleties of his ideas as he stared out over the sea.

The inevitable return to Paris brought hard reality. He entered a world where Chateaubriand was enjoying all the prestige of having

written *Moïse,* readings of which Ballanche had attended at the
Abbaye during the month of June. Furthermore, he needed money
badly; at the end of November, 1829, he had been forced to borrow
four thousand francs from Jean-Jacques Ampère, no rich man
himself.[2] His political faith, too, had been shaken badly by recent
events. The perverse and stupid attitude of Charles X slowly
brought the realization that the Bourbons were about to make
another botch of personal rule. The formation of the Polignac
ministry left no doubt as to the direction in which the government
was heading, one completely objectionable to Ballanche. Since the
House of France had failed to heed countless warnings, Ballanche
decided to let it run its course.

He busied himself with his own affairs. In 1830 appeared his
Oeuvres complètes,[3] unconsciously reminding France how many of
his ideas had been converted to action since the appearance of
Du Sentiment. There had been, of course, much revising. Nothing
seems to have been able to keep Ballanche from adding constantly
to his work, but, for the most part, the *Oeuvres* contained the
essential part of all he had ever written. The notable exception was
Du Sentiment. Ballanche had refused to include it for several important reasons. First, the meaning of the word *sentiment* had
changed since the year 1801, having since assumed a sense not
earlier known. At the least, he would have had to rewrite most of
the book to give it significance for the generation of 1830. More important, however, he feared to draw attention to the fact that *Du
Sentiment* contained a quantity of the same ideas as the *Génie du
Christianisme.* Many would believe that he was trying to crowd
into the glory of his great friend; others would compare dates and
make the re-publication an occasion for sneers at Chateaubriand.
Lastly, any attention drawn to the *Sentiment* surely would bring
grumbles of dissatisfaction from René himself.[4] Compensation, however, came from the very circumstances that had outmoded his
first book. The advice given so freely to the Bourbons in *l'Homme
sans nom* made timely a new edition of it. Many more people read
it than Ballanche had expected, and his fame expanded.

Repetition of what seemed elementary truths to the Lyon philosopher finally won coveted attention. The critics at last decided to take

him seriously now that events had impregnated so many of his apparently vague remarks with meaning. In June, 1830, E. V., of the staff of the *Revue de Paris,* looked with kindly eyes on the *Oeuvres complètes:*

> La publication des *Œuvres complètes* de M. Ballanche, événement plein d'intérêt pour le monde littéraire, produira une sensation non moins vive dans le monde philosophique. La réputation qui appartient comme écrivain à l'auteur d'*Antigone,* bien qu'elle nous paraisse devoir grandir encore est déjà formée. La critique a dès long-temps marqué à ce beau talent une place élevée et distincte. Mais la réputation qui appartient à l'auteur de la *Palingénésie sociale* comme créateur d'un système dont les diverses branches se rattachent à la science religieuse, à la politique et à l'érudition, est encore entourée de quelque mystère. . . . Désormais on ne pourra séparer en M. Ballanche l'écrivain du philosophe. Il acquiert le droit d'être jugé tout entier.[5]

The review was studded with such expressions as "l'harmonie du style" or "de vastes connaissances." E. V. acknowledged him the legitimate heir of Vico, a man to be classed with Lessing and Herder. For once a critic handled Ballanche tenderly and with an attitude of respect.

Yet, although the critics said what Ballanche had always wanted to hear, the sale of the *Oeuvres* made him no richer. He was forced to ask M. de Barante to inquire of the Ministry of the Interior or the Ministry of Public Information whether the government would buy a number of copies, but Barante replied that funds for 1830 had been exhausted and that nothing could be promised until the following year.[6] Ballanche had had to swallow his pride to take such a step, but, as he wrote to Madame Récamier, "la question est donc de savoir si mon nom doit subsister; s'il ne doit pas subsister, je me serais donné bien du chagrin en pure perte."[7]

Thus it was with a jaundiced eye that Ballanche viewed the Bourbons when the July days began. He had been at Dieppe again with Madame Récamier for a short stay in company with the abbé Lacordaire. For the latter's benefit he had given in the city cemetery a reading of a new episode of the *Palingénésie,* the *Vision d'Hébal,* in which the style of the Apocalypse was used for a general plan of the history of the world.[8] When the news of the *Ordonnances* arrived, he sniffed trouble in the wind and departed post-haste for

Paris. At Rouen he met Sainte-Beuve in the coach and together they ended their trip. Travel was slow, broken at every relay by countless small incidents; passengers kept entering or leaving the coach. Ballanche seemed disinterested in the news pouring in from the capital, but inwardly he seethed. When the fate of the Bourbons seemed obvious, he turned to his friend and remarked: "Je crois bien que pour le coup nous allons franchir deux degrés d'initiation à la fois."[9] And he began to laugh.

II

With the Bourbons gone, France changed rapidly. After the Restoration a strong yeast seemed to be working France into great intellectual ferment. Some of the gay frivolity remained. The giraffe at the Jardin des Plantes still drew great crowds, though the new whale threatened to obscure its popularity. But in the main, France leaned to the serious side of life. Lady Morgan, returning to France after a long absence, noted that all values were being subjected to tests. The youth of the nation tended to republicanism, although it lacked the basis of reasoning. Sects of all kinds flourished. In literature, the romanticists and the classicists battled for supremacy on the stage, their struggle complicated by political undercurrents. Royalists, Jesuits, republicans, constitutionalists, and doctrinaires, their very existence denoted a period of transition in which the various attitudes and approaches toward all the great questions were provisional.[10] Most believed the unrest tokened a reawakening of the western world. Billot thought it a Catholic renaissance, but others preferred to consider the time ripe for a new religion. On all sides men groped and searched while the younger generation avidly followed its elders. "Nous étions," wrote Carnot, "à l'affût de toutes les manifestations philosophiques ayant une tendance religieuse. La *Palingénésie sociale* de Ballanche était en haute estime parmi nous; nous poussions nos recherches jusque dans les *Neuf livres* de M. Coëssin."[11]

Amidst the general stir of the times, Ballanche's philosophy came into its own. After 1830 he no longer was simply Madame Récamier's squire, but an author in his own right. 1830 helped him crawl out from Chateaubriand's shadow by giving him much of the confidence he lacked. He regretted little the fallen dynasty; having been its prophet in the wilderness, he wrote its epitaph without nostalgia:

> Une nation nouvelle s'était élevée, était sortie de son silence. . . . Cette nation nouvelle, pleine de force et de puissance, devait être civilisée: on a voulu d'abord la nier; ensuite, lorsque son existence n'a pu être méconnue, on a imaginé de la dédaigner.
>
> Pour la première fois, il a été dit à l'immense majorité d'une nation: Tu est privée de toute espèce de vertu; tu n'as que des vices odieux. Il y a, au milieu de toi, une petite minorité qui seule a des vertus, qui seule est dépourvue de vices: c'est à cette minorité que nous allons te livrer. . . .
>
> Les représentants du passé ont voulu refaire le passé. La société, qui ne sait jamais rebrousser en arrière, s'est arrêtée un instant; mais elle ne s'est arrêtée que pour s'étonner d'une telle démence. . . .
>
> Eh bien, puisque tu ne veux que le passé, réfugie-toi dans le passé et laisse-nous accomplir nos destinées. . . . Eh bien, puisque tu ne veux pas nous civiliser, nous nous civiliserons nous-mêmes.[12]

III

Instinctively, puzzled minds gradually began to turn to the new prophet as the reputation of the *Oeuvres* spread, to seek in his mystic words the answers to their questions. It was the age when Sainte-Beuve desperately hunted a doctrine behind which to shelter himself, when Lamennais evolved the ideas that would bring ex-communication, and when the majority of France's writers began to suspect that they needed intellectual anchors. A contemporary and a friend, Charles Lenormant, noted the astounding fervor with which the men of 1830 greeted the ideas incorporated in the *Oeuvres:*

> Il faut avoir jugé par soi-même de l'impression exaltée que causait la seule présence de M. Ballanche; il faut avoir vu des jeunes gens, qui, après avoir erré dans les ténèbres d'une fausse philosophie, avaient enfin entrevu le port en lisant *Orphée* et la *Palingénésie sociale*, se jeter, pour ainsi dire, à ses pieds, et l'adorer presque comme leur sauveur; il faut avoir été témoin de ces enthousiasmes sincères pour comprendre ce qui empêcha M. Ballanche d'en répudier l'entraîne-ment.[13]

Even by 1830, Ballanche could claim what his friends called a little "church." A group of writers had adopted him as god-father and refused to publish except at his direction.[14] The attention was exciting, but embarrassing.

This same attention came to Ballanche from more established writers, too, men like Senancour. Ballanche had sought him out to exchange philosophical opinions, and, when he felt his reputation solid enough, announced the intention of converting Senancour to Catholicism. For all this difference of opinion, their respect for each other was mutual and great. The ubiquitous Ferdinand Denis reports that Ballanche esteemed *Obermann* so highly that he was prone to state when its title was mentioned, "il y a de grands artistes ignorés."[15]

Another of the same generation, Charles Nodier, had been Ballanche's friend since shortly after the Lyon philosopher's arrival in Paris, and time knitted their friendship even closer. Nodier had for long wandered in search of a belief. Epicurean prior to 1800, then "homme sensible" until the dream offered him an attitude more befitting his temperament and a subject for research less shopworn, he finally ended his career with a defense of French traditions and popular legends. In his old age his perplexed mind found shelter in a Catholicism tinged with illuminism, the Catholicism of Ballanche.[16]

There can be little doubt that some, at least, of Nodier's beliefs came from the philosopher of the Abbaye-au-Bois. Nodier had long known Ballanche's master, Charles Bonnet, and had in his turn tarried over the chain of being. He had not arrived at the concept of the *Palingénesie sociale,* but had once considered embodying Bonnet's ideas in his novels. Thus the two men, Ballanche and Nodier, shared a common fondness for the doctrines of Bonnet which helped cement their own friendship, and, when Ballanche drew from the eighteenth century philosophy for his own books, he entered a new domain, but one in which Nodier could feel partly at home. It is not surprising, therefore, to learn that after the publication of the *Palingénesie sociale,* Nodier acknowledged himself the disciple of his friend rather than that of Bonnet, and that he fostered the spread of Ballanche's ideas with a zeal that transcended friendship alone.[17] Nodier it was who introduced him to a workers' club August 31, 1832, where a pleased Ballanche cheerfully exposed his philosophy of history and its basis in the dogma of fall and rehabilitation.[18] On this occasion he remarked to Ferdinand Denis that he felt more at ease and better appreciated than when speaking before Academicians.[19]

Not only could Ballanche feel the hot spurt of pride when he considered that some of the great men of his generation accepted him as a peer, he could also point with pleasure to some of the contemporary religious movements stemming from his writings. In 1828, the reading of his prolegomena contributed greatly to inspiring a religious turn of mind in the then materialistic school of Saint-Simon. As Saint-Beuve pointed out, the group repeated what Ballanche called the error of the eighteenth century: it persisted in placing the beginnings of society in a savage age. None the less, though accepting different premises, the saint-simoniens were influenced by Ballanche to the extent that they proceeded to exploit the religiosity he had awakened.[20] Some idea of the extent of this subtle relationship may be glimpsed in the letter which Enfantin wrote to Ballanche after the publication of the third volume of the *Oeuvres complètes:*

Monsieur,

J'ai à m'excuser du long retard que j'ai mis à vous témoigner combien j'avais été sensible à votre obligeant souvenir, je voulais lire et relire Orphée et repasser encore une fois les prolégomènes, certain que je pourrais mieux exprimer l'impatience où nous sommes, mes amis et moi, de connaître la suite de votre bel ouvrage.

Le Producteur va incessamment reparaître, et l'un de nos premiers soins sera de faire connaître l'impression que la *Palingénésie* a produite sur les élèves de Saint-Simon; j'espère, monsieur, que nous pourrons justifier alors, mieux que je ne le ferais dans une simple lettre, l'exception que vous avez bien voulu faire en notre faveur; cependant je sens le besoin de profiter de cette circonstance pour vous dire le regret que nous fait éprouver le sage réserve que vous vous êtes imposée dans la publication de cet ouvrage.

Je ne crains pas d'affirmer que les élèves de Saint-Simon sont à peu près les seules personnes qui, occupées d'idées sérieuses, comprendront l'idée régénatrice de la Palingénésie, et sympathiseront avec elle; tous, (et ils sont assez nombreux aujourd'hui) ont lu les exemplaires que vous m'avez envoyés ou ceux que leur sollicitude a su arracher avec peine de quelques mains privilégiées qui ne leur rendraient pas l'hommage d'étude qu'ils méritent. La masse du public lettré, absorbée par des intérêts politiques d'un jour, ou écrasée sous le poids de cette vieille enveloppe dont l'humanité s'efforce de se dépouiller; en d'autres termes, tout ce qui s'appelle libéral ou ultra, tout ce qui vit dans le présent ou dans le passé, et qui n'a pas d'avenir, ne vous lira pas ou vous lira mal; si quelques jeunes littérateurs, qui se disent philosophes, consentent à se donner cette peine, ils verront en vous un *écrivain élégant,* et croiront, en vous nommant ainsi, avoir justement apprécié et même dignement récompensé vos travaux.

Pour nous, monsieur, pour nous qui croyons à une grande régénération sociale, à un avenir promis par Dieu même à l'humanité, à un nouveau développement de la chaîne non interrompue des traditions, l'auteur de la Palingénésie a pris une noble place parmi les hommes dont l'âme généreuse sympathise avec les destinées humaines. Aussi est-ce avec reconnaissance, et permettez-moi de vous le dire avec une respectueuse affection, que nous avons lu vos ouvrages, et les mêmes sentiments nous animeront lorsque, vous adressant non une critique mais une prière, nous demanderons au poëte des grands souvenirs de nous révéler surtout ses espérances, et de faire succéder une hymne de bonheur à l'élégie.[21]

Ballanche answered politely, informing Enfantin that volume would treat the question of human destiny. The present he considered too fugitive to bother with; enough people were already at work dissecting contemporary times. His reply acknowledged the compliments, but it gave no evidence that flattery would lead him into the camp of the saint-simoniens.[22]

The golden age of Saint-Simon offered few delights to so confirmed a Catholic. In 1834, at a time when Lyon again knew the uneasy stirring of labor's revolt against the intolerable conditions imposed on it, Ballanche credited a good share of the blame for the unrest to the saint-simoniens:

Ma pauvre ville de Lyon est au fond d'un abîme d'où elle ne peut plus sortir. . . . Les doctrines saint-simoniennes et les passions politiques, en précipitant le mouvement, ont amené l'irrémédiable catastrophe. . . . Maintenant on dirait que la force et l'intelligence aient émigré de la classe supérieure dans la classe inférieure, laquelle, dans cette circonstance, n'a pu être vaincue que par l'intervention violente de toute la force dont le gouvernement dispose.[23]

IV

Ballanche's greatest joy at his growing reputation and influence, however, came from the reaction of the young men to his doctrines.

Even more baffled by events than their elders, they eagerly paged through the philosophers in pursuit of an ideology suitable for their times. Some, like Théophile Gautier, read the Lyonnais and rejected him. In 1833, the second generation of romanticists was attempting to *épater le bourgeois* with *les Jeunes-France*. Gautier then thought little of mysticism, for in his short stories he deliberately poked fun at pedantic philosophers. One of his tales he called a *conte panthéistique et palingénésique,*[24] but the term was all he had borrowed from Ballanche, whom he held in low esteem. In the preface of the *Jeunes-France,* Gautier jeeringly wrote, "Je vous jure sur ce qu'il y a de plus sacré . . . , qu'il n'y a pas plus d'idée dans ma préface que dans un livre quelconque de M. Ballanche."[25]

Others, however, more than compensated for the scorn of the Gautiers. Quinet frequented the society of Madame Récamier and, in the course of visits to the Abbaye, became fast friends with Ballanche. Each Sunday he visited the famous salon for, as he told his mother, "c'est ma meilleure soirée."[26] To her he sent the *Orphée* of this "excellent homme . . . que j'aime fort."[27] And later, in his first lesson at the Faculté des Lettres de Lyon, April 10, 1839, he placed his course under the patronage of Ballanche, who, he told the pleased burghers, was "les plus spirituel des écrivains de nos jours."[28]

It is awkward to treat the question of direct influence and borrowing in Ballanche's case because of the difficulty of seizing his ideas. Yet there were many who looked to him as the master, as the two young men who wrote poems entitled Ballanche, one of them in nine chants. Auguste Brizeux took from Ballanche the line, "Les Athéniens ont crée l'art, et l'art est la noble couronne du génie plébéien" for the basis of *Les Deux Statuaires,* which he dedicated to Auguste Barbier.[29] Back in Lyon a group of devout young enthusiasts pondered his every word. The philosopher Blanc Saint-Bonnet labored mightily to squeeze into *De l'unité spirituelle ou de la société et de son but au delà des temps* a summa of the doctrine of the master; André Pezzani likewise found in the *Oeuvres* material for his *Dieu, l'homme, l'humanité et ses progrès.* Paul Chenavard, the painter, conceived and composed from the *Palingénésie* an immense synthesis of the history of humanity, while Victor de

Laprade, later to meet and maintain his respect for his model, meditated *Psyché*.[30] When the latter came to Paris, he appointed himself Ballanche's guardian and could be seen escorting *le père* on visits to Lamennais. Laprade became the friend of Alfred de Vigny and in his rôle of disciple explained to Vigny some of the mysteries of Ballanche's ideas.[31] Frédéric Ozanam, powerful in the Catholic circles of Lyon, immediately placed himself under the protection of Ballanche when he travelled to Paris in his turn. When the mentor benignly lectured on the fact that "toute religion renferme nécessairement une théologie, une psychologie et une cosmologie," Ozanam excitedly wrote to Ernest Falconnet, "n'est-ce point là la métaphysique transcendentale dans laquelle viennent se résumer toutes les connaissances humaines?"[32] And it was Ozanam who ranked the *Oeuvres* with the *Summa* of Saint Thomas and the *Æneid*, who stated that French literature contained no pages that could surpass *Antigone*.[33]

Ballanche's works even reached out beyond the frontiers of France, sometimes to work in a manner that would have astounded their author. Three Poles, Hœne Wronski, Mickiewicz, and, above all, Sigismond Krasinski, incorporated into their writings many of Ballanche's ideas. Their works, introduced clandestinely into Poland at peril of death were read behind locked doors by ardent young patriots. Modified and adapted to the needs of the situation, his philosophy kept alive the hope of revolutionary Poland before the very faces of watchful Cossacks, Wronski, Mickiewicz, and Kransinski fed to their compatriots a mixture formed principally of six of Ballanche's favorite theses:

1. The providential law of initiation, demanding the sacrifice of the initiator, consoled Poles for past injustices and promised hope of certain resurrection;

2. In opposition to Rousseau, Ballanche postulated that a nation is the product of a historic evolution in which its culture dominates the political fact and, on the basis of this principle, he foresaw the emancipation of Poland;

3. As a corollary to this, Ballanche maintained that the unity of a nation continued regardless of its political form;

4. Consequently, social institutions exist at the whim of time;

5. The man of genius brings, as a *voyant,* continuity and initiation to his people;

6. Though Ballanche fundamentally stood for pacific means of settling differences, he had justified any revolution that purported to obtain civil liberty for the people. This portion of his doctrine, on plebeianism and revolution, was the most successful of those exported to Poland.[34]

From Germany, more receptive to Ballanche's philosophy than France, came word of a reputation of major proportions. Edouard Gans, Hegel's friend and publisher, wrote to Madame Récamier December 21, 1830, to acknowledge the gift to the Berlin jurisconsult of the *Oeuvres* and in the course of his letter mirrored the German respect for the Lyon philosopher:

> On trouve bien souvent dans notre temps des écrivains qui ont la conscience qu'un mouvement s'opère, que des progrès se préparent. . . . Il y en a des très peu (sic) qui aiment les progrès de l'humanité par des raisons religieuses. . . . M. Ballanche appartient à cette dernière classe peu nombreuse qui, par sa profondeur même, est beaucoup plus admirée que comprise. Quant à moi, j'adopte et avec une conviction intime les idées de M. Ballanche qui se rapportent à la philosophie de l'historie.[35]

V

Some of the influence that Ballanche exerted on his contemporaries passed fleetingly or merged so subtly with other tendencies that the fixed contours of the elements borrowed disappear into an attitude or an affection. Sainte-Beuve, certainly, had carefully considered Ballanche's contribution to philosophy before he finally chose Lamennais as his mentor. The critic had probably met the little man from Lyon either at the Arsenal, at Senancour's, or at one of the numerous salons he frequented between 1828 and 1830 and at which Ballanche was an honored guest. Perhaps the strange Ferdinand Denis introduced them. Certainly, their meeting did not take place at the Abbaye, for here Sainte-Beuve was *persona non grata* because of some harsh statements made about the demi-god of the salon.[36] Ballanche, however, refused to permit the feuds of others to effect his own friendships. Chance threw them together again when they met in a coach while rushing to Paris in July, 1830. Finally, towards the end of 1833, Madame Récamier relented and

admitted Sainte-Beuve to her home as a regular visitor, thus bringing
the critic into constant contact with the philosopher. Ballanche's
fondness for Sainte-Beuve increased with the discovery that the
latter read him with pleasure. For this reason, on March 24, 1830,
he thought it necessary to explain to Sainte-Beuve the constitution
of his *Oeuvres:*

> Il n'y a pas longtemps que je sais la nature des sentiments que
> vous avez l'exprême bonté de me porter. Je l'ai appris d'abord par
> M. David et en dernier lieu par Nodier que j'ai le malheur de voir
> si rarement. Soyez certain, monsieur, que je connais bien tout le prix
> d'un suffrage tel que le vôtre. Je vous rends grâces mille fois et je
> vous prie de vouloir bien agréer l'expression de toute ma reconnais-
> sance.
>
> Non, monsieur, vous n'êtes point incompétent pour juger certaines
> choses. J'ai dû commencer par placer mon système d'idées dans la
> sphère du mythe avant de le placer dans la sphère de l'histoire. Cet
> ordre chronologique, je ne pouvais m'empêcher de le suivre, mais
> j'aurais été plus facilement compris si j'avais donné le troisième
> volume avant le second. Je n'ai senti cet inconvénient que lorsque
> l'impression de ce second volume a été finie. Je serais obligé de faire
> un supplément soit au premier volume soit à la préface du second;
> ce supplément éclairera les deux premiers volumes et préparera au
> troisième. Votre modestie, monsieur, vous a donné le change sur un
> défaut du livre, défaut qui tient, comme je viens d'avoir l'honneur
> de vous l'expliquer, à ce que je n'ai pas songé à intervertir l'ordre
> de la publication et que surtout n'ayant pas interverti cet ordre
> je n'ai pas pensé que je devais à mes lecteurs quelque développement
> de plus dans la préface. J'espère que tout sera réparé. Plus tard, si
> le livre doit être donné tout à fait au public je serai instruit par
> l'expérience de cette première publication toute confidentielle.
>
> J'attends, monsieur, avec une bien vive impatience le volume de
> poésies que vous avez la bonté de me promettre et je me sens davantage
> tout fier de ce que vous avez bien voulu y placer mon nom.[37]

Once the guest of Madame Récamier, Sainte-Beuve felt the charm
of the Abbaye. Always in search of literary material, he determined
to use his friends as subjects for pen-portraits and, since Ballanche
obviously stood second only to Chateaubriand as the great man of
the Abbaye, what more natural than to write of him, especially now
that his reputation was expanding prodigiously. The article appeared in the *Revue des Deux Mondes,* September 15, 1834, giving so
kind an appreciation of Ballanche that the benevolence of the critic

seeps through his phrases. He treated Ballanche as a great man in explaining his philosophy with a thoroughness that revealed close acquaintance with it.

Sainte-Beuve's liberal friends howled with rage when they read the article. The *National* frothed at the thought of wasting so much affection and attention on an *ultra,* a friend of Chateaubriand. The maledictions reached such a crescendo that, on October 1, 1834, Sainte-Beuve fled from Paris for Précy-sur-Oise, where he remained for fifteen days in the hope that tempers would cool in the fresh breeze of time. From there, on October 8, he wrote to Jean-Jacques Ampère:

> Je ne serais même pas venu du tout ici sans une affaire qui s'annonçait d'abord comme plus grave qu'elle n'est devenue. Je vivais de cette vie que vous me savez à Paris, plus seul que jamais par l'absence de tous mes amis. . . . En un mot, je séchais dans cette poussière de notre aride automne quand l'article enfin écrit sur le bon M. Ballanche à déchaîné contre moi un orage difficile à prévoir et trop long à raconter. Le numéro de la *Revue* de 1er septembre chez Vieusseux pourra vous indiquer le point de départ de la querelle qui n'est que trop grotesque. Mais la politique de nos énergiques amis de l'opposition républicaine s'en est mêlée et j'ai été jugé suspect d'une véhémente ardeur de Restauration. Bref, j'ai reçu une lettre que je garde précieusement, signée Raspail et Bastide, écrite de la main de ce dernier, à la sollicitation de M. de Beauterne (je vous parle comme à un homme qui a lu la *Revue*) qui était passablement provoquante. Mais je deviens sage et je n'ai pas un seul instant hésité: de plus j'étais menacé, à ce qu'on me disait, d'un autre cartel de N. . . . , qui prenait fait et cause pour les régicides (fils pieux!) que j'avais effleurés sans m'en douter à propos de *l'Homme sans nom.* Je n'ai pas voulu me prêter à cette manière de me faire passer par les armes comme un déserteur èt j'ai quitté Paris un beau matin, la veille même du jour où l'on représentait *Moïse* à Versailles. Mon absence, le bon sens qui revint après la première folie, les observations de nos amis du *National* ont apaisé et je crois terminée l'affaire. Mais l'impression en reste toujours; en somme, j'ai payé à ce sujet l'arriéré de *Volupté* et la peine de mon rapprochement avec les doctrinaires, car c'est ainsi que mes meilleurs amis politiques, Leroux etc., appellent mon désir d'être à l'Ecole Normale. . . . Un mot de M. Ballanche m'a fait savoir tout son aimable intérêt; quant à lui, il a d'abord été consterné autant que vous pouvez le croire de cette bataille de Lapithes qui a failli se livrer autour et au sujet de son temple de Delphes.[38]

Sainte-Beuve had been sanguine when he imagined that the incident would be dropped at the end of a few weeks. An excited Paris
labelled the clash *l'affaire Sainte-Beuve* while critics and authors
heated tempers by enthusiastically taking sides. Furthermore, compli-
cations arose in the shape of Coëssin, mentioned in the article in a
manner decidedly not to his liking. Bastide and Raspail backed
Coëssin in the latter's efforts to obtain reparation from the critic.
Sainte-Beuve became so furious at the stupidity of the entire proceedings that he resigned all connections with the *National,* even
refusing to enter its offices to collect money due him.

The *Revue* entered the debate in an attempt to rescue all concerned from the tragi-comic. Buloz inserted in the *Chronique* of
October 1, 1834, a note in which he attempted the rôle of peacemaker:

Une phrase de l'article de M. Sainte-Beuve sur M. Ballanche,
inséré dans notre dernier numéro, a donné lieu à une réclamation
fort vive à propos de laquelle nous croyons devoir donner quelque
explications.

En parlant des systèmes philosophiques et religieux que M. Ballanche avait pour ainsi dire côtoyés sans y pénétrer et des penseurs
contemporains qu'il avait visités à diverses époques sans se faire
leur disciple, on disait:

"Il (M. Ballanche) lut les Neuf livres de Coëssin dès 1809, et
dans un voyage qu'il fit à Paris, il visita un prophète d'une époque
pontificale; mais l'esprit envahissent du sectaire le mit d'abord sur
ses gardes, M. Ballanche voulant avant tout rester lui-même."

M. Coëssin a adressé à ce sujet à l'auteur de l'article une lettre
dont il demandait l'insertion *textuelle et sans aucune addition,
changement ou retranchement.* Notre impartialité nous eût fait un devoir d'accéder à cette demande, si quelques passages et expressions de la
lettre ne nous avaient paru d'une convenance contestable par rapport
à l'auteur de l'article, à M. Ballanche et au recueil que nous
dirigeons. . . .

L'auteur de l'article croit devoir déclarer qu'il n'a nullement voulu
dire en employant le mot de *sectaire* que M. Coëssin fût sectateur
ou fondateur *d'une secte quelconque condamnée par l'Eglise,* ce
qu'il ignore tout à fait.[29]

This was a handsome explanation, but not the end of the affair.
The Monday morning following the publication of this issue of the
Revue, a M. de Beauterne, although a follower of Ballanche, arrived

at Buloz' office with an imperious demand for the insertion of Coëssin's letter. When Buloz refused, de Beauterne announced that he would see Sainte-Beuve at the *Revue* the next Sunday. Buloz, one of the staff, Pierre Leroux, and Doctor Paulin attended the conference. The words exchanged carried so many barbs that, in the evening, de Beauterne demanded a duel. Tuesday a new challenge appeared, when Sainte-Beuve was accused of having sneered at patriotism, but the critic refused the challenges, considering the affair a question of the liberty of the press, a view which the *Revue* thought correct. A note from the editor simply stated that the critic would answer the attacks as he wished and at his leisure. The scandal finally died of its own weight. Coëssin's letter did not appear for several months, when the editors buried it in a four page supplement.[40] By that time both de Beauterne and Sainte-Beuve had calmed down sufficiently to estimate the true value of their tea pot tempest.[41]

The *affaire Sainte-Beuve,* though it might well have killed the friendship between Ballanche and the critic, instead furnished them with added reason for mutual esteem. Sainte-Beuve maintained a sharp interest in Ballanche's writing, as he demonstrated when, in July, 1835, he wrote to Jean-Jacques Ampère: "Tâchez qu'il nous donne quelques belles pages; rappelez-lui que c'est à Dieppe dans un cimetière, je crois, qu'il a lu, pour la première fois, cette *Vision d'Hébal* que nous relisons. Serrez-lui tendrement la main pour moi."[42] Differences of opinion there were between Sainte-Beuve and Ballanche, as when the comte Jean Hervé de Kergolay made the unfortunate error of sending Mme d'Hautefeuille's *Une Vie brisée* to Sainte-Beuve as the work of an unknown author, with a request for criticism. The honest reply shocked the sensitive author. Ballanche intervened December 1, 1836, to soothe Mme d'Hautefeuille's feelings, finding the work "très belle et très originale . . . son jugement me paraît dépourvu de sens. Je crois que Balzac eût mieux jugé."[43] Yet, notwithstanding these differences, Sainte-Beuve kept intact his original appraisal of Ballanche. As late as 1859 he could write: "Tous ceux qui ont écrit sur lui l'ont loué. . . . Génie plus qu'à demi-voilé, on n'y entrait qu'en y mettant du sien; on ne le comprenait qu'en l'achevant."[44]

VI

Sainte-Beuve contributed also to the spread of Ballanche's fame by sharing his intimate knowledge of the Lyon philosopher's doctrines with George Sand. She had refused to appear at the Abbaye in 1831, but inevitably encountered Ballanche as he trotted from one salon to another. Furthermore, when George Sand became friendly with Liszt, she found Ballanche to be one of the musician's favorite authors. His works stood unblushingly on the shelves beside Montaigne, Voltaire, Lamennais, and Lamartine.[45] Later, in 1836, when George Sand occupied an apartment next to Liszt and Madame d'Agoult, she had ample occasion to meet the philosopher and to find in him material on matters of mysticism. Since Madame d'Agoult loved to be surrounded by celebrities, she conceived the idea of establishing a powerful literary and political salon. Thus the Hôtel de France became the center of a select circle where Heine, Mickiewicz, Chopin, Nourrit, Lamennais, and Ballanche all rubbed shoulders.[46]

Ferdinand Denis helped Sainte-Beuve in this difficult task. On November 5, 1836, he recorded in his amazing *Journal* a conversation he had just had with George Sand:

> J'ai beaucoup causé avec George Sand. Elle a dit des choses pleines d'âme et d'intelligence sur Senancour, Ballanche et Lamennais, ses trois grandes sympathies, mais Senancour est le prophète de ses oeuvres. Elle s'est plaint de l'avoir trop imité dans Lélia et de n'être pas assez forte pour aller près d'un tel homme. B[allanche] lui a paru moins digne peut-être de cette vive sympathie parce qu'il est plus admiré. Elle le connaissait peu et quelques mots ont suffi pour le grandir dans son âme.[47]

Their advice evidently impressed her for, in 1840, George Sand sent Sainte-Beuve an appraisal of Ballanche that betrayed more than a simple curiosity for the publications of the philosopher of the Abbaye-au-Bois.

> Ballanche qui, à défaut des termes poétiques, n'hésite pas à employer les termes philosophiques modernes . . . Nul n'admire Ballanche plus que nous. Cependant nous ne pouvons nous défendre de considérer comme un notable défaut, cette ressource technique qui l'a affranchi parfois du travail de l'artiste et qui détruit l'harmonie et la plastique de son style, d'ailleurs si beau, si large et si coloré d'originalité primitive.[48]

The passage was suppressed in the original letter but reintroduced in an article for the *Revue des Deux Mondes* in 1840.

That same year Sainte-Beuve sent further advice to his literary god-daughter which specified Ballanche as a model to be followed:

> Cette ébauche du Centaure me frappe surtout comme exprimant le sentiment grec grandiose, primitif, retrouvé et un peu *refait* à distance par une sorte de réflexion poétique et philosophique. Ce sentiment-là par rapport à la Grèce, ne se retrouve dans la littérature française que depuis l'école moderne. Avant l'*Homère* d'André Chénier, les *Martyrs* de Chateaubriand, l'*Orphée* et l'*Antigone* de Ballanche, quelques pages de Quinet (*Voyage en Grèce* et *Prométhée*), on en chercherait les traces et l'on n'en trouverait qu'à peine dans notre littérature classique. . . .[49]

Not that George Sand always received from Ballanche the attention due a possible disciple. Frequently she dined with Ballanche, Nourrit, Lamennais, and Liszt, but in the excitement of fencing with their favorite ideas, the men sometimes forgot her. One such memorable dinner she recorded in the *Histoire de ma vie:* "Un dîner où Liszt avait réuni M. Lamennais, M. Ballanche, le chanteur Nourrit et moi, lui [Sainte-Beuve] paraissait la chose la plus fantastique qui se pût imaginer. Il me demandait ce qui avait pu être dit entre ces cinq personnes. Je lui répondais que je n'en savais rien, que M. Lamennais avait dû causer avec M. Ballanche, Liszt avec Nourrit, et moi avec le chat de la maison."[50]

VII

Like George Sand, Lamartine had been exposed to the doctrines of Ballanche, though his acquaintance with them spans a much longer time. He seems first to have met Madame Récamier in 1822 at the home of the duchesse de Devonshire, where he was heartily welcomed as an impeccable royalist. On his return from the years in Italy, he was pleased to note that Madame Récamier had received him at the Abbaye "en homme attendu depuis dix ans."[51] There he soon found in Ballanche someone who could talk with authority of the mysticism that had then begun to infuse all Lamartine's poetry.

As in the case of George Sand, it is difficult to prove absolutely any direct influence. Certainly the men had much in common, not only their strikingly similar visions, but the contours of their thought. As far back as the *Méditations,* Lamartine had flirted with illuminism and the occult. The *Mort de Socrate* parallels in more than one way the *Mort d'un platonicien.* Common to them are the theory of the *voyant,* the same conception of the after life.[52] And in *la Chute d'un ange,* when the old patriarch expounds his gospel to Cédar, more than one phrase echoes *Orphée* and the *Palingénésie.* Lamartine, like Ballanche, has the habit of making austere old sages his mouthpieces. The rôle of the hermit who leads the poet to Lebanon recalls that of Thamyris in *Orphée,* while Adonaï teaches his visitors the primitive arts of society, marriage, property and legislation, just as Orpheus had done. Both hold the same theory of language; and the basic idea of the *Chute d'un ange is* that of *épreuve* and *expiation.*[53]

After the first meeting they remained in close touch with each other. The letters Ballanche sent to his protégée, Mme d'Haute-feuille, are studded with references to M. and Mme de Lamartine. In June, 1835, for instance, he asked Mme d'Hautefeuille to give "notre affection à M. de Lamartine et à sa noble et douce femme. Mme Récamier les aime beaucoup, et moi je leur suis tendrement attaché."[54] For his part, Lamartine reciprocated the affection and the esteem for intellectual ability. In February, 1836, he wrote to Sainte-Beuve about a project for a journal which he was consider-ing and stipulated that Ballanche should be included on the staff:

> . . . parlerons-nous de presse politique? C'est bien vil. Cependant j'en ferai si vous voulez. Organisez cela, mais à condition que vous, Ballanche, To [c] queville, Beaumont, Carné, Pagès, etc., nous écrirons ensemble, car là serait une force, en moi seul il n'y a qu'un instinct droit et rapide des choses.[55]

The idea hung fire, then expired. Later, in January, 1839, it was revived again by Lamartine, a fact which Ballanche duly reported to Mme d'Hautefeuille along with his misgivings. By this time Lamartine had evolved politically a bit farther than Ballanche cared to follow.[56]

Carefully Ballanche watched Lamartine's career, sensing that the acts of his friend would affect France more than those of the ordi-nary statesman. Sometimes he had occasion to talk politics with

Lamartine, at the Abbaye, or when they met at the home of Mme d'Hautefeuille, but more often he merely read of his exploits, always full of a feeling that Lamartine's fate was bound up with a *palingénésie*. In 1840 he beamed proudly at the position Lamartine had taken in the Chamber, but two years later he was still waiting for the poet to make some great move.[57] When, however, Lamartine began to slip away from the Right, Ballanche expressed strong disapproval. "Selon moi, Lamartine aurait dû garder sa situation, ne pas quitter des fossiles pour aller trouver d'autres fossiles," he told Mme d'Hautefeuille.[58] Then the publication of the *Girondins* convinced the Lyonnais that his faith had been misplaced. He deliberately refrained from reading the book, yet the casual conversation of others and their comments on Lamartine's call to revolution confirmed his worst fears.[59]

In the surge of events, Lamartine forgot his friends temporarily as he basked in the view of all Europe, the statesman-poet, the man to whom it had been given to direct the romantic revolution. But later, when poor and rejected by a bourgeoisie that refused tolerance to his social schemes, he found leisure to sum up his relations with Ballanche:

> Ballanche n'avait rien reçu de la nature pour séduire ni pour attacher: d'une naissance honorable mais modeste, d'extérieur disgracieux, d'un visage difforme, d'un langage embarrassé, d'une timidité enfantine, d'une simplicité d'esprit qui allait jusqu'à la naïveté, Ballanche ne se faisait aucune illusion sur cette absence de tous les dons naturels; mais il sentait en lui le don des dons: celui d'admirer et d'aimer les supériorités physiques ou morales de la création. Il savait se désintéresser complètement de lui-même, pourvu qu'on lui permît d'adorer le beau: le beau dans les idées, le beau dans l'âme, dans le talent, dans le visage. . . .

> Tel fut Ballanche; je l'ai beaucoup connu; j'ai assisté, au pied de son lit, à ses dernières contemplations de l'une et l'autre vie; je l'ai vu vivre et je l'ai presque vu mourir dans cette petite mansarde de la rue de Sèvres d'où il pouvait voir la fenêtre en face de son amie, madame Récamier. Ballanche laisse dans le coeur de ceux qui l'ont connu l'image d'un de ces rêves calmes du matin, qui ne sont ni la veille ni le sommeil, mais qui participent des deux. Ce n'était pas un homme, c'était un sublime somnambule de la vie.[60]

VIII

As he watched in Lamartine the expression of a more liberal political philosophy, so Ballanche examined in Lamennais an evolution toward a fusion of democracy and religion. Not that he agreed with Lamennais. Ballanche preferred Gallicanism to complete dependency on Rome. Since Gallicanism seemed to him capable of conserving the individuality of his beloved France, he fought ultramontanism as harmful to his conception of affairs.[61] Napoleon he had once seen ruthlessly suppressing individual rights and he wanted no more of it.

Yet there existed common ground on which the two men could meet. Just as Lamennais veered toward the people after the ordonnances of 1828, trumpeting his new ideas in *Des progrès de la Révolution et de la guerre contre l'Eglise,* so did Ballanche, in a quieter manner, abandon royalty. Each chose the people and, in his own way, tried to show them the inner meaning of Christianity.

Like so many of his generation, Ballanche had heartily endorsed Lamennais when he began to argue in favor of the Church. Ferdinand Denis reports that one day, October 22, 1831, when Sainte-Beuve, still a friend of Lamennais, spoke at Ballanche's home of the author of the *Essai,* "de son ignorance des écrits nouveaux, de sa puissance de pensé, qui devinait en quelque sorte ce qu'il n'avait pas voulu lire,"[62] Ballanche countered with an expression of deep respect for Lamennais. He sought out the priest and, as one of the great Catholic lay philosophers of his time, exchanged ideas with him.

Even when Lamennais became more papist than the Pope, Ballanche maintained his friendship while watching wide-eyed the attempt of the proud Breton to argue first Leo XII, then Gregory XVI, into becoming the sole source of Church power. In August, 1832, the encyclical *Mirari vos* warned of the approaching schism. Then Gregory XVI issued the *Singulari nos* in disapproval of the *Paroles d'un croyant* and the rupture was complete. The new apostle had outstripped his church. Officially, Ballanche made a statement in the *Revue Européenne* in which he praised and blamed in a mild manner:

On peut considérer ce livre, en certains endroits et même dans tout son ensemble, comme une peinture mystagogique dont les emblèmes quelquefois doux, plus souvent terribles, ne doivent être pris au pied de la lettre. Ainsi, dans les *Paroles d'un croyant,* tout doit être apprécié en dépouillant chaque chose des proportions gigantesques, exagérées, indéfinies, d'une séance d'initiation. Toujours les grandes visions, les puissantes évocations, les prosopopées plastiques d'une énergique synthèse, mêlent dans l'esprit l'épouvante et l'espérance.[63]

Privately he put his finger on what he considered the fault of the book. Mme d'Hautefeuille, knowing the friendship between the two men, wondered what a Catholic philosopher would say of a book in which a great and fervent abbé flouted the Holy See. The reply was explicit: "Je ne le considère point comme un prophète de l'avenir, mais comme un prophète du présent."[64]

Ballanche felt none of the bitter disappointment that stunned Sainte-Beuve. He carefully kept his ideological differences with Lamennais removed from the sphere of friendship. In this way he could continue to admire Lamennais even though disapproving of his book. Lamennais sensed this faithfulness and gratitude prompted him to write Ballanche a letter of explanation:

Je vous remercie mille fois de votre souvenir, mon bien cher ami, ainsi que des excellentes choses que renferme la lettre que L . . . m'a remise de votre part. . . . Je suis catholique et je veux l'être sans que cela m'oblige à adopter [la ligne] suivie par les hommes de la hiérarchie, ni en général leurs opinions en ce qui ne touche pas la foi. . . . Et qu'est-ce que le Christianisme sinon la religion du fils de Dieu fait homme? L'humanité ne saurait rester dans l'état où elle est maintenant. La nuit s'achève; attendons le jour; il paraîtra bientôt.[65]

Gently, through his letters, Ballanche began to wage a war of ideas with Lamennais, hoping to convince him of his error. He pointed out that Christianity offered the only means of progress, that it alone constituted the law of man. To this Lamennais heartily agreed, but he refused to share Ballanche's optimism. When the Lyon philosopher stated that all needs could be satisfied by the application of the Gospels to daily life, Lamennais intimated that his own case proved the aversion of authority to any progressive interpretations. Neither could he grant a fusion of science and religion, nor of sociology and religion. The Church seemed to him to have retrograded in a manner that threatened its whole structure. On the question of politics, the two spoke different languages. Ballanche hinted that the clergy might better leave politics alone, but Lamennais demurred. Why restrain a few? "Puis, qu'est-ce que la politique si ce n'est l'ensemble des moyens par lesquels on peut réaliser dans l'ordre pratique les idées véritablement sociales?"[66]

Though he never succeeded in changing Lamennais' ideas, Ballanche persisted in demonstrating that religious differences could not separate them. Then came the *Affaires de Rome*, which shook Ballanche so much that he refused to write the criticism of it that he had originally planned. "Il est trop nul philosophiquement et logiquement," he confided to Mme d'Hautefeuille. "En outre, sa situation est triste comme santé et comme fortune. Je ne le vois point, et il ne me sort pas de devant les yeux."[67] By this time, too, Lamennais had become cooler toward Ballanche. On December 17, 1837, Ferdinand Denis wrote in his *Journal:*

> Il [Lamennais] lit tout, disait-il, il lit volontiers un *Almanach,* mais jamais il n'a pu lire Ballanche. C'est une grande rivière calme épanchée, dont l'œil perd de vue les rives. C'est un mélange de Fénelon et des Incas. Avec tout cela, il accorde la correction et la science du style. Je crois, moi, à une lecture plus fréquente.[68]

Little by little, ideological shifts opened a wide chasm between the two. To Ballanche, Lamennais appeared the ruin of a once-great man, though he always kept great respect for him. In 1834, in the first flush of pity, he had chided the abbé Gerbet, once the disciple of Lamennais, for adhering to the encyclical. Later he changed his mind. By 1839 he preferred Gerbet, though the memory of the exalted words of Lamennais often sent a twinge through him.[69] The publication of the *Questions politiques et philosophiques* in 1840, however, almost obliterated this remorse, and the appearance the next year of the *Discussions critiques et pensées diverses sur la religion et la philosophie* made him abandon Lamennais for lost. Hurt, he told Mme d'Hautefeuille that, health permitting, he intended to study the question of human responsibility, the problem that Lamennais had failed to solve.[70]

It might well be expected that Ballanche would become intoxicated from the heady drafts of success that were served up to him after 1830, but, to the contrary, he retained for the most part an unperturbed equanimity. Not even when a stranger came to Paris solely to say, "Monsieur, c'est de vos ouvrages que sortira la théologie de l'avenir!", or when Nodier bluntly called him "un homme divin," did he do more than flush with embarrassment.[71] To tell the truth, his expanding renown frightened him; he sensed that more was expected of him than fell within his powers. Occasionally, the timid little man from Lyon let himself indulge in a moment of fierce pride. In February, 1832, Ferdinand Denis noted that Ballanche had finally perceived his own fame. Denis observed that during the past six months Ballanche's name had become a commonplace in Paris. Pleased, Ballanche admitted that "comme vous me le dites, depuis six mois surtout je sens que mon nom a commencé à se répandre avec mes idées. J'en ai toujours désespéré."[72] A few months later he came down to earth with a thud. Sorrowfully, he told Denis that in all probability a long time would pass before *Orphée* was understood. Denis consoled him by remarking that, to understand the *Oeuvres*, one had to be a poet and a historian, and a visibly brightened Ballanche begged his friend "de dire cela quelque part, et je vous en prie parce que cela doit être dit et que vous le sentez."[73]

Once again, in 1834, after the resounding fall of Lamennais, he felt the hour had come to impose on France a solid philosophy. His customary modesty so deserted him that he even called himself a prophet of the future.[74] Chateaubriand watched with amusement signs of Ballanche's growing intoxication with himself, even dubbing him *l'hiérophante.* This second flight into foolishness lasted slightly longer than the first because Ballanche thought that at last he could overtake and surpass René. One day, after the publication of one of Chateaubriand's last brochures, Ballanche solemnly stopped Sainte-Beuve to ask, "Monsieur, ne pensez-vous pas que le règne de la *phrase* est près de finir?" His tone implied that the reign of the idea, that is, his reign, was about to begin.[75]

Ballanche's ego, however, soon subsided, leaving him the same gentle, genial philosopher, content to pontificate only before a select inner circle which dutifully acknowledged that "M. Ballanche est *l'homme le plus avancé* de l'Abbaye-au-Bois."[76] Perhaps this return to normalcy worked against him. From 1835 on, although greatly interested in the religious renaissance that was sweeping over France, he remained motionless when it became evident that a leader was needed for the movement. Nor did he indicate any practical solutions to problems, perhaps haunted by the fate of Lamennais, who once had thought he could lead French Catholicism to a secure port.[77] Certainly he could have occupied Lamennais' place, or, at least, one like it. As Ampère put it, "avec moins de candeur et plus d'ambition, il aurait pu être chef de secte." But one of the most famous Catholic lay philosophers preferred to be content with the admiration of his friends. "Si mon nom me survit," he wrote to Madame Récamier, ". . . je serai le philosophe de l'Abbaye-au-Bois, et ma philosophie sera considérée comme inspiré par vous . . . Cette pensée est une de mes joies."[78]

CHAPTER VIII

La Vision d'Hébal—La Ville des Expiations—Articles

I

THE success of the *Oeuvres complètes* moved Ballanche to continue in 1831 the publication of the various manuscripts tucked away in his desk. Now that fortune had blessed him, he reasonably expected the same good luck from another. Accordingly, on May 1, he had printed and distributed to his friends the *Vision d'Hébal,* an episode taken from the yet unpublished *Ville des Expiations.* The little volume went as a gift to all subscribers to the *Oeuvres,* in appreciation of their faith in the author and as a sign that his abilities had not vanished. Later, he promised, the episode would be replaced in its original setting, though time gave him the lie.[1]

Hébal concerns the strange fate of a young Scottish boy, gifted with second sight and cursed with the weakest of bodies. His adolescence, like that of Ballanche, had yielded relentless suffering. He had reached maturity with a nervous condition that sometimes induced somnambulism or catalepsy, in which his sharpened senses reacted swiftly to the surrounding atmosphere, making him feel that its physical disturbances occurred within himself. More than once hallucinations tricked him into believing he was talking to someone long dead. In this manner he traveled abroad, spoke to the heroes of antiquity, or solved the enigmas of the past. All beings and objects spoke to him; from them, like Lamartine and Michelet, he learned the secrets of the universe, visiting in the fashion of Séraphita the regions of pure intelligence.[2] Like so many of the romanticists, he sensed himself in immediate personal contact with the chain of human destinies that threaded through history. Occasionally, his mind dimly glimpsed a past existence, felt itself mystically united to universal man.[3]

Each visitation of this strange power seemed to bring Hébal

nearer death, but he struggled for life until he could once express the magnificent things he had seen. He fought so well that, about the time of his majority, his health strengthened and the vertiginous accesses of vision disappeared. For several years, he remained comparatively normal, retaining from the days of illness only a penchant for solitary meditation.[4] Idle hours were filled with the hungry reading of the philosophers in a continual search for the answers to the problems of metaphysics. Then, one day, as Hébal puzzled over the question of man's relationship to the material world and the world of intelligence, watching a clock all the while, there came the inevitable comparison between the workings of the universe and the functioning of clocks. Outside, a summer sky darkened; the clock played the *Ave Maria* and whirred expectantly before striking nine. Hébal felt himself in the grip of a vision, but, this time, a synthesis of all the visions previously experienced. His various metaphysical gropings led him into the clear and he saw

> une magnifique épopée idéale à-la-fois successive et spontanée.
>
> Et cette épopée prit une forme dithyrambique. La strophe, comme dans la poésie lyrique primitive, représentait le ciel des fixes; l'antistrophe le ciel des mobiles, le temps et l'éternité, le fini et l'infini, l'épode résumait l'harmonie des deux mouvements. Comme Pythagore, il voyait une noble sirène jouant de la lyre à l'extrémité de chaque cercle des sphères célestes, et la cadence majestueuse de la sphère se mariait à la cadence de toutes les autres, et les sept notes fondamentales des nombres produisaient un concert sans fin, une danse éternelle.[5]

Ino the few pages that hold the vision of Hébal, Ballanche managed not only to repeat all previous statements, but to review the history of mankind from before the Fall to the Day of Judgment. Much of the book reiterates the ideas of the *Oeuvres,* for Hébal's vision closely approximates that described in *Orphée.* There is the same tireless emphasis on the doctrines of sin and retribution.

And yet new elements do appear. Chronologically, the *Vision* should have preceded the *Palingénésie* because here, for the first time, Ballanche discussed the reasons for the creation. Following Plato, he stated that God manifested himself in reality for his own pleasure, as positive evidence of his perfection. From then on, Ballanche accepted the usual explanation of the Fall. When some of his creatures erred, God created for them a habitat and a form.

The earth he cast into infinity as a part of a slow-forming universe. Over a period of centuries, the atmosphere formed, the animals came, though for a long time the creation had seemed aimless, peopled with creatures eating and being eaten. Hébal understood that man received at birth the capacity to choose between good and evil. Man, supposedly, was to act on the world and help complete it. The explanation for the peculiarities of life lay, for Ballanche, in the fact that man refused to aid Providence. For this, the Creator established a series of tests to replace the one man had originally failed.

The rest of Hébal's vision summed up the history of mankind. He saw men cover the earth, grow proud, and suffer the punishment of the Flood. Chastened, humanity spread again over the world and the reign of history began. Before Hébal, passed the Jewish prophets, Greek warriors, and the Roman conquerors. Everywhere life symbolized the struggle between *le principe stationnaire* and *le principe progressif*. Then Christ came, bringing the promise of redemption and Hébal watched the apostles disseminate the gospel, stared as a lusty Christianity defeated the onrush of the Mohammedans. Charlemagne, the Crusaders, Galileo, and Columbus flickered by, to make way for Calvin, Descartes, and Napoleon; but when the Restoration came, Ballanche could not restrain from interjecting his own disgust: "les vieux rois se sont retirés dans l'exil; et ils ont excité une pitié profonde, car on a compris qu'ils avaient été sans intelligence, qu'ils avaient méconnu leur mission."[6] His sympathies now lay, not with the Bourbons, but with nations like Poland, struggling to be freed.

Hitherto Ballanche had hesitated to discuss the future, fearful of exposing himself to the ridicule heaped on so many pseudo-clairvoyants. Now, however, Hébal's dream swept him into events to come. In strange sentences, arranged as though for chanting, rhythmic and powerful, he predicted the future of the West:

Un nouveau rideau est tiré, un dernier sceau est brisé.
Et le passé raconte l'avenir.
Et une voix se fait entendre: Qui dira l'avenir?
Et une autre foix dit: Celui qui sait le passé sait aussi l'avenir.
L'Europe se constitue donc de nouveau.

> Et un frémissement général se fait sentir dans toute la création.
>
> Le sang qui a arrosé le Golgotha proclame enfin l'abolition de la peine de mort, et dit l'impiété de la guerre.
>
> Et la solidarité devient la charité.
>
> La loi est fondée sur l'identité de l'essence humaine.
>
> Le christianisme achève son évolution; il règne sur le monde, mais d'un règne pacifique. . . .
>
> L'Occident triomphe. . . .
>
> L'islamisme succombe dans la lutte.[7]

On the last horizon of humanity, man completed the creation, thereby achieving the spiritualization of matter. The animals disappeared, all life being assimilated by man. A hushed Hébal watched the agony of the universe as Quinet's Ahasvérus would do. The earth staggered in its orbit, all life wiped from its surface. In the dream, the dreamer died and his soul saw the earth spin into a corner of the universe where, at a sign from God, the dead awoke to berate the Creator: "Pourquoi la guerre, les dévastations, l'esclavage, les castes et les classes? Pourquoi les sacrifices humains, les superstitions, les infamies?"[8] And the answer pealed forth: "Pourquoi m'avez-vous abandonné?"[9] Lightning powdered the earth and its dust settled throughout infinity. Man had withdrawn to another world.

> De nouveau, l'idée contemple d'idée.
>
> L'âme n'a plus de lieu . . .
>
> La capacité du bien et du mal a produit la liberté dans le bien . . .
>
> L'homme a accompli la loi de son être.
>
> Il connaît le but de la création.
>
> Il se connaît lui-même.
>
> Il connaît Dieu.[10]

The vision ended on the last stroke of nine. Hébal had finally found the answer he desired, but discovered that words lacked the precision and strength to convey his meaning to others. Death came at a moment of bitter triumph.

II

The strange form of the book, its concentrated philosophy, its powerful Biblical prose, and some new ideas, proved that Ballanche had not settled into the rut of repetition after the publication of the *Oeuvres*. The form, that of a vision, offered nothing novel. Its parent, the dream, had brought Nodier fame. But here Ballanche had expressed the thought of a lifetime in such a way that the discerning Sainte-Beuve would later write: "Pour moi, le plus complet, le plus fidèle et satisfaisant résumé de sa doctrine est encore la *Vision d'Hébal* où le prisme poétique réfracte pourtant chaque idée."[11]

Actually, the *Vision* dated from 1824, though Ballanche did not begin to set down his ideas until five years later. This gave him priority over the younger romanticists who were to make his statements commonplaces, and explains to a large extent why he chose to back the *Cénacle* rather than follow the course of least resistance by accepting neoclassicism as the national literary doctrine.[12] Ballanche repudiated capital punishment long before romanticism accepted this position. Long, too, before the *Marseillaise de la paix,* he denied the social value of war, hoped that some day man might decide to forbear from the savage joy of self-slaughter. These hopes Hébal had seen realized in the far future, but the optimistic philosopher believed they might sooner be converted into fact.

In the matter of theology, Ballanche remained for the most part impeccably within the fold, but in one instance, he made statements calculated to raise the eyebrows of the conservative. His explanation of evil simply stated that man had sinned, therefore, punishment must follow. The tale of the Garden of Eden received only a casual mention. Actually, Ballanche refrained from questioning too closely the intent of the Creator in permitting plagues, diseases, wars, and hate; God gave evasive answer when the dead demanded an explanation of evil. In one instance, Ballanche stepped apart from the majority of his co-religionists: He came out more clearly than ever, explicitly and implicitly, with the idea that Christianity must evolve with social institutions to maintain its proper place within the structure of society. While not heresy, the opinion sent some uneasiness through the rigidly orthodox who, at this time, were anxiously watching Lamennais run a hectic course. Most of these traditionalists cared little for the statement that the end of time would prove that "la capacité du bien et du mal a produit la liberté dans le bien."[13] It smacked too much of the republicanism that frightened them so much.

III

The publication of the *Vision* brought Ballanche more public attention than had previous books. Now that the *Oeuvres* had established the Lyonnais as a leading literary figure, the critics took notice of his writings. The affair Sainte-Beuve turned up before most of them found time to review the *Vision*, with the result that some of the comment verged on the bitter. The *Impartial de Fribourg* belied its own name by hurling maledictions on Ballanche's innocent head. A young lady of the city had gone mad for reasons generously attributed to him and to the *Vision*. The editors' anger was in no way eased when a pamphlet appeared in praise of the philosopher, blithely entitling the nineteenth century *l'ère de Ballanche*. A. M. O'Mahony fulminated; the *Fribourgeois* danced in anger. But Ballanche dismissed their rantings with charitable excuses. He cherished rather the article by Sainte-Beuve and the statement of the *Revue du Progrès Social* which declared the *Vision* "une œuvre platonique de la plus grande portée." Triumphantly, he exulted that this would shock *l'invariable,* to whom could be quoted the phrase of Galileo: *et pourtant elle se meut!*[14]

Most of the journals had gone to war over the question of the position of Catholicism in the state, or had renewed the battle of liberalism versus conservatism. Ballanche's book served them as the point of departure in a broader argument. Saint-Chéron, in the *Revue Encyclopédique,* summed up the primary reason for liking or disliking the *Vision* in his review:

> . . . [Ballanche] prétend faire entrer toute l'humanité nouvelle, telle qu'elle vit à cette heure, violemment dégagée du catholicisme, dans le dogme chrétien, sans l'affaiblir, sans le violer; il prétend concilier, sans la conception d'une unité nouvelle, d'un Dieu nouveau, les éléments en lutte depuis trois siècles, l'autorité et la liberté, le catholicisme et le protestantisme, le spirituel et le temporel, l'église et l'état.[15]

Saint-Chéron, however, stood well on the side of Ballanche. To him, the author of the *Vision* had created "l'épopée de l'univers," a book compounded of the *Apocalypse, Genesis,* and the *Discours sur l'histoire universelle.*[16]

Nul n'a mieux senti le caractère palingénésique de notre époque, la nature de l'émancipation universelle qui se prépare . . . nul n'a jeté plus d'idées neuves et fécondes. La lecture de ses ouvrages est enivrante par le charme d'une exquise sensibilité, d'une délicatesse pleine de grâce. . . . Sa poésie est vague quelquefois, mais c'est le vague de l'infini dans le sein duquel roulent des mondes.[17]

Chateaubriand, too, commented on the *Vision,* though not in so outrageous a manner. Ballanche had sent him a copy at Geneva, where the great man was basking in the admiration of the city.

J'aime prodigieusement vos siècles écoulés dans le temps qu'avait mis la sonnerie de l'horloge à sonner l'air de l'*Ave Maria.* Toute votre exposition est magnifique; jamais vous n'avez dévoilé votre système avec plus de clarté et de grandeur. A mon sens, votre *Vision d'Hébal* est ce que vous avez produit de plus élevé et de plus profond; vous m'avez fait réellement comprendre que tout est contemporain pour celui qui comprend l'éternité. Vous m'avez expliqué Dieu avant la création, la création avant l'homme, la création intellectuelle de celui-ci, puis son union à la matière par sa chute quand il crut se faire un destin de sa volonté.[18]

What Chateaubriand did not mention was that the book contained not only the intellectual history of the author, but his actual autobiography. The very name Hébal is a shortened anagram of Bal[lanc]he, one he henceforth used in letters to intimates. Hébal, like Ballanche, had been sickly from birth; he shunned crowds, read omnivorously, and puzzled over the origin of evil. This desperate concern with the reason for good and bad had early marked him as a precursor of romanticism, although by 1832 he appeared merely to have entered into a literary current by virtue of a disinclination to publish until a manuscript had aged sufficiently. Even the dreams, the terrible abysses into which Hébal's mind plunged, stemmed from the days of his own illness. Ampère relates that Ballanche once reminiscently remarked that in his youth, while seized by a nervous ailment, he had listened to himself moan and cry in a distant room, and M. Dupré states that one day, in the middle of a bridge over the Saône, Ballanche actually fell into the trance described in the *Vision,* seeing on the sky the ensemble of human history.[19]

IV

The *Vision* belonged to a work of much greater scope, the *Ville des Expiations,* which goes back to the excursion to the Grande

Chartreuse.[20] However, the first detailed plan of the work seems to date from August, 1820. On the 26th of that month, Ballanche had written to Amélie Récamier:

> Je viens de faire le plan d'un livre sur les prisons. Dominé par la pensée que la peine de mort finira enfin par disparaître de nos codes barbares, je veux que l'on bâtisse une ville qui sera appelée la *Ville es Expiations*. Cette ville sera destinée uniquement à recevoir tous les condamnés de la France. Il faut que j'associe à ce travail un architecte pour qu'il me fasse les dessins de tous les édifices nécessaires à la *Ville des Expiations*. L'inconvénient de cet ouvrage, c'est qu'il me coûtera beaucoup d'argent à exécuter. Mais je ne puis pas me dispenser de faire cette dépense, parce que les gravures sont nécessaires pour faire saillir mes idées, parce que aussi il est bon de montrer qu'elles ne sont pas chimériques. Il me faut aussi des devis estimatifs. Vous saurez, Mademoiselle, que les Israélites avaient non pas des villes d'expiation, mais des villes de refuge. Mon idée je crois, vaut mieux que celle de la colonisation. J'aurais là un collège de Missionnaires. J'aurais une école de geôliers. J'aurais une magistrature particulière. J'aurais des établissements d'instruction spéciale, des frères de la doctrine chrétienne, des soeurs de la charité. J'aurais des ateliers pour occuper ceux des prisonniers qui pourraient être occupés. Les condamnés auraient des moynes d'améliorer leur sort. Ils verraient leurs fers s'alléger à mesure qu'ils le mériteraient. Que sais-je? Peut-être les hommes les plus exécrables pourraient-ils parvenir un jour à sortir de la Ville des Expiations pour rentrer dans le monde des honnêtes gens. J'userai de tout ce qui peut servir à civiliser et à polir cette section de la société qui peut-être n'a besoin que d'être faite à l'instinct social. Je formerais un collège de médecins accoutumés à étudier la science sous le rapport moral. Il ne faut point parler de cette idée jusqu'à ce qu'elle puisse recevoir les développements dont elle a besoin. Elle passerait pour le rêve d'un songe-creux et il ne faut pas la discréditer d'avance.[21]

By 1823, the *Ville* was ready for publication, but Ballanche still refused to send it to the printer. On February 25 of that year, Bredin complained of his friend's chronic slowness: "Et cette *Ville!* elle est toute bâtie et cependant elle ne voit pas le jour."[22] During the trial of the ministers of Charles X in 1830, Ballanche revised the manuscript considerably, setting aside Hébal's vision, but he never did relinquish the main parts of the *Ville,* except to allow portions to dribble into the hands of *La France Littéraire.*[23] His friends protested at what seemed gross negligence, but Ballanche put them off with promises, working over the book with loving kindness. On April 18, 1834, he assured Mme d'Hautefeuille that he was constructing the *Ville* to cement the break which the riots and repressions at Lyon had sent running across France.[24] But the demon of discontent pricked him. New thoughts crowded the old from his mind; what had been written yesterday asked to be revised in the light of today. In June, 1835, he wrote to a bewildered Mme d'Hautefeuille that he had begun all over again. "Cette pauvre *Ville des Expiations,* je l'arrache de ses vieux fondements, je dis vieux, car à l'heure qu'il est, il y a près de vingt ans qu'elle a été faite une première fois. . . . Savez-vous que de voir disparaître autour de moi de belles réputations si bien établies, me donne une fière tâche?"[25] The manuscript finally hibernated in Ballanche's boxes until his death when, with other papers, it passed to the Bibliothèque de Lyon.[26]

In the master plan of Ballanche's work, the *Ville* follows *l'Homme sans nom,* which was supposed to serve it as introduction. *L'Homme sans nom* tells the story of the sin and expiation of an individual, his rehabilitation through meditation and self-prescribed penance. The *Ville* rests on the same thesis of punishment, but attempts to sketch a system of penal servitude vastly different from the crude barbarism then in force. As Ballanche wrote in the *Prolégomènes pour la Ville des Expiations:*

> Il s'agit maintenant, comme une des conséquences les plus importantes du christianisme, d'abolir à jamais cette doctrine qui a trop long-temps regné sur la terre, doctrine qui consiste à croire que le châtiment doit être infligé pour l'utilité de l'association.[27]

Rather, the peace-loving burgher from Lyon thought, criminals should be given new points of view and fresh confidence.

The *Ville* logically constituted the culminating point of Ballanche's teachings. The four volumes of the *Oeuvres* constantly repeated that life is a striving for goodness, the reconstruction of humanity to a greater state from which it had fallen. In this work, Ballanche attempted to describe how France could hasten progress. He had, of course, never vaunted the executioner like de Maistre. His heroes had always been victims: Orpheus, Antigone, Inès de Castro, Jeanne d'Arc, and Louis XVI. To him, progress meant the abolition of caste, a struggle in which the people, the active principle, defeated the aristocracy, the passive principle. The social greatness of Christianity was that it established a religious equality from which must inevitably spring civic equality. These, too, were his own ideas, born of the reaction of a gentle mind to the growing materialism of the age of Louis-Philippe and to the starkly remembered violence of the Terror and subsequent revolutions.

Like his other books, the *Ville* stems directly from Ballanche's religious beliefs. The abolition of capital punishment is far from its sole thesis. Ballanche attacks, like the romanticists, the entire problem of evil. He wished to conciliate the doctrine of the inviolability of human life with that of the security of society. What man destroys, he must rebuild. Therefore, to accomplish a two-fold purpose, he proposed building a city made sacred by the resumption of the ancient right of asylum:

> Elle est une cité stationnaire par son principe éternel, progressive par son alliance toujours subsistante avec les destinées générales du genre humain; elle doit être la représentation continue de l'ancien monde civil, du monde civil actuel, du monde civil de l'avenir, du monde religieux qui embrasse tout le genre humain dans ses voies préparatoires.[28]

The city would be composed of two sections, an outer one for the rehabilitation of criminals, and an inner one to house a college of priests skilled in judging quarrels between nations, or between governments and their peoples.

The plan of the work calls for nine books, the first three of which explain the intent of the scheme. Books IV and VI analyse the outer city, its exact functioning and the place of the criminals. Book V is composed of digressions, while book VII is completely recondite, dealing with a visit to the mysterious temple that dominates the city. The *Ville* ends here, though it seems obvious that book VIII must have been the *Vision,* since this is the only place where that episode can logically be inserted. Some fragments are left of book IX, which was intended to justify the unity of Ballanche's thought.

The idea of a city of expiation unfolds in story form. Ballanche assumes that the city exists and that envious foreign sovereigns have sent envoys to France to study the administration of the colony.

He himself acts as one of these visitors, assiduously investigating all phases of the city, even unearthing the fact that its construction cost but one-fourth the money expended for the two Allied invasions of France.

Patient questioning reveals the careful planning of the administration of the *Ville Haute.* A dictator rules by decrees which are in turn interpreted by a High Court consisting of five tribunals, each charged with the cases of part of the population: neophytes, colonists, guards, soldiers, or savants. Soldiers garrison the town, three thousand infantry and one thousand cavalry, housed in their own quarters and possessing their own arsenal and drill grounds. A commercial section stands off to one side to keep its chatter from the city, opened only from dawn to dusk, after which the inhabitants are locked in. In another section, Ballanche established, perhaps under the influence of Lamennais, a *collège de frères de la doctrine chrétienne.* Vast hospitals, a seminary, and a normal school for prison wardens complete the Upper City.

The *Ville Basse* contains that part of the colony consecrated to neophytes come for voluntary expiation. Composed of twelve parishes or sixty villages collectively entitled *le Désert,* it is divided mathematically in an almost mystic respect for numbers. Each village contains sixty houses, all in the form of tents. There is one room to a house, one person to a room, and one book for each inhabitant, the *Manuel du chrétien.* Every night the prisoners are locked in; each week lots are drawn to determine the village and house to be occupied. The sexes live separately, though age groups are kept together. The city sparkles in its cleanliness and, since even talk of politics and war is forbidden, quiet hangs over its many lawns and gardens. All this Ballanche had planned in an attempt to make the city mirror "la loi monotone et triste des vicissitudes humaines, . . . la loi imployable des nécessités sociales . . . il faut que tout y avertisse incessament que rien n'est stable, et que la vie de l'homme est un voyage dans une terre d'exil."[29]

The life of one neophyte corresponds precisely to that of another. When a man is condemned to the city, he appears for initiation in the manner of the ancients. Received in a black robe, covered with chains, he hears a catalogue of his crimes. The fetters are then removed and the rules explained. For thirty days, the convict stays in a prison called *le tombeau,* then is led out to be washed and clothed in a white robe. A new life begins, for which he is provided with a new name and age. The prisoner is warned never to reveal his identity under pain of punishment and the dictator begins a weekly account of his actions. When the inhabitants are summoned for an introduction to the newcomer, they welcome him and quiet descends on the city. The law demands a silence broken only at dawn and dusk, at which times the neophytes sing and pray at the thresholds of their homes.

Once inside the colony, a neophyte can communicate with the outside world. His mail undergoes censorship, but only for his own protection. He can study, too, if he so desires, except that no science is permitted without the express permission of the masters of science, no truth promulgated without the consent of the teachers. Everything is decided by the authorities, but the corps of censors is charged with remaining in intimate contact with the movement of contemporary ideas in order to understand the times. Occasionally, prisoners weaken under the regime, at which time the others encourage, even reprimand them.

Life within the city has attained a fine degree of standardization. The neophytes are kept separated, no talk being allowed even at meals or in the hospitals. Personal linen is changed every day, bed linen every week. The law requires every prisoner to bathe once a fortnight, and guards scatter perfumes everywhere. Most of the routine of daily life is accompanied by music; there are concerts even in the middle of the night.

As they merit promotion, the neophytes progress from one part of the city to another. If his conduct seems exemplary, a prisoner may leave the villages and become an *habitant,* that is, own a fixed home. He may also take a wife, though celibacy is generally the rule. Next, he passes to the upper city where he may exercise a profession, and finally, he is given permission to own a business or a farm. The delicate difference between a business and a profession Ballanche maintained because he believed that "la plus grande moralité qui résulte de la société, c'est la propriété."[30]

Whenever a neophyte completes his expiation and wishes to re-enter the world, the entire city rejoices. At a ceremony, the rehabilitated sinner regains his name. If, on the contrary, an inhabitant maintains bad habits to the extent of dying impenitent, the news is sadly announced. At time of death, whether or not the prisoner has been contrite, he is buried within the confines under his assumed name.

As is to be expected, the entire thesis of the *Ville* rests on the idea that Christianity asks rehabilitation through education, not punishment. The prisoners pray often, read their *Manuel* continuously. At times, they can be heard to exclaim: "La terre que nous habitons a été maudite à cause de nous; les végétaux ont contracté des qualités malfaisantes. L'air a perdu sa pureté. Les animaux ont participé à l'anathème. Eux aussi sont déchus."[31] Since the city must teach the inhabitants that "la vie de l'homme est un voyage dans une terre d'exil,"[32] the names of the various villages are significant: Bonté de Dieu; Réparation de la nature humaine; Expiation par l'oppobre; Repentir, seconde innocence. The names of the justices include: Providence qui veille à chacun des cheveux de notre tête; Providence qui s'occupe de la parure des lis, while the prefect bears the magnificent title of: Soleil qui luit sur les bons et les méchants. Plaques on the wall carry sententious phrases for the edification of the passer-by: "La liberté, c'est le moi humain."[33] Most of these, however, are couched in the strange phrases for which Ballanche showed such partiality:

> Les anciens, synthèse;
> les modernes, analyse;
> l'avenir, retourn à la synthèse.[34]

Some are borrowed from the great writers of the past, from Homer, Dante, Corneille, and Shakespeare. Conspicuously absent is Voltaire. Other plaques inject some of Ballanche's favorite opinions into the minds of the neophytes. One sign warns bluntly that "Boileau aurait voulu pétrifier la littérature," while another simply announces, "Jean-Jacques Rousseau: des émotions et non des pensées."

The upper city, however, differs markedly from the sections inhabited by the prisoners. After a stay of several months, Ballanche

visits the secret inner temple of the college of priests. His description of the church inevitably recalls the sanctuary into which
Thamyris was introduced in *Orphée* for his introduction to the
mystic doctrines of the Egyptians. The theology that the priests
explain to Ballanche parallels, too, what had been revealed to
Orpheus. Most of it would not frighten the *bien-pensants,* but
occasionally an opinion seems colored with the occult. Contemporaries were not surprised when Ballanche reiterated the doctrine
of temptation and expiation, and their irritation was only political
which sprang from his statement that "la moralité entre dans les
peuples par la liberté."[35] But many a puzzled reader wondered what
kind of priest would calmly discourse on "la théogonie cabirique et
platonique."[36]

V

Ballanche's attitude in the *Ville des Expiations* represented an
enormous stride forward in the consideration of the treatment of
criminals. For centuries, France had clung to a penal system based
on the maintenance of class privilege. The clergy and the nobility
punished evil-doers as a threat to their own security. A maze of
courts ground out sentences of appalling barbarity, not with the
intent to reform, but to strike bleak terror into any who dared
tamper with the *status quo.* Executions became public festivals and
criminals were maimed and tortured for the slightest breach of the
law.

Not until 1791, did there appear any evidence of a change in the
official attitude toward criminals, though initial attempts at reform
ended futilely. For the prisoner, the Terror offered only unhygienic
living conditions and comparative license to enjoy himself before
visiting the guillotine, but under Napoleon, the first timid reforms
were made. From 1810 on, the imperial government poked a cautious finger into the detention system, founding departmentally-
owned penitentiaries. And yet the quality of its mercy was not
well strained. At Toulon, Brest, and Rochefort, the Minister of the
Navy kept under his control large gangs of convicts sentenced to
forced labor. Here the discipline erred on the side of severity.
Chains kept most of the prisoners docile, while the constant threat

of the bastonnade curbed the small minority of the unruly and the stubborn. The only paternalism demonstrated was the provision that, after reaching the age of sixty, convicts might spend their remaining days in an ordinary prison.

Strangely enough, it was the conservative government of the Restoration which made the first real attempt to ameliorate the lot of prisoners. On April 9, 1819, a royal ordonnance modified the system of handling feeding in the prisons and, that same year, there was founded the *Société royale des prisons*. This society, while not basing its work on the principle of repression, nevertheless did not shift to the modern premise of rehabilitation. Reform it wanted, but reform founded on religious meditation. Through Christianity and the use of humane treatment, the members hoped to convert criminals to model citizens. Thus regulations were changed to provide high pay for prison work, provided the inmate desired to work. Excellent food was prepared and contacts with the exterior were abused and tolerated. The use of tobacco became standard procedure; money was even loaned to those temporarily out of funds. The age was so golden for prisoners that shocked taxpayers indignantly cried scandal when they learned of the conduct permitted in the name of Christianity. And yet, for all its preaching, the *Société royale* did leave with France a lasting reform. The young were henceforth segregated from older habitual criminals in institutions of their own.

Under the July Monarchy, the urge for change finally culminated in a complete revision of the penal code. Forthright and positive burghers even permitted the introduction into the law of the concept of attenuating circumstances. More important, in 1836 and 1841, commissions began investigations into the idea of cellular regime. Discipline became less severe, and in 1848, the romantic revolutionaries abolished forced labor and suppressed the death penalty for political crimes.

When the *Ville des Expiations* is examined in the light of this change in attitude toward criminals, its measure of originality becomes evident. Begun shortly after the Terror, the *Ville* precedes the considerable romantic literature of criminal reform that flowed from the presses during the reign of Louis-Philippe. Ballanche early foresaw a situation badly in need of correction and acted to ameliorate it. The kind-hearted philosopher from Lyon began to mull over plans for a different approach to the problem of correction, with the result that the *Ville* stands as a first in this particular kind of romantic creation.

Given the character and temperament of Ballanche and the knowledge that the manuscript of the book dates from 1820, one year after the foundation of the *Société royale des prisons,* the content of the work can be well appreciated. Like the members of the *Société,* Ballanche frowned on repression, preferring instead, correction through meditation. With a tremendous faith in the innate goodness of man, he firmly believed that a criminal would reform if shown that his actions were anti-social and anti-Christian. Long before the government began to consider the value of cellular incarceration, Ballanche had built his city around a modification of this idea, even separating prisoners into age groups. Passionately, he espoused the belief that a prisoner could be returned as a useful member of society, and to spare the condemned as much as possible, he advocated obliterating the criminal's identity until society had been repaid.

Why, then, had he not published his proposals for reform? The answer to this again lies in Ballanche's habit of procrastination. The *Ville* had been kept private until the moment suitable for its publication had passed. The Restoration looked with favor on such projects as the Christian city of the Lyon philosopher, but with the passing of the Bourbons, a more practical administration took charge. Again there came to the fore the concept of repression, this time not for class privileges, but for property rights. The bourgeois monarchy preferred to handle the problem of crime cautiously and, lacking Ballanche's faith in man, worked carefuly from a conservative position. While maintaining the principle of repression as a bulwark against any challenge to mine and thine, it timidly sought a new system without challenging the premises of the old. In such an atmosphere, one dessicating to anything overtly religious, Ballanche knew his city could never rise. Consequently, to avoid the jeers of the practical and the vengeful, he let the manuscript stay in the privacy of his desk.

VI

After 1830, Ballanche's literary output declined considerably, partly because of growing ill health, partly because of other interests. At this time, there came some compensation for the loss of some of Madame Récamier's affection to Chateaubriand. Mme d'Haute-feuille, née Anne-Abbe-Cornélie de Beaurepaire, became a second Récamier, someone to whom he could turn for praise, someone who would worry wholeheartedly about him. She had married the Comte Charles d'Hautefeuille on January 15, 1823, and since the Count frequented some of the same circles as Ballanche, his wife eventually met the philosopher of the Abbaye in 1827. Mme d'Hautefeuille had read *Antigone* and *l'Homme sans nom,* and she had been all the more impressed by them because she cherished ambitions to become a great writer herself. Drawn to Ballanche through his books, she tried unsuccessfully to arrange a second meeting through friends. Finally, taking her courage in her hands, she wrote to him, beginning thereby a long and close friendship.

Ballanche happily accepted Mme l'Hautefeuille as a disciple. It pleased him to act as the supreme judge of another's work, to guide without fear of rebellion. Dutifully, Mme d'Hautefeuille prepared her first work under his direction, a *nouvelle, la Vie brisée.* A great many letters passed back and forth with questions and answers until, in 1836, the story had been finished. Ballanche showed it to Sainte-Beuve as the work of an anonymous author, but the great critic remained singularly unimpressed.[37] For this reason, Ballanche kept closer watch on Mme d'Hautefeuille's first novel, *l'Ame exilée,* published under the pseudonym of Anne-Marie.[38] The plot of the story is uninspiring, though intended to be edifying:

> Une jolie jeune fille meurt d'une maladie de langueur, un miracle la rend à l'amour de sa mère, mais elle est triste sur la terre parce qu'elle a vu les cieux; on l'unit à son prétendu et elle en profite aussitôt pour trépasser définitivement.[39]

Mme d'Hautefeuille's success failed to equal that of the better known writers, but it was sufficient to encourage her to continue. Ballanche, therefore, became for the rest of his life a friend and a master, working with her on any difficulties encountered, then struggling to convince the press of the value of her novels.

The association with Mme d'Hautefeuille so pleased Ballanche
that he continually attempted to form a close friendship between
her and Madame Récamier. Why not, he thought, make friends of
the two women who constitute my universe? In this he made a
major tactical error. Mme d'Hautefeuille gladly consented to share
in the spotlight at the Abbaye, but Madame Récamier rejected the
idea coldly. There could be no other throne in the Abbaye-au-Bois.
She had worked too hard and too long to tolerate a younger rival,
especially one that had already bewitched Ballanche. Mme d'Hautefeuille frequented the Abbaye when in Paris, but the friendship
between the two women remained entirely official, something that
caused the naïve philosopher much puzzlement.

Mme d'Hautefeuille seemed to have brought Ballanche a measure
of good fortune. His cup filled when, in 1831, Chateaubriand recognized his existence as a major writer by considering his work in the
Etudes historiques. To be sure, the compliments verged on the
tepid, but the mere fact of their existence where all could read them
compensated for many a heartache. Chateaubriand grouped Ballanche in the company of the distinguished Herder and Vico, and
obligingly told the public that

> L'histoire vue de si haut ne convient peut-être à toutes les intelligences;
> mais celles même qui se plaisent aux lectures faciles trouveront un
> charme particulier dans la *Palingénésie sociale* de M. Ballanche. Un
> style élégant et harmonieux revêt des pensées consolantes et pures:
> il semble que l'on voie tous les secrets de la conscience calme et sereine
> de l'auteur, comme à la tranquille et mystérieuse lumière de son
> imagination. Ce génie théosophique ne nous laisse rien à envier à
> l'Allemagne et à l'Italie.[40]

Ballanche repaid the compliment when, in June, 1832, Chateaubriand was arrested for plotting against the safety of the state. The
duchesse de Berry had disembarked in Provence in a mad attempt
to win back the nation to the Bourbons. Appointed a member of
her secret government, Chateaubriand had sent two notes to per-
suade her to desist. The messenger, Berryer, fell into the hands of
the police at Angoulême, and, on June 16, the prefect of police
sent men to arrest Chateaubriand. Ballanche promptly rallied to
his friend. The entire Abbaye used its considerable influence to
keep René from harm, even persuading Bertin to write an article

in the *Journal des Débats* demanding the liberty of the great writer.

When Chateaubriand prudently left Paris for Switzerland, to be followed shortly by Madame Récamier, Ballanche found himself functioning as a clearing house for all news and gossip. Thus it was he who forwarded the news of the condemnation of the *Avenir,* with comments on the action of Rome to show that he had not relinquished his right to criticize:

> Vous avez pu voir par les journaux que M. de Lamennais et ses amis, pour ne pas être en opposition avec le pape et en contradiction avec eux-mêmes se retirent de la polémique qu'ils avaient entreprise. Ils renoncent en même temps au journal l'*Avenir* et à l'Association pour la liberté religieuse. Ceci est, à mes yeux, un grand événement, sous le rapport que le catholicisme semble de plus en plus se séparer de nous. Les gallicans vont peut-être essayer de relever un drapeau mais ils auront si peu de monde derrière eux que ce sera une vraie pitié. . . . Au reste, ce qui arrive pour la société religieuse arrive également pour la société civile et politique. Le pouvoir n'a plus en lui la force d'assimilation et de représentation d'idées.[41]

Faithfully he repeated to Madame Récamier his disappointment that men whom he knew, Saint-Marc Girardin, for instance, should fail to speak of him in their articles, or that the *Débats* should publish studies on Roman history without crediting the use of his theories. He consoled himself by regaling her with an account of a visit with Nodier to a workers' study group. By this time Ballanche had become so partial to workers that he considered insulting a remark by Saint-Marc Girardin that the rise of the modern proletariat could be compared to an invasion of barbarians.

VII

Though aging, Ballanche had not by any means relinquished thoughts of further publication, though countless occupations kept him from his desk. Now that Madame Récamier lived far away in Constance, with M. and Mme. de Chateaubriand, he had leisure to add to his literary edifice:

> J'ai, depuis longtemps [he wrote to Madame Récamier on August 30], le projet de faire un petit volume qui aura pour titre: *La mort symbole de l'immortalité.* Ce livre est tout fait, car il se compose de différents épisodes de mes ouvrages: la Fille de la Sunamite (Orphée); Mort d'Œdipe (Antigone); la Sibylle du vieux monde (Orphée); Mort d'Eurydice (Orphée); Mort d'Erigone (Orphée); Mort d'Antigone

(Antigone); Mort de Virginie (Formule générale); Mort d'Orphée
(Orphée). Tous ces épisodes sont des peintures de la mort, mais de
la mort qui produit la vie. Aussi toutes ces morts sont douces,
aimables, harmonieuses et même, pour plusieurs, le cérémonie funèbre
se présente sous l'emblème d'une pompe nuptiale. En même temps
que je m'occupe de la pensée de ce petit volume, tout d'affection,
j'arrange dans ma tête un autre petit volume, mais celui-là est à faire;
c'est la *Tapisserie-Fée*. La mort y sera aussi le symbole de l'immortalité.
Je songe toujours à mon volume de *Méditations* mais ce sera le dernier
acte de ma vie, mon testament. Vous voyez que j'ai encore de la laine
à ma quenouille et que c'est toujours de la laine blanche, blanche
comme l'apparition de votre personne pure et sacrée.[42]

La Tapisserie-Fée appeared that same year in the *Revue de Paris*,
the only short story Ballanche ever published.[43] The strange tale
recalls the fantastic plots of Nodier, while still carrying the same
philosophical message as Ballanche's other work. Though in
nouvelle form, there appears the same incapacity for dialogue, the
same long, didactic speeches, but, on the credit side of the ledger,
the same ability to describe, to intimate more than the words stated.

The story recalls the days when Ballanche traveled south to meet
Madame Récamier. At Trieste, in Le Lion-Endormi, the inn-keeper
regaled him with the story of a magic tapestry in a near-by castle.
Wreckers are to demolish the old château and the tapestry, the
work of a famous magicienne, will probably dissolve. Ballanche left
by the light of the moon to see this curiosity.

The thesis of the short story appears from the description of what
Ballanche sees in the design of the hanging. While staring at the
picture of a farmhouse, he is startled to have a young girl step from
its door, and finds himself asking who she is:

Je suis la fille de ta vision [she answers]: je suis, j'ai été, je serai, ainsi
que toi-même tu es, tu as été, tu seras. Je viens de la région qu'habite
toute pensée avant d'être une parole; et cette contrée, que tu entrevois
à peine, est une idée, un mirage de ton esprit, qui représente l'abrégé
du monde.[44]

The young girl pursues her tasks, gathering flowers for two crowns,
one for a dying old man, another for her wedding. She climbs high
on some rocks to cry mystic warnings to the cities below. Ballanche
asks the meaning of these words; she gives an explanation:

Depuis que l'homme existe toujours sur la terre, toujours deux armées sont en présence, et toujours animées d'une fureur égale. L'activité humaine est au prix d'un combat terrible. La guerre éternelle n'est suspendue que par des trèves. Les principes opposés, aux temps palingénésiques, subissent des transformations qui leur laissent la même vie et la même antipathie. C'est la lutte de l'Orient et de l'Occident, du patriciat et du plébéianisme, du destin et de la volonté, du sacerdoce et du génie militaire, de la puissance spirituelle et de la puissance temporelle, de l'autorité et de l'examen, de la tradition et de la spontanéité, de la science et de la croyance. Tu sais cela aussi bien que moi, puisque c'est ta pensée que j'exprime. Puis elle ajoute: 'Les deux armées n'en viendront pas aux mains. Un chef s'avance au milieu de l'espace qui les sépare, comme dans cette fameuse bataille décrite par le grand poète indien. Et ce chef va dire la loi d'harmonie qui établira la nouvelle trève des deux armées.[45]

Like Séraphita, the girl disappears skyward in search of the new leader. Dawn breaks, finding Ballanche full of the sense of contrast in life and with renewed hope that evil might disappear.

VIII

In 1833, Ballanche's health weakened more than usual; he was confined to bed, where he could brood over the events occurring outside. Cholera had come to Paris as an uninvited guest. He could see the long convoys of bodies filing down the streets in dreary uninterrupted procession. No relatives escorted them; passers-by shrank against the wall when necessity forced them to approach the ghastly line of carts, wagons and carriages. Workers threatened the sky with upraised fists, then shrugged away their anger as soon as the cortège had passed.[46] M. and Mme. Lenormant attempted to cheer him up, but the first years of the bourgeois monarchy had piled up within him a distaste for contemporary values that could not be drained away in a moment of laughter. From a bed he wrote his misgivings to Bredin, pouring out the black mood that blanketed him:

Bon ami, je suis fort attristé de tout ce qui se passe autour de moi, et la société me paraît bien malade. Toutefois, j'espère en la Providence, elle a des ressources qui échappent à nos regards. . . .
La noblesse a mis plus de quatre siècles à se ruiner; moins de quatre ans ont suffi à la bourgeoisie pour se dégrader et s'avilir. . . .
Le sentiment moral s'en va; la littérature n'a plus d'honnêteté; les

écrivains, à quelques exceptions prés, font marchandise de leur plume;
que leur importe la vérité? Les journaux ne songent qu'à flatter les
passions des partis, sans tenir aucun compte du vrai et du juste. . . .
Maintenant, il est manifeste que nous rétrogradons rapidement.[47]

Few, it seemed, could be called principled and art appeared to have
soiled the cradle of the romantic reform.

To offset this spreading gloom, Ballanche published a second edition of the *Œuvres*.[48] Sainte-Beuve, extremely conscious of Ballanche's work now that he frequented the Abbaye, jotted down some
compliments for the author on March 1, 1833:

> Chacun pourra désormais suivre la pensée de M. Ballanche sous les
> diverses formes et dans l'ordre de génération où elle s'est produite:
> on désirera vivement surtout l'achèvement de cet édifice grandiose, dont
> on aura traversé le péristyle et dont on aura vu se dessiner l'enceinte.[49]

Another bright moment came that year as the gift of the monarchy.
In 1833, Guizot, then Minister of Public Instruction, completely of
his own accord, awarded Ballanche a literary pension of eighteen
hundred francs a year. At first Ballanche refused, not wishing to
accept money from a government of which he disapproved. Besides,
there were so many others in more desperate want. But Madame
Récamier insisted until Ballanche reluctantly accepted the gift. He
really needed it. The funds inherited from his father had slowly
disappeared, generously shared with others or spent fantastically
for privately printed editions, for plans of the *Ville des Expiations,*
or handed over to inventors with strange machines. Like many of
the romanticists, Ballanche lacked a sense of money value, which
caused him to forget that his funds were limited. Madame Récamier
had been wiser than he in forcing acceptance of the pension.

The tragic sights around him and the necessity of having to thank
Guizot had a curious effect on Ballanche. He slashed out in anger,
but this time he selected for a target the Czar of all the Russias.
Now that he had moved closer to democracy, now that he had been
cured of all affection for the Bourbons and their kind, he decided
to support the victims of oppression in other lands. And this effort
was to be his swan song. He began in October, 1833, a series of
articles in *le Polonais* to aid Polish exiles in a seemingly hopeless
fight against Russian domination. He called down the wrath of the

faithful on the Czar with a warning that Russia had remained behind the times. Though wishing to become a European nation, the bear that walks like a man still tried to maintain aristocratic prerogatives.[50] Europe, he fumed, could only protest at the barbarous confiscations carried on by troops the French could well remember, the Cossacks. France herself was to blame for permitting an old friend to be persecuted by the colossus of the north. Property and family had become mockeries.[51]

Until 1835, Ballanche maintained a steady stream of protest directed at the Czar's policy. While Lamartine orated magnificently to the Chamber on the fate of the "sick man of Europe," Ballanche insinuated that the bear might march down to outwit the French. Let Russia establish forts on the Dardanelles and the French would soon discover what an error they had made in permitting so much power to slip from their hands.[52] The Russians should be excluded from the European confraternity and kept from the carcass of the Turk.[53] Ballanche never did relinquish hope that Poland would rise again, though he did see the futility of his campaign. Therefore, in his last contribution to *le Polonais*, in March, 1835, the little philosopher left his friends with a note of hope; it was all he could offer them.[54]

CHAPTER IX

The Last Years—The Inventor—The Academy

I

AFTER the gloomy year 1833, Ballanche settled down in the placid life of the Abbaye, content now to grow old. He might have lapsed again into morbid thoughts had not the solemn readings of the *Mémoires d'outre-tombe* taken his mind from these troubles. Before a select committee comprising Ballanche, Montmorency, Noailles, La Rochefoucauld, Ampère, Quinet and Sainte-Beuve, René read the story of his life.[1] These sessions meant more to Ballanche than to the others, for Chateaubriand had begun to speak of Madame Récamier. René had decided to place beside his own a portrait of the woman with whom he had so long been associated. Ballanche watched suspiciously lest liberties be taken with her reputation. Chateaubriand could give himself to the public, but Madame Récamier was not to be dragged from privacy without her express permission. As her determined protector stated, "Je suis là pour ajouter aux soins de l'auteur, pour veiller aux susceptibilités de celle qui en est l'objet."[2]

Perhaps unconsciously thinking of his situation with regard to Madame Récamier, Ballanche published early in 1834 a collection of letters written by Mlle de Condé in 1786 and 1787.[3] Paris pricked up its ears in the belief that the book was a political manifesto. Interest quickened as readers attempted to devine the names prudence had deleted. Even Lamennais became intrigued with this new game. On November 23, 1834, he asked the baron de Vitrolles:

> . . . avez-vous lu les Lettres écrites en 1786 et 1787, que Ballanche vient de publier? Comme tout se sait, on doit savoir les noms que l'éditeur a dû taire. Je serais curieux de les connaître, parce qu'ils appartiennent, au moins l'un des deux, à notre province. Ces lettres me paraissent, au surplus, beaucoup trop louées dans la préface.[4]

Those who saw in the publication of the letters a tribute to the Ancien Régime were quick to flay Ballanche with jeers at his contention that the princess had lived only two happy days. They laughed deeply at his panegyric of her love and purity. The mockery reached such a pitch that the normally even-tempered Ballanche struck back with unexpected vigor in a brochure entitled *De la publication des lettres écrites en 1786 et 1787*.[5] Hypocrisy, hate, envy, and impudence tried, he said, to soil the letters; on all sides men worked to ruin morality. Wound up with indignation, Ballanche loosed a torrent of invective on the pseudo-intellectuals of an age that specialized in negation:

> . . . à vous la honte et le ridicule, têtes perdues à travers le choc des crises perturbatrices au dernier point, qui ne laissant pas de ressentir une certaine émotion et même quelque admiration à la lecture des ineffables lettres, n'avez plus qu'à appeler l'inconséquence au secours de la méchanceté, pour vous mettre en droit de frapper du reproche. . . .[6]

His anger attained splendid proportions because of the error of his opponents in mistaking a compliment to purity for a declaration of ultra-royalism. In truth, as he admitted to Loménie:

> J'ai été très consulaire, mais pas du tout impérial; j'ai vu avec bonheur la restauration de l'Eglise, mais j'ai été effrayé pour elle de la voir renaître pompeuse comme jadis et liée à l'Etat par la reconnaissance: je l'aurais mieux aimée libre de se relever sans appui et d'elle-même avec sa croix de bois. Le Consulat et l'Eglise hors de l'Etat, voilà quel était mon idéal en politique et en religion.[7]

Not all Paris mocked Ballanche. Adolphe Mazure stepped in to back the outraged author by publishing in *la France Littéraire* a flattering portrait of the philosopher of the Abbaye, with special emphasis on precisely the traits at which the liberals had sneered in the *Lettres*. "M. Ballanche a des rivaux, il n'a pas de maîtres. . . . M. Ballanche . . . est un fleuve majestueux, qui ne passe et ne tarit jamais."[8] The words were balm to a little man harassed by the cynical chuckles of political opponents.

Ballanche's anger quieted with the compliment, then turned to dismay when, in 1835, Madame Récamier fell ill, frightening the two men who constantly watched over her. Her sight weakened, fever set in from lack of sleep, and she began to cough. Could it be tuberculosis? That winter, on cold mornings, Ballanche and Chateau-briand stood in the courtyard waiting for the doctor to depart from his daily visit. They dared not ring for fear lest Madame Récamier guess their worry, but hid from view of her windows to pounce on the physician as he opened the door. This companionship in terror brought them closer together, perhaps, than any other event in their past; for the moment, jealousies and rivalries were forgotten in a common worry.

Happily for them, Madame Récamier recovered without serious after-effects and the men could continue the former tenor of their lives. Ballanche slipped back with a sigh to his reading and counsel-ing. Mme d'Hautefeuille, Adolphe Dumas, and a host of others occupied much of his time. Now that his reputation had begun to spread, there was even talk of an illustrated edition of his complete works. Some of the younger generation, he felt, still had faith in the principles for which he stood.[9] Accordingly, he planned to work on the *Vision d'Hébal,* spurred by the news that there had appeared at Angers an English translation of *Orphée.* Surprisingly, sufficient subscribers came forward to subsidize the work when the translator was unable to finance the publication.[10]

The next year he again found himself the object of flattering at-tention. Edouard Gans, permitted to enter the sanctuary of the Abbaye-au-Bois, returned to the *Revue de Paris* to write a reverent article on *le Salon de Madame Récamier.* As befitting his rank in literature, Chateaubriand received first mention, but it was pleasing to Ballanche to be discussed at great length with affection. What author would resent being told that "l'histoire du temps passé nous apparaît sur ses lèvres comme un breuvage magique dans un vase d'or"?[11]

But the very passive enjoyment with which Ballanche tasted praise revealed that time had begun to pull at his coat tails. Gone was the fierce pride in success. Little by little the disappearance of con-temporaries had brought a reminder that he could no longer plan elaborately for the future. On June 10, 1836, André-Marie Ampère died, leaving Ballanche heartsick. In memory of his great friend, he prepared a eulogy for the *Journal des Débats,* but the editor cav-alierly ignored the article. Again in August death called, this time for his sister. Ballanche felt conscience-stricken not to have been with her. He had closed the eyes of his mother and father and, as the survivor of the family, should have attended his sister. He drew cold comfort from the fact that death had spared her acute suffering when he pointed out cheerlessly to Mme d'Hautefeuille that her life had been "une triste preuve que la vie elle-même est une expiation, car, certainement, elle n'avait rien à expier pour elle."[12]

To slough off the depressing thought of a diminishing circle of friends and relatives, Ballanche worked over a new selected edition of his books. He spent many hours planning two volumes of thirty-three books, one volume on the ancient world, another on the modern. He hoped to arrange them in the form of a last will and testament.[13] Didot prepared special type in November of the same year and Ballanche carefully selected a fine paper. To be sure, the money came from the author's pocket. Ballanche had little except for Guizot's pension, but the death of his sister had given him properties left to them jointly, which he immediately sold to pay old debts. With undiminished optimism, he saw himself out of the financial woods: "Je pourrai payer ce que je dois, faire les derniers frais que j'aurai à faire pour mes livres. Et j'entrerai dans un repos parfait."[14] But like so many projects, this one never reached culmination. Ballanche found himself poorer than ever, and his time occupied at the Abbaye listening to the *Mémoires d'outre-tombe*. Three years later he was still talking of publication, but he never actually finished the work.

The almost constant state of poverty in no way dampened Ballanche's hopes of making a fortune. A favorite dream called for repurchasing for three or four hundred thousand francs the *Mémoires* which Chateaubriand now regretted having sold. Yet, even with these plans, he held no illusions about approaching old age. "Notre pauvre vie s'en va goutte à goutte [he wrote to Madame Récamier]. . . . J'ai eu quelques beaux jours auprès de vous, cela me suffit. . . ."[15]

He could console himself with a new honor. On June 7, 1837, the *Moniteur* published a list of promotions to the Legion of Honor inspired by the marriage of the duc d'Orléans to the Princess Helen of Mecklenburg-Schwerin. Characteristically, Ballanche protested on finding himself included among the *chevaliers* along with Sainte-Beuve, de Tocqueville, and Paulin Paris; he could think of no reason for the award.[16] But an ever-watchful Madame Récamier insisted until he reluctantly decided to keep the medal. However, the honest philosopher felt obliged to recount his scruples to Mme d'Hautefeuille:

> M. de Salvandy, en m'écrivant une lettre officielle pour la Légion d'honneur, y avait joint une lettre très aimable de lui. J'ai bien fait trois lettres de réponse et je n'en ai envoyé aucune. Cette décoration me paraît une stupidité pour moi dans ce moment. Depuis longtemps je n'ai rien publié, ce qui ôte le motif de l'occasion. Je suis en dehors de toutes choses, je ne vais nulle part. A quoi donc peut me servir le ruban? Je ne l'ai pas encore mis. Il faudra bien qu'un jour je fasse une visite à M. de Salvandy. Ce jour-là je mettrai le ruban, puis ce sera fini.[17]

On June 25, he finally thanked M. de Salvandy for the distinction, but added stubbornly that, since he had done nothing of note for some years, he considered the decoration a tardy acknowledgment of former deeds.[18]

II

Most of Ballanche's admirers puzzled over his disappearance from the literary scene. By his own admission, he had published nothing of importance for a long time, and nothing else seemed likely to come from him. Many simply decided that his vein had given out and that the aging man now intended to rest in the warmth of an expanding fame. This may have been partially true, but there was another stronger reason. Despite precarious health, Ballanche had turned inventor. Such dabbling in science plus a mania for de luxe editions, explained why his sizeable fortune had disappeared, forcing him to the disagreeable position of having to watch every penny.

His preoccupation with science had been evident long before 1837. In 1813, Ballanche had perfected for his father a new method of melting type and had even momentarily considered establishing a foundry at Paris. In the prolegomena for *Orphée,* he had observed that "peut-être aussi que les préoccupations de la science m'auraient rendu moins propre à un certain ordre de méditations,"[19] but actually, he had been too intent on spreading his philosophy to spend much time on science. After 1830, however, when there came the realization of the end of his mission, that he could do nothing but wait to see if his ideas would live, he turned to experimentation.

In this, Ballanche was reacting to the Industrial Revolution in true nineteenth century style. Though theoretically the eighteenth century had seen the introduction of mechanization, it was the nineteenth that felt its full impact. In 1819, Oersted experimented with the telegraph and his work was continued by Ballanche's close friend, André-Marie Ampère. In the course of experiments, Ampère formulated the general law of electro-magnetic attraction and repulsion. By 1843, other men had produced a practical instrument and the next year Paris and Rouen were linked by telegraph. The progress made on the steam engine was even more impressive. In the eighteenth century these had been curiosities, but, by 1839, two thousand were in productive use, and the Jacquard loom had given Lyon an era of prosperity. Shipping also profited from these technical advances. In 1816, Jouffroy d'Abbans launched a steamboat on the Seine and, that same year, the *Elise* crossed the Channel. Fourteen years later, France could boast of fifteen steamships. Likewise, the spread of the railroad contributed to the rapid change in French technology. The Restoration granted the first concession in February, 1823, from the Loire to Pont d'Ain, and the railroad began operation five years later. Shortly thereafter, in 1832, the Sainte-Etienne-Lyon Railroad astonished France by installing a steam locomotive. So successful was it that Louis-Philippe authorized networks that soon changed the complexion of the country.

It is to be noted that Ballanche's friendship with Ampère spurred him to emulate the famous scientist in the hope that he, too, would earn world-shaking renown. Furthermore, though catholic in his experiments, Ballanche worked principally on a new motor for use in ships and locomotives. The curious philosopher realized that speed in transportation was of primary interest to industrialists.

In pursuit of this motor, Ballanche managed to dissipate so much money in weird experiments that by August, 1836, Madame Récamier became uneasy. His affairs, she told Mme Lenormant, had come to a sad state. He had become the Don Quixote of mechanics. But Ballanche persisted. He drew up plans for a revolutionary omnibus, but a hydraulic machine claimed almost all his attention.

With the designs and the explanations ready, he told Mme d'Haute-feuille in August, 1839, that he hoped to apply for a patent in a month. The great test would come with submission of the idea to a committee then considering methods to replace the Versailles water system. The aqueduct from Marly had lately functioned so poorly that the government judged imperative a new system of piping water. Acceptance of his machine would yield a prize of 400,000 francs. A sanguine Ballanche already began to count the money.[20]

The invention did not turn out as hoped, but Ballanche kept his faith. The theory seemed sound and he hired two mathematicians to check it algebraically. The only remaining difficulty was to find a mechanic to help solve some of the practical problems.[21] He had trouble discovering a young Montgolfier, for by July 25, 1840, the work had progressed little.

Finally, by September 10, the machine was so near completion that he hoped to begin tests. His motor now promised to generate so much power that he hesitated continuing until its precise strength could be ascertained. By this time, too, he had decided to use it in a new kind of boat. He let Mme d'Hautefeuille in on the secret be-cause to her would fall the honor of launching the first craft at Saint-Vrain.[22] He allowed enthusiasm to carry him away. The in-vention would outmode steam, and the monograph in which he expected to describe it surely would win him a seat in the Académie des Sciences. Breathlessly he piled dream on dream. Then the Académie Française could do what it wished. He would present himself, but he intended to remain imperturbable even in the face of an improbable refusal. All this, he assured Mme d'Hautefeuille, within three months; she needn't worry about finances, for soon he would have more than enough money. The excess he planned to share with friends and to use for the publication of the great scien-tific works of the Middle Ages. "Je persiste," he ended, "dans mon projet de la restauration de la science."[23]

To the eager inventor, work went slowly, but nothing could rush matters. Countless trivialities slowed down a job that should have been finished in a month. Long he labored on new apparatus with the aid of a single worker until finally trials could be made.

Then, on August 22, 1841, he admitted the terrible news; the machine had failed. Twice he ran tests. The first time an eery cracking sounded and, to remedy any weakness, he had the foundation reinforced. Then he started the motor confidently, only to have it leap through the roof, base and all. Such a disaster would have crushed an ordinary man, but Ballanche only admired the terrible strength of his creation. He knew now that the motor could generate more power than a steam engine; all he had to do was master its energy. It lay in ruins but he could rebuild. Think of it. Six men could scarcely lift the monster and at the second run it had left the ground. Ballanche felt dizzy with expectation.[24]

The world-shaking motor came to naught, but during the course of a fantastic career as inventor, Ballanche did realize some successes. Noted as a pacifist, he none the less invented a new cannon, a model of which was installed at Versailles. More remarkably still, he had foreseen and worked on some ideas which others would carry to conclusion. He poured his small fortune into the moulds scraped out of the ground for his apparatus, doomed to envisage what would be, but incapable of creating it himself.[25]

III

So deeply did Ballanche immerse himself in inventing that he gave little time to writing. However, at the Abbaye he studied Chateaubriand's work carefully for, in 1839, René resumed the portrait of Madame Récamier, even to the detriment of the *Mémoires*. Ballanche functioned as a member of the group that ruled on the inclusion of material. It was such a delicate task that Ballanche once snorted, "Je suis entouré de personnes qui traitent fort mal ceux qui ne partagent pas leur enthousiasme."[26] Discussions inevitably arose as to the suitability of some sections and when Chateaubriand doubted his own scruples, Ballanche proposed Mme d'Hautefeuille as an impartial reader. Mme d'Hautefeuille agreed, but the manuscript was probably not sent to her until late in July. Her observations are unknown though soon she began to speak of writing her own biography of Madame Récamier. Chateaubriand's portrait took form, at all events, and was incorporated into the *Mémoires* as book XI, part III.[27]

By now Ballanche's health had become progressively worse, and he lived for the most part on a diet of milk and vegetables. The doctor ordered short, but frequent walks, moderation in all things. Ballanche obeyed as best he could, but when health forbade work in the shop, the irrepressible little man worked on what he called his *Théodicée*. Alone in his room he had been gripped by a passion for modern history, partly because he believed France needed good historians. Only three men could be named as measuring up to his standards: Chateaubriand, Guizot, and Augustin Thierry.[28] Ill health and the demands of inventing, however, prevented completion of the task. As the months passed, he complained continually that his writing had to be postponed, even though Mme d'Hautefeuille carried him off to Saint-Vrain in 1840 so that he could classify his notes while recuperating. Here he played chess to his heart's content and his health improved under lavish care, but ambition left him proportionately as he grew stronger.[29]

Ballanche had retired even from active participation in politics. Formerly, he had delighted in ceaseless offers of gratuitous advice to France's rulers. Now he retained only a constitutional right to dislike the government. And this he did heartily. The reign of King Pear appeared shabbily materialistic, a slovenly imitation of former glories. Thiers postured in Parliament, but Ballanche remained cold to his wiles. And when the fortifications of Paris were completed, he wondered, like many a fellow citizen, whether the new walls protected the Parisians or their king. By April, 1841, he was certain that Louis-Philippe's famous royal umbrella would disappear: "Aurons-nous le prince Louis ou le gamin Thiers [he inquired of Mme d'Hautefeuille]? Charles X, par le licenciement de la garde nationale, avait livré Paris à M. le duc d'Orléans. A qui vont arriver ces clefs?"[30] Commerce may have improved under the duc d'Orléans, but France had lost so much prestige that Ballanche feared for her future; what it held, he dared not guess. Legitimacy was dying in exile; quasi-legitimacy continued to ruin itself; but a republic seemed impossible.

IV

In 1842, Ballanche's last wish was granted. The Académie Française, wooed over many years, opened reluctant arms to receive him. The chase had been long and arduous, but Ballanche finally attained the distinction of officially becoming an immortal. Yet the triumph came so late in life that it had lost almost all flavor.

Immediately after the publication of the *Oeuvres,* Madame Récamier had begun to work for his election to the Academy. Perhaps it was she who persuaded Sainte-Beuve to write in favor of a candidacy for Ballanche, or perhaps the critic himself considered his Abbaye friend great enough for the honor. At all odds, on December 11, 1834, Sainte-Beuve notified Buloz of his intention to send the next day a short article on the vacancy at the Academy. Thus, under the signature G[ustave] P[lanche], the *Revue des Deux Mondes* inserted two pages on *M. Thiers à l'Académie Française.*[31] The note ended with the following advice to the Academicians: "Qu'elle [the Academy] appelle dans son sein M. Ballanche et M. Hugo; qu'elle rende une éclatante justice à l'auteur d'*Antigone.*"[32]

Sainte-Beuve's propaganda made Ballanche feel good, but it failed to convince the voters. On January 16, 1835, he judged his chances good for the seat of Parseval-Grandmaison, a famous poet of the Empire, but hedged on a possible disappointment. At all events, successful or not, candidacy would bring a good meed of publicity.[33] Messieurs the Academicians could not agree on a choice, and final decision was postponed until February, but the first results convinced Ballanche he had little chance. This he attributed to the levity with which some of his friends had at times publicly treated the forty immortals.[34]

The blunt Academic refusal of Ballanche's company had one salutary effect: it sent him scurrying to produce other qualifications. Though joking at the idea of ever being elected, he none the less solemnly told Mme d'Hautefeuille that his new books would see him in.[35] The next January (1836), without any new books, he trotted assiduously on another round of calls. Sainte-Beuve regretfully informed Adolphe Dumas that Molé would win, but added that Ballanche was considering a translation of the Bible, a fitting use of his extraordinary style.[36] The unpredictable Academicians selected Dupaty, February 18, 1836, with the result that some of the newspapers screamed with rage at the choice of such a successor for Lainé. The *Revue de Paris* of February 21, commented bitterly on the *bona fides* of the new member:

Trois candidats d'un nom imposant se présentaient: L'un philosophe de l'école symbolique de Vico, qui a cherché à pénétrer les mythes de l'Orient, qui a jeté un manteau aux plis flottants et majestueux sur le squelette amaigri et desséché du rationalisme du dernier siècle, l'homme modeste, de saveurs douces, véritable sage à la façon antique ou plutôt nouvel anachorète des premiers temps du christianisme, c'était M. Ballanche. Le second candidat était un homme politique éminent . . . [M. Molé]. Le troisième candidat était M. Victor Hugo. . . . Lorsque l'on interroge son voisin sur les titres de M. Dupaty . . . l'un vous répond, la *Leçon de Botanique;* l'autre des épithalames officiels; le troisième, capitaine de la garde nationale. . . . Ce choix a produit quelque étonnement.[37]

No whit daunted by refusals, Ballanche became a consistent candidate for election. So relentlessly did he pursue the elusive and coy Academy that his patience was finally rewarded in 1842. By this time, he had managed to collect a number of sure votes: Cousin, Chateaubriand, Lamartine, Hugo, and Nodier. The latter especially would cast his ballot for Ballanche at every occasion, while Chateaubriand considered it a duty to the Abbaye to fight for his friend. This time two seats had fallen vacant, those of M. de Cessac and M. Duval, and so strong a claim did Ballanche now have that Alphonse Karr whispered to Paris in *Les Guêpes:*

L'Académie, la vieille coquette, semble ne vouloir céder qu'à un de ces *beaux feux,* qu'à une de ces longues passions sur lesquelles mademoiselle de Scudéri faisait dix volumes. Il faut lui faire longtemps la cour pour obtenir ses faveurs. . . . D'après toutes les probabilités, M. Pasquier succédera à M. de Cessac, et M. Ballanche à M. Duval.[38]

Madame Récamier worked tirelessly in favor of her candidate, soliciting votes through the power of her salon and her famed hospitality. Ballanche hoped for success as he watched her struggle with smiling, but non-committal, academicians,, or urge Chateaubriand to secure the votes of his friends. Politics and the Abbaye vogue for Rachel passed into the background as Madame Récamier's determination to elect her philosopher became an obsession. In this atmosphere, Ballanche knocked on famous doors, hat in hand, courting elusive fortune in the maze of Academic politics. This time he succeeded. Ballanche excitedly reported to Mme d'Hautefeuille on February 17, 1842, that M. Pasquier had won by a majority of twenty-three votes, he by seventeen.[39]

The election, however, could not escape some cries of dissatisfaction, especially from editors who resented the selection of an old habitué of the Abbaye salon. Shortly after the great event, there appeared a small satirical dictionary that dealt with contemporary celebrities. Fortunatus, the unknown author, pretended to have come to judge leading personalities. Concerning Ballanche, he noted that "Tout récemment, on a embaumé ce profond vieillard déjà antique; on l'a ficelé de bandelettes et déposé dans une niche à l'Académie, avec cette étiquette: Ballanche-Logogriphe." Yet, for all his biting humor, he bought back his words with a kindly remark for the quiet old man: "Et pourtant les ombres de La Fontaine et de Fénelon lui ont souri."[40]

The reception at the Academy on April 28, 1842, stood out as a brilliant social function, if not one of vivid intellectual fireworks. M. de Barante had been selected to reply to Ballanche's speech, and the entire Abbaye assembled in support of its philosopher. Chateaubriand appeared at a public function for the last time. A pleased Ballanche reported that his election had been well-received by the socially-minded, many of whom came to see him installed. Even his maid, Fanny, seemed pleased.

Ballanche's speech approached the cautious, as befitted a newly-elected Academician. Caught by one of his spells, his acceptance was read by the historian, Mignet, while the successful candidate smiled happily from his seat. The discourse treated mostly of Duval's life, though the new immortal admitted that the works of his predecessor were unfamiliar to him.[41] Once he did depart from a prosaic relation of Duval's work to chide the latter on his part in the battle of romanticism. Though Ballanche knew that the issues on which he touched still stung the Academy into sharp debate, he nevertheless scolded the classicists for obstructing the new æsthetics.

> M. Duval, vous le savez, Messieurs, fut en effet très vif dans la querelle entre les classiques et les romantiques. J'ose dire ici qu'il ne savait pas, et que le temps où s'agitait la question avec le plus de violence ignorait également le problème qu'il s'agissait de résoudre. Et ces problèmes qui embrassent l'homme tout entier . . . ne se prêtent à des théories trop timides, ni à des spéculations trop aventureuses, ni à de vagues doctrines.[42]

The speech ended with a bow for the manner in which Chateaubriand had backed him, and the modest academician added that his only hope to glory lay in being carried along by his great friend.[43]

The baron de Barante answered suavely, if with a touch of condescension that betokened a pat on the head. He gracefully complimented the new colleague, though labelling his doctrines "naïves." He pointed out that the Academy had hoped to receive an exposition of Ballanche's system, but this task had been avoided.[44] Perhaps it was, as Ballanche had written, that he could not read far enough into the future to foresee even the lives of their children. And yet, despite this carping and subtle criticism, de Barante welcomed the member-elect to the brotherhood as gently as could be expected, with enough rolling oratory to make the Abbaye feel that its champion had been greeted with all proper ceremonies.

The Academy now filled the moments in Ballanche's day not set aside for the Abbaye or inventions. He attended meetings religiously though exercizing little influence on its actions. The honorarium of fifteen hundred livres enabled him to renounce his pension. He had no desire to be obligated to Guizot, whom he disliked personally, or to Thiers, whom he thought a vain little man in love with war. Rather, he sympathized with the romantic socialism and pacifism of Lamartine, the only deputy whose opinion he was anxious to know. This did not throw him into the arms of the Republicans, for he remembered too clearly a youth spent under the Terror.

His vote, however, gave him the opportunity to start driving a wedge into the Academy's door for writers hitherto ostracized for romanticism. Despite the fact that he believed the Academy partial to mediocrities, he began a one-man crusade in favor of Alfred de Vigny, persevering even when his choice was rejected in favor of M. Patin. With Ballanche voting, the younger generation could claim a friend among its judges. In recognition of this, Vigny noted in his *Journal* about this time: "Aujourd'hui, le bon Ballanche me dit que sa voix est à moi lorsqu'il aura le droit de voter.—Il cause en paix et agréablement avec moi. Honnête et bon vieillard, il a l'air satisfait et heureux.—Dans un salon, dit-il, sur quarante hommes, chacun prend les siens; je ferai de même, et vous aussi, à l'Académie: nous prendrons les nôtres."[45]

IV

His health bad, Ballanche passed the summer of 1842 with Mme d'Hautefeuille at Saint-Vrain, where he could review his life. He had attained the summit of desire, only to glance down into gloom. The salon at the Abbaye had lost its first rank. Chateaubriand had become more imperious in demands for praise and services, yet protested each time Madame Récamier tried to introduce new faces. Ballanche insisted on retaining an intimate circle, closed to all outsiders. This made Madame Récamier's task easier, yet permitted decay to set in, reducing the famous salon to a group of oldsters shrouded in memories of greater days.[46]

More attentions showered on Ballanche now that he had been officially stamped great. At Neuchâtel, Switzerland, he was told, children were made to learn *Antigone* by heart.[47] Louis de Loménie sketched a portrait of him in the *Galerie des contemporains* that would have pleased any writer. Enthusiastically, de Loménie stated that

> S'il y a au monde des âmes plus ardentes, des génies plus grands, des existences plus larges, des voix plus puissantes, que l'âme, le génie, la vie et la voix de ce lyrique penseur, nulle vie, du moins, ne fut plus pure que la sienne, nul coeur ne brûla d'un plus sincère amour pour l'humanité, nul génie n'aborda des sphères plus élevées, nulle voix ne revêtit de plus consolantes pensées d'un langage plus harmonieux.[48]

Nevertheless, all this glory could not hide the fact that time, the magnificent abstraction of which he had written so much, was beginning to close down on him and his friends as it had on Orpheus. Chateaubriand's health sank visibly, and Ballanche, closer to him with increasing years, worried over approaching death. It took so little time to shrink a man into a mockery of himself. Besides, the *Vie de Rancé* made him suspect that René had adopted the tone of "la réaction catholique," that he was merely trying to "s'encapuchonner."[49] Consequently, the quiet old man withdrew into black thoughts, trying desperately to find reason for optimism in evidences of a religious revival and the strides of science.

His last years found him more bitter politically than ever, now that, in his own words, he led the life of a vegetable. He had abandoned the once beloved game of chess, favoring solitude, except when he could be with Madame Récamier. His affairs had become a muddle from costly experiments. All he had left was indignation. Each day he read the *Constitutionnel* to work himself into a proper fury, then raged at the government. In everything, he saw the bony hand of Voltaire:

> Voyez [he wrote Madame Récamier]: on a beau dire et beau faire, je suis obligé de le reconnaître, en fin de compte, l'Université est voltairienne. La nation officielle, c'est-à-dire la Chambre des députés et les Collèges électoraux sont voltairiens. Voltaire est l'expression de l'esprit français et Voltaire, c'est la dissolution de tout lien de famille et de toute espèce de moralité. Voltaire, et les feuilletons sont un choléra morbus qui passera, je l'espère. Dieu nous soit en aide.[50]

Part of the Abbaye sought relief from the urgent pressure of the present in travel, in the constant movement that drugs unpleasant thoughts. Chateaubriand voyaged to Bourbonne-les-Bains, to the Néothermes. He considered a trip to the Pyrenees, even to China, with Madame Récamier and "le mandarin ès lettres, le grand Ballanche."[51] But Ballanche vegetated, growing deaf and feeling futile even at the Academy. His health had sunk so low that he found little pleasure in attendance there. At first, he sat through all proceedings, but his deafness prevented hearing what was said and he usually fell asleep to the consternation of the speakers, left to choose between the heat and their oratory as the cause of his peaceful slumber.[52]

Outside his rooms, religious discussion raged as writers attempted to defend the faith or to build personal beliefs. Ballanche happily carried to the Abbaye news of what he interpreted as a Catholic revival. He counselled friends to read Saint Augustine, all the while burying himself in a study of Pascal. In the conflict between Descartes and Pascal, he had unquestionably chosen the latter. Notes from his reading heaped scorn on Descartes and "MM les universitaires."[53] He felt an affinity for Pascal, the religious writer and the inventor. Both had fought the good fight for a world in which spiritual values might prevail; both had desired the establishment of a real Christian ethics.

This renewed concern for his beliefs prompted in 1845 an article for the *Correspondant* on Alexandrian philosophy. Perhaps the last disciple of this school, Ballanche wanted to show Alexandria as a city predestined "à fondre l'Occident dans l'Orient, à les rajeunir tous les deux en les retrempant l'un dans l'autre."[54] The theme of his work had carried down to the present article almost through every one of his books, and had blossomed only a few years earlier in *la Tapisserie-Fée*. In addition, the subject claimed the merit of actuality since the University and the clergy were presently occupied in exchanging blows over religious and philosophical questions. Ballanche upheld the thesis that Alexandria had served as the intellectual center of the world while Rome had been its political hub. Wholeheartedly he defended the contributions of the city against those who belittled it, a defense that furnished him with an excellent occasion for sharp asides at grammarians and pedants.[55]

After 1846, Ballanche experienced a steady decline in health; his mind remained young, but his body refused to be whipped into further activity. The first sign of the end of his world came when Madame de Chateaubriand died on February 9, 1847, forcing on the Abbaye the realization that few days remained to it. Ballanche struggled to make their last moments happy by having Chateaubriand and Madame Récamier come to live with him, but the plan fell through, Madame Récamier and René preferring their solitude. Although each began to take better care of himself, Chateaubriand especially, illness came again when Madame Récamier went blind and had to submit to an operation for cataracts. Despite the success of the surgery, a worried Ballanche visited her constantly with little consideration for himself, even though his own health deteriorated rapidly under the strain. To make him more miserable, Lamartine apparently deserted their common principles in the *Histoire des Girondins*, and Ballanche immediately began to plan to correct the impression given by the *Girondins* with a volume of his own.[56]

But anxiety over Madame proved his undoing. On Friday, June 4, 1847, he fell victim to a pleurisy which the doctor diagnosed as fatal. He had walked to the Abbaye once too often. Friends poured in to sit apprehensively in an ante-chamber. Victor de Laprade arrived hurriedly and Madame Récamier, learning that Ballanche was calling for her feverishly, tore the bandages from eyes to rush to him, thereby preventing her own cure. For a week Ballanche lingered.

The following Friday night he asked permission to kiss Madame Récamier's hand, the only favor he had ever solicited of her. The next morning he received Extreme Unction. He died the same day, June 12, 1847, about three o'clock in the afternoon, murmuring to the weeping Madame Récamier: "Je m'endormirai dans le sein d'une grande espérance et plein de confiance dans la pensée que votre souvenir et le mien vivront d'une même vie."[57] It was the closest he had ever come to a declaration of love. The priest who had heard his confession sobbed with the mourners, "Cet homme est un ange; ses paroles m'ont fortement ému."[58]

Since Ballanche was the last of his family, Madame Récamier and the group at the Abbaye claimed him for their own. Monday, June 14, 1847, Lenormant and Jean-Jacques Ampère led the cortège to the Abbaye, followed by a large number of eminent men, including Villemain and Dupaty. Chateaubriand wept unashamedly. Ballanche was buried with the Récamier family in the Cimetière du Nord, at Montmartre. Alexis de Tocqueville read a discourse for the Academy, while Ballanche's disciple, Victor de Laprade, represented the city of Lyon.

The death of her friend had so exhausted Madame Récamier with her constant vigil that Chateaubriand carried her away from Paris. Ampère followed them to Normandy to prepare the volume which they hoped would popularize and perpetuate the works of Ballanche. Here the three reread his letters in search of passages to be quoted.[59] To the end, Madame Récamier fought for the reputation of her philosopher, but already the Catholics were deserting the principles of Ballanche. The youth of the day found him too stodgy; only the older men remembered him with affection. Alexis de Saint-Priest, for instance, came to submit to Madame Récamier a eulogy of Ballanche which he had prepared for the Academy.[60] Madame Récamier, however, did not mourn long. On May 13, 1849, she suddenly succumbed to an attack of cholera, and was buried next to Ballanche, a few feet from André-Marie Ampère. But even after death, she had taken care to keep Ballanche alive for his countrymen. The famous picture of *Corinne* went to the municipal museum of Lyon in her name and that of the city's famous writer.

CONCLUSION

Almost immediately after his death, Ballanche's reputation plummeted into the oblivion reserved for the almost great. Sainte-Beuve sang his requiem with a final judgment: "Ballanche vient de mourir; il a eu en partage une douce gloire, et il en a joui. Il me rappelle ce verset de l'Ecriture (Mattieu, V, 4): *Beati mites, quoniam ipsi possedebunt terram!*"[1] Then the century proceeded to let the dust gather on his books.

Appreciation never came, even though a few connoisseurs worked to keep his memory alive. Ballanche had failed to distinguish himself as the leader of a coterie; he had persistently kept to the middle way and, hence, received no great hate, great love, nor the respect of immortality. As a compromiser, he had consistently attempted to unite classicist and romanticist, for which he was rewarded with the contempt of both and the indifference that blights reputation. Each side scorned him because he favored a progress based on slow and careful exploration. Later, young writers, ambitious to conquer new worlds, dismissed him and his kind as timid souls with one cautious hand on tradition and the other tentatively on the future.

And yet, for all this lack of understanding, he did not disappear completely. From time to time, a few inquisitive men resurrected his work with pleasure and profit. Maurice de Guérin found in *Orphée* material for a *Bacchante;*[2] Rimbaud sought and discovered in the *Œuvres* some of the theories that lie back of the *Illuminations,* while Sully-Prudhomme admittedly knew and liked his writings. In Lyon, a group of disciples perpetuated the thinking of the master in their own works.

Ballanche really has a place in French literature in his own right, not as the friend of Madame Récamier and Chateaubriand. First, he spoke for much of the middle class, and it was the middle class that ultimately resolved the conflict between the classicist and the romanticist, choosing from both the elements it judged best suitable to its welfare. And, secondly, as an individual, he contributed in no small way to the cause of the new literature. From the beginning, he had chosen the side of the nineteenth century. When the future leaders of romanticism were still schoolboys, he was helping prepare for them ideas they would thanklessly accept for their own: fresh literary doctrines, political and social reforms, and a new version of an old philosophy. From him, too, they would inherit concern for the nation's social structure. In his historical researches, he had taken a long look at France's institutions and had decided that the poet-Messiah should be concerned with the ills of society rather than with the nymphs of an alien mythology. This incursion into pre-sociology gave him a strong sense of the realization of the growth and decay of all things, a feeling which he gave to others, along with a faith in what man could make of himself and his environment. The revolution of 1848 was in part of his making.

Most of the credit for these legacies Ballanche lost by his habit of retaining manuscripts overlong. While he was still concerned with interminable corrections and revisions, the ideas he had developed and gratuitously discussed were picked up by others who were destined to overshadow Pierre-Simon. For him was reserved the thankless and forgotten rôle of precursor of romantic thought.

BIBLIOGRAPHY

BIBLIOGRAPHY

(Unless otherwise specified, the place of publication is Paris)

Ampère, André-Marie et Jean-Jacques. Correspondance et Souvenirs. 2 vols., Hetzel, 1875.

Ampère, Jean-Jacques. "Ballanche" (Mélanges d'histoire littéraire, vol. II). Calmann-Lévy, 1876.

Anonymous. "Du Sentiment, dans ses rapports avec la littérature et les arts," *Journal de Paris*, 27 germinal, 3 and 4 floréal an X.

—— Lyon et Paris en avril 1834, précédé . . . d'une notice historique sur Lyon et le siège qu'il a soutenu en 1793. Lyon: Chambet, 1834.

—— "Souvenirs et correspondance de Madame Récamier," *Quarterly Review*, January and April, 1860.

Baldensperger, Fernand. Alfred de Vigny. Hachette, 1912.

—— Le Mouvement des idées dans l'émigration française. 2 vols., Plon, 1924.

Ballanche, Pierre-Simon, "Alexandrie," *Le Correspondant*, 1845.

—— "L'Avenir," *Le Polonais*, janvier-juin 1834.

—— Compte-rendu des travaux de l'Académie royale des sciences, belles-lettres et arts de Lyon pendant l'année 1816. Lyon: Durand, 1822.

—— De la publication des lettres écrites en 1786 et 1787. Didot, 1835.

—— Discours de M. Ballanche, prononcé dans la séance du 28 avril 1842, en venant prendre séance à la place de M. Duval-Pineu. (Recueil des discours, rapports et pièces diverses lus dans les séances publiques et particulières de l'Académie Française, 1840-49, 1ʳᵉ partie). Didot, 1850.

—— Du Sentiment considéré dans ses rapports avec la littérature et les arts. Lyon: Ballanche et Barret, 1801.

—— "Essais de palingénésie sociale," *Revue de Paris*, 1829, tomes, 2, 4, 6.

—— "Fragments de la Formule Générale," *Revue de Paris*, 1829.

—— Inès de Castro. Stock, 1904.

—— Lettres d'un jeune Lyonnais. Lyon: Ballanche, 1805.

—— "Un Mot sur des articles publiés dans le Polonais sur l'avenir de la Russie et de l'Europe," *Le Polonais* janvier-juin 1835.

—— "Un Mot sur la question d'Orient," *Le Polonais*, juillet-décembre 1834.

—— "Un Mot sur les confiscations exercées en Pologne," *Le Polonais*, juillet-décembre 1833.

—— Oeuvres. 4 vols., Barbezat, 1830.

—— "Palingénésie sociale, épilogue," *La France Littéraire*, I, 1832.

—— "Pologne et Russie," Le Polonais, janvier-juin 1834.
—— "La Providence et le destin," Le Polonais, janvier-juin 1835.
—— "La Russie et la Pologne," Le Polonais, janvier-juin 1834.
—— "La Tapisserie-Fée," Revue de Paris, 1832.
—— "Variétés," Le Polonais, juillet-décembre 1833.
—— Le Vieillard et le Jeune Homme. Edited by Roger Mauduit. Alcan, 1929.
—— La Ville des Expiations. Edited by Amand Rastoul. Bibliothèque Romantique, 1926.
—— "La Ville des Expiations. Episodes tirés du livre V," La France Littéraire, II, 1832.
—— "La Ville des Expiations. Traditions générales de l'humanité," La France Littéraire, V, 1833.
—— "La Ville des Expiations. Organisation de la ville et mode de réception de ceux qui y sont admis," La France Littéraire, XIX, 1835.
—— La Vision d'Hébal, chef d'un clan écossais. Didot, 1834.
Balzac. Correspondance, 1819-50. (Œuvres complètes, vol. XXIV.) Calmann Lévy, [1876].
Barante, le Baron de. Réponse au discours de M. Ballanche. (Recueil des discours, rapports et pièces diverses lus dans les séances publiques et particulières de l'Académie Française, 1840-49, 1ʳᵉ partie.) Didot, 1850.
Barzun, Jacques. Romanticism and the modern ego. Boston: Little Brown, 1943.
Biographie nouvelle des contemporains. "Ballanche," Librairie Historique, 1821.
Biré, Edmond. Les Dernières Années de Chateaubriand. Garnier, 1905.
Blum, Eugène. "Un Sociologiste inconnu: essai sur Ballanche," La Critique Philosophique, 30 juin 1887.
Boas, George. French philosophies of the romantic period. Baltimore: Johns Hopkins Press, 1925.
Bonnerot, Jean. Bibliographie de l'œuvre de Sainte-Beuve. Giraud-Badin, 1937.
Bonnet, Charles. Contemplation de la nature. 2 vols., Amsterdam: Rey, 1769.
—— La Palingénésie philosophique. 2 vols., Genève: Bruyset, 1770.
Brizeux, Auguste. Œuvres. Garnier, [1910].
Buche, Joseph. "Ballanche et Victor Hugo: une source des Misérables," Revùe d'Histoire Littéraire de la France, 1927.
—— "Un Conflit de conscience entre trois amis: Ampère, Ballanche et Bredin," Mémoires de l'Académie de Lyon, 3ᵉ série, XIV, 1914.
—— L'Ecole mystique de Lyon. Alcan, 1935.
Calippe, abbé Charles. "Un Essai de rapprochement entre l'Eglise et l'Etat. Ballanche," Annales de Philosophie Chrétienne, octobre 1901-mars 1902.
Champfleury. Les Vignettes romantiques. Dentu, 1883.
Chateaubriand. Correspondence générale. 5 vols., Champion, 1912-24.

―――― Etudes historiques (Œuvres complètes de Chateaubriand, IX.) Garnier, [1901].

―――― Mémoires d'outre-tombe. 6 vols., Garnier, 1925.

―――― Œuvres complètes. Garnier, 1901.

Clement, N. H. Romanticism in France. New York: Modern Language Association, 1939.

Constant, Benjamin. Lettres à Madame Récamier. Calmann-Lévy, 1882.

―――― Lettres à sa famille. Stock, 1931.

Cuisenier, André. Jules Romains et l'unanimisme. Flammarion, 1935.

Delécluze, E. J. Souvenirs de soixante années. Lévy, 1862.

Denis, Ferdinand. Journal. Edited by Pierre Moreau. Plon, 1932.

Dupuy, Ernest. Alfred de Vigny, ses amitiés, son rôle littéraire. 2 vols., Société Française d'Imprimerie et de Librairie, 1910.

Durry, Marie-Jeanne. La Vieillesse de Chateaubriand. 2 vols., Le Divan, 1933.

Erdan, Alexandre. La France mistique (sic). 2 vols., Coulon-Pineau, sd.

E. V. "Variétés: Œuvres complètes de M. Ballanche," Revue de Paris, 27 juin 1830.

Faguet, Emile. Politiques et moralistes. 3 vols., Boivin, sd.

Féletz, Ch.-M. de. Jugements historiques et littéraires. Librairie classique de Périsse frères, 1840.

Frainnet, Gaston. Essai sur la philosophie de Pierre-Simon Ballanche. Storck, 1904.

Gans, Edouard. "Le Salon de Mme. Récamier," Revue de Paris, XXV, 1836.

Gautier, Théophile. Les Jeunes-France. Charpentier, 1919.

George, Albert. Lamartine and romantic unanimism. New York: Columbia University Press, 1940.

Gérando, la Baronne de. Lettres. Didier, 1880.

Giraud, Victor. "Pour le centenaire du Génie du Christianisme," La Quinzaine, 16 avril 1902.

Goncourt, Edmond et Jules de. Histoire de la société française pendant la Révolution. Flammarion, [1928].

Gottschalk, Louis. The Era of the French Revolution. Boston: Houghton Mifflin, 1929.

Gunzburg, Nico. Les Transformations récentes du droit pénal interne et international. L'Eglantine, 1933.

Haussonville, le Vᵗᵉ d'. Sainte-Beuve. Lévy, 1875.

Herriot, Edouard. Madame Récamier et ses amis. 2 vols., Plon, 1905.

Hugo, Victor. Les Misérables. Hetzel, sd.

Huit, Charles. La Vie et les œuvres de Ballanche. Vitte, 1904.

Hunt, H. J. The epic in XIXth century France. London: Blackwell, 1941.

Jasinski, René. Les Années romantiques de Théophile Gautier. Vuibert, 1929.

Karénine, Wladimir. George Sand. 3 vols., Plon, 1912.

Karr, Alphonse. Les Guêpes. 3 vols., Lévy, 1858.
La Gorce, Pierre de. Histoire religieuse de la Révolution française. 5 vols., Plon, 1912-23.
Lamartine, Alphonse de. Cours familier de littérature. 28 vols., Chez l'auteur, 1860.
Lamennais. Correspondance inédite avec le baron de Vitrolles. Edited by Eugène Forgues. Charpentier, 1886.
Laprade, Victor de. Ballanche, sa vie et ses écrits. Lyon: Boitel, 1848.
────── "Union de la métaphysique à la poésie" (Questions d'art et de morale). Didier, 1861.
Larat, Jean. La Tradition et l'exotisme dans l'œuvre de Ch. Nodier. Champion, 1923.
Latreille, Camille. Chateaubriand. Le Romantisme à Lyon. Fontemoing, 1905.
Lemaître, Georges. From cubism to surrealism in French literature. Cambridge: Harvard University Press, 1941.
[Lenormant, Mme Amélie]. Mme Récamier and her friends. Boston: Roberts, 1875.
────── Souvenirs et correspondance tirés des papiers de Madame Récamier. 2 vols., Lévy, 1859.
Lenormant, Charles. "Ballanche," Le Correspondant, avril-juin 1847.
Leroux, Pierre. La Grève de Samarez. 2 vols., Dentu, 1863.
Levaillant, Maurice. Chateaubriand, Mme Récamier et les Mémoires d'outre-tombe. Delagrave, 1936.
Loménie, Louis de. Galerie des contemporains. 10 vols., Bureau Central, 1841.
Lovejoy, Arthur O. The Great Chain of Being. Cambridge: Harvard University Press, 1936.
Marcellus, le comte de. Chateaubriand et son temps. Lévy, 1859.
Marquiset, Alfred. Ballanche et Mme d'Hautefeuille. Champion, 1912.
Maze-Censier, G. "Camille Jordan et ses correspondants," Revue Politique et Parlementaire, 10 janvier, 10 février, 10 juillet, 10 septembre 1897.
Mazure (de Poitiers), Adolphe. "Ballanche," La France Littéraire, XI, 1834.
Merlet, Gustave. Tableau de la littérature française, 1800-1815. Didier, 1878.
Michaut, G. Senancour, ses amis et ennemis. Sansot, 1909.
Michelet, Jules. Lettres inédites. Presses Universitaires, 1924.
Moreau, Pierre. "Ferdinand Denis et les romantiques," Revue d'Histoire Littéraire de la France, 1926.
Morgan, Lady Sydney. La France en 1829 et 1830. Stuttgart: Hoffman, 1830
Mossé, Armand. Les Prisons et les institutions d'éducation corrective. Recueil Sirey, 1929.
Nodier, Charles. Mélanges de littérature et de critique, vol. I. Raymon, 1820.

——— Les Tristes. Demonville, 1802.

Ozanam, Frédéric. Lettres. 2 vols., Lecoffre, 1881.

——— Mélanges. 2 vols., Lecoffre, 1859.

Pascal, Félicien. "Un Prophète de l'avenir: Ballanche," *Le Correspondant*, 25 janvier 1927.

Prat, Alphonse. "Le Romantisme de Ballanche," *La Quinzaine*, 16 mars 1902.

Quinet, Edgar. Lettres à sa mère. 2 vols., Germer-Baillière, [1876].

Revue Nationale de Belgique. "Ballanche." 1847.

Saint-Chéron, Alex. "La Vision d'Hébal," *Revue Encyclopédique*, janvier-mars 1832.

Saint Hilaire, Jules Barthélemy-. Victor Cousin, sa vie et correspondance. 3 vols., Hachette, 1895.

——— La Philosophie des deux Ampère. Didier, 1866.

Saint-Priest, Alexis de. "MM. Ballanche et Vatout" (Etudes diplomatiques et littéraires, 2 vols.), 1850.

Saint-Simon and Enfantin. Œuvres. 2 vols., Dentu, 1865.

Sainte-Beuve. Causeries du Lundi, I, V, X, XI, XIV, XV. Garnier, sd.

——— Correspondance générale. Edited by Jean Bonnerot. 3 vols., Stock, 1935.

——— Mes Poisons. Plon, 1926.

——— Portraits contemporains, II. Calmann-Lévy, 1889.

——— Portraits littéraires, I. Garnier, sd.

——— Premiers lundis, II. Lévy, 1875.

Salomon, Michel. Charles Nodier et le groupe romantique. Perrin, 1908.

Sand, Georges. Lettres à Alfred de Musset et à Sainte-Beuve. Calmann-Lévy, 1897.

Senza. "En marge de la vie de Lamartine," *Vie des peuples,* mars 1924.

Sirich, John Black. The revolutionary committees in the departments of France. Cambridge: Harvard University Press, 1943.

Starkie, Enid. Arthur Rimbaud. New York: W. W. Norton, nd.

Tronchon, Henri. La Fortune intellectuelle de Herder en France. Rieder, 1920.

Vaudon, Jean. "Ballanche," *Le Correspondant*, 25 octobre, 10 novembre 1883.

Vauthier, G. "Premiers Relations entre Chateaubriand et Ballanche," *Revue d'Histoire Littéraire de la France*, 1922.

Viatte, Auguste. Claude-Julien Bredin. De Boccard, 1927.

——— Les Sources occultes du romantisme. 2 vols., Champion. 1928.

——— Victor Hugo et les illuminés de son temps. Montreal: Editions de l'Arbre, 1942.

NOTES

INTRODUCTION

[1] *Portraits contemporains,* II. Calmann-Lévy, 1889.
[2] In the *Mélanges d'histoire littéraire,* II. Calmann-Lévy, 1876.
[3] *Ballanche.* Lyon: Boitel, 1848.
[4] "Ballanche," *Le Correspondant,* April-June, 1847.
[5] *Galerie des contemporains.* 10 vols., Bureau Central, 1841.
[6] Vol. II. Boivin, nd.
[7] *Cf.* Eugène Blum, "Un Sociologiste inconnu," *La Critique Philosophique,* June 30, 1887; Joseph Buche, "Ballanche et Victor Hugo," *Revue d'Histoire Littéraire de la France,* 1927; abbé Charles Calippe, "Un Essai de rapprochement entre l'Eglise et l'Etat,' *Annales de Philosophie Chrétienne,* October, 1901-March, 1902; Alphonse Prat, "Le Romantisme de Ballanche," *La Quinzaine,* March 16, 1902.
[8] La Vie et les œuvres de Ballanche. Vitte, 1904.
[9] Essai sur la philosophie de Pierre-Simon Ballanche. Storck 1904.
[10] 2 vols., Plon, 1905.
[11] *Ballanche et Mme d'Hautefeuille.* Champion, 1912.
[12] *The epic in nineteenth century France.* London: Blackwell, 1941.

CHAPTER I

[1] Born May 4, 1773.
[2] March 16, 1775-July 23, 1836.
[3] Now n° 7, rue Centrale.
[4] The name was spelled Balanche on the birth certificate. *Cf.* Rastoul, *Ville des Expiations,* Intro., p. xiii.
[5] Frainnet, *Ballanche,* p. 8.
[6] The *Annuaire du Doubs* of 1889 mentions a Blaise-Ballanche-Richard, 1622-1685, a painter of frescoes, who was born at Morteau, then called the Combe d'Abondance.
[7] Guillaume-François, septuagenarian, died October 26, 1751.
[8] Joseph Buche, *L'Ecole mystique de Lyon,* p. 2.
[9] Rastoul, *Ville des Expiations,* Intro., p. xiv.
[10] Lenormant, *Ballanche,* p. 812.
[11] Anon., *Lyon et Paris en 1834,* pp. 52-53.
[12] *Cf.* Goncourt Brothers. *Histoire de la société française pendant la Révolution,* pp. 26, 232, 235.
[13] *Lyon et Paris en 1834,* p. 35.
[14] Huit, *Ballanche,* p. 8.

[15] *Lyon et Paris en 1834*, p. 55.

[16] *Ibid.*, pp. 55-56.

[17] *Ibid.*

[18] Pierre de la Gorce, *Histoire religieuse de la Révolution Française*, III, 303-304.

[19] Frainnet, pp. 9-10.

[20] Rastoul, *Ville des Expiations*, Intro., p. xvii.

[21] Frainnet, p. 10.

[22] Jean Vaudon, "*Ballanche*," p. 251.

[23] Sainte-Beuve, "*Ballanche*," p. 4.

[24] Rastoul, *Ville des Expiations*, Intro., p. xx.

[25] Buche, *Ecole mystique*, p. 8.

[26] *Cf. Du Sentiment*, passim.

[27] *Discours de réception*, p. 251.

[28] *Du Sentiment*, pp. 284-87.

[29] Frainnet, pp. 16-17.

[30] Vaudon, "*Ballanche*," p. 239.

[31] *Du Sentiment*, Notes, p. 284.

[32] Gustave Merlet, *Tableau de la littérature française*, pp. 4-5.

[33] De la Gorce, *Histoire religieuse*, V, 24-25.

[34] *Discours de réception*, pp. 250-51.

[35] *Du Sentiment*, p. 185.

[36] Frainnet, p. 21.

[37] Lyon: Ballanche et Barret; Paris: Calixte Volland.

[38] *Du Sentiment*, Intro., pp. 12-13.

[39] *Ibid.*, pp. 126-27.

[40] *Ibid.*, pp. 56-57.

[41] *Ibid.*, p. 144.

[42] *Ibid.*

[43] *Ibid.*, p. 107.

[44] *Ibid.*, Notes, pp. 286-87.

[45] *Ibid.*, p. 3.

[46] *Ibid.*, Intro., pp. 4-6.

[47] *Ibid.*, p. 44.

[48] *Ibid.*, p. 48.

[49] *Ibid.*, p. 121.

[50] *Ibid.*, p. 101.

[51] *Ibid.*, p. 155.

[52] *Ibid.*, p. 153.

[53] *Mes Poisons*, p. 180.

[54] *Cf.* René Jasinski, *Les Années romantiques de Théophile Gautier*.

[55] *Du Sentiment*, pp. 156-157.

[56] *Ibid.*, pp. 180-181.

[57] *Journal de Paris*, 27 germinal an x.

[58] *Ibid.*, 4 floréal an x.
[59] *Mes Poisons*, III.
[60] Abbé de Féletz, *Jugements historiques*, p. 407.
[61] *Ibid.*, p. 408.
[62] *Ibid.*
[63] *Ibid.*, p. 409.
[64] Frainnet, p. 21.
[65] J.-J. Ampère, *Mélanges*, "Ballanche," pp. 15-16.
[66] Frainnet, p. 24.

CHAPTER II

[1] Samedi, 4 floréal.
[2] My italics; *Du Sentiment*, p. 182.
[3] Ampère, *Mélanges*, "Ballanche," p. 13.
[4] *Cf*, Herriot, *Mme Récamier*, I, pp. 271-272.
[5] The material concerning the title of the *Génie* is taken principally from Victor Giraud, "Pour le centenaire du *Génie du Christianisme*," *La Quinzaine*, April 16, 1902.
[6] *Du Sentiment*, p. 311.
[7] Giraud, "Pour le centenaire du Génie," p. 521.
[8] *Cf.* Joseph Buche, *Ecole mystique*. The material used here in support of this theory is drawn from chapters 7-9.
[9] *Ibid.*, p. 65.
[10] Sainte-Beuve, "Ballanche," pp. 13-14.
[11] For the complete details of the first relations between Chateaubriand and Ballanche, *cf.* G. Vautier, "Premières relations entre Chateaubriand et Ballanche," *Revue d'Histoire Littéraire de la France*, 1922, xxix, pp. 268-87.
[12] *Ibid.*, pp. 269-70. Letter to Beuchot, 16 ventôse an xi.
[13] *Ibid.*, p. 271.
[14] *Ibid.*
[15] *Ibid.*, p. 275.
[16] *Ibid.*, p. 279, April 4.
[17] *Ibid.*, pp. 280-81.
[18] *Ibid.*, p. 283.
[19] *Ibid.*, p. 284.
[20] The *Bulletin* appeared regularly from the first day of the year XI (September 25, 1802) to the last day of 1809.
[21] Some of its articles were signed by Ballanche. *Cf.* Frainnet, pp. 31-32.
[22] *Cf. Rastoul, Ville des Expiations*, Intro., xxii.
[23] The society, dissolved in 1793, had been revived on June 8, 1800, by order of Veruinac, prefect of the Rhône, as the *Athénée*.
[24] Frainnet, pp. 18-19.
[25] Demonville, 1802, Intro., p. ii.
[26] Frainnet, p. 25.
[27] Rastoul, *Villes des Expiations*, Intro., p. xxviii.

[28] Buche, *Ecole mystique*, pp. 46-47.
[29] Auguste Viatte, *Claude-Julien Bredin*, p. 8.
[30] Buche, *Ecole mystique*, p. 47.
[31] *Ibid.*, p. 91, 1819.
[32] Frainnet, p. 26.
[33] Buche, *Ecole mystique*, pp. 85-86.
[34] Viatte, *Bredin*, p. 31.
[35] Lyon: Ballanche père et fils, 1805.
[36] Ballanche proudly catalogued the stupendous facts. Easter Thursday, twelve hundred communicants; Good Friday, the Pope himself actually blessed thirty thousand chaplets, crosses, and medals.
[37] *Lettres*, p. 36.
[38] Not much is known of Ballanche's visit to Coppet. Later, however, he did leave a pen portrait of Mme de Staël that shows how highly he considered her. Cf. *infra.*, p. 107.
[39] *Œuvres*, I, 27.
[40] *Ibid.*, p. 32.
[41] *Correspondance et souvenirs d'André-Marie et de Jean-Jacques Ampère*, I, 19-21.
[42] Frainnet, pp. 19-20.
[43] Rastoul, *Ville des Expiations*, Intro., p. xxvii.

CHAPTER III

[1] Frainnet, pp. 32-33.
[2] Rastoul, *Ville des Expiations*, Intro., p. xxxi.
[3] Sainte-Beuve, "Ballanche," pp. 17-18.
[4] Frainnet, p. 33.
[5] *Ibid.*, pp. 33-35.
[6] *Neuvième fragment, Œuvres*, I, 507, 31 mars 1830.
[7] Rastoul, *Ville des Expiations*, Intro., p. xxxvi.
[8] Ampère, *Correspondance*, I, 29.
[9] I, 28 mai 1808; II, 23 juillet 1808; III, 24 août 1808; IV, 5 novembre 1808; V, 24 décembre 1808; VI, 28 janvier 1809; VII, 20 septembre 1809; VIII, 25 octobre 1809.
[10] *Œuvres*, I, pp. 497-98.
[11] *Ibid.*, p. 492.
[12] *Ibid.*, p. 493.
[13] Sainte-Beuve, "Ballanche," p. 8.
[14] Vauthier, "Chateaubriand et Ballanche," pp. 279-80, letter of April 18, 1809.
[15] Probably June or July. Charles Huit states that the reading occurred Tuesday, August 27, 1811, but Frainnet claims the manuscript proves otherwise. Cf. *Inès de Castro*, Intro., pp. 8-12.
[16] *Ibid.*
[17] The manuscript was not published until 1904, when Gaston Frainnet edited it.

[18] *Inès de Castro*, note, p. 74.

[19] *Ibid.*, note, p. 46.

[20] Sainte-Beuve, "Ballanche," p. 44.

[21] Ampère, *Correspondance*, I, 80. For further details on Ballanche as an inventor see *infra*, chapter IX, pp. 252-57.

[22] *Du Sentiment*, p. 114.

[23] Buche, *Ecole mystique*, pp. 109-10.

[24] Herriot, *Madame Récamier*, I, 300.

[25] *Ibid.*

[26] Herriot, *Madame Récamier*, I, 273-277.

[27] Vaudon, "Ballanche," p. 253.

[28] Madame Lenormant, *Madame Récamier and her friends*, p. 102.

[29] *Œuvres*, I, 37.

[30] Frainnet, p. 55. Letter of February 19, 1813.

[31] *Ibid.*, p. 50.

[32] *Cf.* the preface to *Antigone*, *Œuvres*, I.

[33] *Cf.* preface to the first edition.

[34] *Œuvres*, I, 41.

[35] *Ibid.*, p. 42.

[36] Eugène Blum, "Un Sociologiste inconnu," p. 405.

[37] Nodier, *Mélanges*, p. 276.

[38] *Ibid.*, p. 282.

[39] Sainte-Beuve, "Ballanche," pp. 19-20.

[40] *Ibid.*, p. 20.

[41] Later Emile Faguet expressed himself more openly: "Ce n'est qu'un *Télémaque* très prétentieux." (*Politiques et moralistes*, II, 141).

[42] *Cf.* preface to *Antigone*.

[43] *Mélanges*, p. 293.

[44] Rastoul, *Ville des Expiations*, Intro., p. xl.

[45] Comte de Marcellus, *Chateaubriand et son temps*, pp. 317-18.

[46] Herriot, *Madame Récamier*, II, 3.

[47] *Ibid.*, II, 6.

[48] G. Maze-Censier, "Camille Jordan et ses correspondants," pp. 146-47.

[49] Herriot, *Madame Récamier*, II, 9.

[50] *Ibid.*, II, 11.

[51] Mme Lenormant, *Souvenirs et correspondance tirés des papiers de Mme Récamier*, I, 291.

[52] *Comte rendu des travaux de l'Académie Royale de Lyon*, 1822, p. 46.

[53] *Ibid.*, p. 12.

[54] Ampère, *Correspondance*, I, 98-100, letter of October 24, 1816.

CHAPTER IV

[1] Marquiset, *Ballanche et Mme d'Hautefeuille*, p. 9.

[2] Lenormant, *Souvenirs de Mme Récamier*, I, 199-200.

[3] *Lettres de Benjamin Constant à Mme Récamier*, p. 24.

[4] *Ibid.*, p. 26.

[5] Jean Larat, *La Tradition et l'exotisme dans l'œuvre de Ch. Nodier*, p. 28.

[6] Charpentier, 1834.

[7] Champfleury, *Les Vignettes romantiques*, p. 46.

[8] Charles Bonnet (1720-1793) had intended to study law, but an accident turned him toward the natural sciences. When his eyes began to grow weak, he spent much of his time in meditation, the results of which he published in *La Palingénésie philosophique* and *Contemplation de la nature*.

[9] Michel Salomon. *Charles Nodier et le groupe romantique*, pp. 208-9.

[10] Viatte, *Bredin*, pp. 34-35.

[11] Rastoul, *Ville des Expiations*, Intro., xliii.

[12] Merlet, *Tableau de la littérature française*, p. 13.

[13] *Essai, Œuvres*, II, 75.

[14] Paris: Didot, in-8°, 420 pp.

[15] *Essai*, p. 23.

[16] *Cf.* Sainte-Beuve, "Ballanche," pp. 25-26.

[17] *Essai*, pp. 153-54.

[18] *Ibid.*, p. 174.

[19] *Cf. ibid.*, pp. 169-70.

[20] *Ibid.*, p. 269.

[21] *Ibid.*, p. 211. Ballanche contended that this view could only lead to the repulsive statement that man had evolved from an oyster.

[22] *Ibid.*, p. 271.

[23] *Ibid.*, pp. 162-63.

[24] *Ibid.*, pp. 179-80.

[25] *Ibid.*, p. 184.

[26] *Ibid.*, pp. 182-83.

[27] *Ibid.*, pp. 265-66.

[28] Enrichissez-vous par l'épargne et par le travail.

[29] *Essai*, p. 355.

[30] *Ibid.*, p. 372.

[31] *Ibid.*, p. 41.

[32] *Ibid.*, pp. 46-47. With this conception, it is to be noted, Ballanche contributed materially to introduce into romantic literature the principle of variation of evolution as opposed to the fixity of classicism. *Cf.* A. Prat, "Le Romantisme de Ballanche," p. 193.

[33] *Essai*, p. 243.

[34] *Ibid.*, pp. 27-28.

[35] *Ibid.*, p. 38.

[36] *Ibid.*, p. 72.

[37] *Ibid.*, p. 260.

[38] *Ibid.*, p. 127.

[39] *Ibid.*, p. 196.

[40] *Ibid.*, p. 87.

[41] *Ibid.*, p. 342.
[42] *Ibid.*, pp. 42-43.
[43] *Ibid.*, pp. 327-28.
[44] *Ibid.*, p. 344.
[45] *Ibid.*, p. 345.
[46] Cited from the *Essai* by Vaudon, "Ballanche," pp. 551-52.
[47] *Essai*, p. 182.
[48] *Cf. ibid.*, pp. 311-13.
[49] *Ibid.*, pp. 65-66.
[50] *Ibid.*, pp. 273-74.
[51] *Ibid.*, pp. 45, 147.
[52] *Ibid.*, p. 53.
[53] *Ibid.*, pp. 351-358.
[54] *Cf.* Sainte-Beuve, "Ballanche," p. 23.
[55] Boas, *French philosophers of the romantic period*, p. 118.
[56] Prat, "Romantisme de Ballanche," p. 190.
[57] Vaudon, "Ballanche," pp. 158-60.
[58] Sainte-Beuve, "Ballanche," pp. 28-29.

CHAPTER V

[1] Herriot, *Madame Récamier*, II, 54.
[2] *Ibid.*, p. 53.
[3] Viatte, *Bredin*, p. 153.
[4] Herriot, *Madame Récamier*, II, 60-61.
[5] *Ibid.*, pp. 61-62.
[6] *Ibid.*, pp. 65-66.
[7] *Ibid.*, I, 163.
[8] *Ibid.*, 163-64.
[9] Vauthier, "Chateaubriand et Ballanche," pp. 285-86.
[10] Viatte, *Bredin*, letter of September 24, 1819.
[11] *Vieillard*, ed. Mauduit, p. 27.
[12] Sainte-Beuve, "Ballanche," pp. 32-33.
[13] *Vieillard*, ed. Mauduit, p. 46.
[14] *Ibid.*, p. 14.
[15] *Ibid.*, p. 65.
[16] *Ibid.*, p. 75.
[17] *Ibid.*, p. 101.
[18] *Ibid.*, p. 136.
[19] *Ibid.*, pp. 120-121.
[20] Rastoul, *Ville des Expiations*, Intro., xliv.
[21] Viatte, *Bredin*, note, p. 118.
[22] Later, in 1835, he edged closer to the convent, inhabiting 21, rue de Sèvres, in the building housing the curé of the parish. Finally, shortly before his death, he came two houses closer to the convent, to number 17, immediately across from

the Abbaye and high enough to be able to see into its courtyard.

[23] Biré, *Dernières Années de Chateaubriand*, pp. 206-7; Durry, *Vieillesse de Chateaubriand*, I, 321-22.

[24] Sainte-Beuve, *Mes Poisons*, pp. 74-75.

[25] Durry, *Vieillesse de Chateaubriand*, I, 388-89.

[26] *Mémoires d'outre-tombe*, ed. Biré, VI, 258-59, Appendix III.

[27] Vaudon, "Ballanche," p. 235.

[28] Marquiset, *Ballanche et Mme d'Hautefeuille*, pp. 15-16.

[29] Herriot, *Madame Récamier*, II, 92.

[30] *Ibid.*, p. 93.

[31] *Ibid.*, p. 89.

[32] Lenormant, *Souvenirs de Madame Récamier*, II, 6-7.

[33] *Ibid.*, pp. 27-28.

[34] The idea of the book dated back to the Hundred Days and perhaps even to 1813, when Ballanche returned from Italy.

[35] The catalogue of the Bibliothèque Nationale contains no reference to a separate edition of 1820. Probably it was circulated privately in small number. Later, Didot issued an edition in 1822.

[36] *Œuvres*, I, 445-46.

[37] *Ibid.*, III, 242-43.

[38] *Ibid.*, I, 465.

[39] Sainte-Beuve, "Ballanche," pp. 35-36.

[40] Paris: Didot, in-8°, 208 pp.

[41] *Œuvres*, I, 305.

[42] *Ibid.*, pp. 331, 334.

[43] Sainte-Beuve, "Ballanche," pp. 36-37.

[44] *Œuvres*, I, 384.

[45] Tome II, 53-54.

[46] The following material on Ballanche and Victor Hugo is taken, for the most part, from Joseph Buche, "Ballanche et Victor Hugo," *Revue d'Histoire Littéraire de la France*, XXXIV, 173-88.

[47] Biré, *Victor Hugo après 1852*, pp. 126-28.

[48] *Ibid.*, p. 132.

[49] *Les Misérables*, I, chapter IX, p. 51.

[50] *Ibid.*, p. 55.

[51] *Ibid.*, p. 56.

[52] *Ibid.*, p. 62.

CHAPTER VI

[1] Levaillant, *Chateaubriand, Mme Récamier et les Mémoires d'outre-tombe*, p. 322.

[2] *Ibid.*, p. 323.

[3] *Causeries du lundi*, XIV, 317, note.

[4] Lenormant, *Souvenirs de Madame Récamier*, II, 42.

[5] Rastoul, *Ville des Expiations*, Intro., p. xlvi.

[6] Lenormant, *Souvenirs de Madame Récamier*, II, 61.

[7] Ampère, *Correspondance*, I, 360.

[8] Herriot, *Madame Récamier*, II, 158.

[9] Lenormant, *Souvenirs de Madame Récamier*, II, 64-66.

[10] *Ibid.*, II, 67.

[11] Herriot, *Madame Récamier*, II, 180.

[12] Rastoul, *Ville des Expiations*, Intro., pp. xlvii-xlviii.

[13] *Correspondance*, I, 421, February 5, 1827.

[14] Paris: Didot, 1827. The 1827 edition was later greatly enlarged in 1830 for inclusion in the *Œuvres complètes*. Cf. *Œuvres*, III, 4.

[15] Published in 1828 by Didot.

[16] *Œuvres*, III, 9-10.

[17] Part of the work seems to have antedated even the stay in Rome. In a letter to Ballanche, July 9, 1822, Bredin writes that "il est impossible de mieux caractériser l'époque actuelle du monde que tu ne le fais par l'épithète Palingénésique. . . . L'impression du volume est-elle commencé? La préface étant faite, je ne vois pas ce qui aurait pu l'arrêter." (Viatte, *Bredin*, pp. 177-78.) Since the only volume Ballanche published in 1822 was the *Elégie*, which had no preface, it appears likely that Bredin referred to the *Palingénésie*, which did not appear until five years later.

[18] *Œuvres*, III, 5-7.

[19] Cf. *ibid.*, 63. Bonnet, like Leibniz and Malebranche, defended the theory of the pre-existence of *germes*.

[20] Lovejoy, *The great chain of being*, pp. 55-56; cf. also George, *Lamartine and romantic unanimism*, pp. 31-33.

[21] Lovejoy, *Chain of being*, pp. 72-73.

[22] *Ibid.*, p. 186.

[23] *Ibid.*, pp. 198-99.

[24] *Ibid.*, p. 252.

[25] *Palingénésie philosophique*, II, 52.

[26] *Ibid.*, II, 423.

[27] *Contemplation de la nature*, I, 84.

[28] *Œuvres*, III, 11-12.

[29] *Ibid.*, p. 33.

[30] *Ibid.*, pp. 37-39.

[31] *Ibid.*, pp. 106-8.

[32] *Ibid.*, pp. 71-72.

[33] *Ibid.*, pp. 110-111.

[34] *Ibid.*, p. 206.

[35] *Ibid.*, p. 74.

[36] *Ibid.*, p. 354.

[37] *Ibid.*, pp. 123-25.

[38] Blum, "Un sociologiste inconnu," p. 412.

[39] *Œuvres*, III, 294-295.

[40] *Ibid.*, III, 191.

[41] *Ibid.*, III, 66.

[42] *Ibid.*, III, 196.

[43] *Ibid.*, III, 195.

[44] *Ibid.*, III, 140.

[45] *Ibid.*, III, 399-400.

[46] *Ibid.*, III, 235.

[47] *Ibid.*, III, 349.

[48] *Ibid.*, III, 359.

[49] *Ibid.*, II, 285.

[50] For further details on Ballanche and the nineteenth century epic, *cf.* Hunt, *The epic in nineteenth century France*, pp. 85-91.

[51] *Cf. infra*, p. 201.

[52] Prat, "Le Romantisme de Ballanche," p. 203.

[53] Viatte, *Bredin*, p. 231.

[54] *Œuvres*, III, 148-50.

[55] *Ibid.*, III, 334-36.

[56] The material on Ballanche and Herder is drawn principally from Henri Tronchon, *La Fortune intellectuelle de Herder*.

[57] *Œuvres*, III, 259.

[58] Buche, *Ecole mystique*, p. 150.

[59] *Ibid.*, p. 158.

[60] Paris: Didot, 1829.

[61] Following past performance, he had held onto the manuscript for at least eight years before making it public. On April 15, 1820, Bredin had written to Ballanche: "J'ai enfin reçu des nouvelles *d'Orphée*. Ampère m'écrit qu'il a entendu le premier des trois chants sur les initiations, il en a été ravi. J'espère que vous n'avez pas fait de grands changements à votre esquisse." (Viatte, *Bredin*, p. 111.) Granted Ballanche's slowness in writing, the first plan must date back to shortly after his arrival in Paris.

[62] *Œuvres*, IV, 43-44.

[63] Three fragments of the *Formule générale* were published in the *Revue de Paris* in 1829.

[64] Viatte, *Bredin*, p. 33.

[65] *Ibid.*, p. 25.

[66] *Ibid.*, p. 111.

[67] *Ibid.*, p. 209.

[68] *Ibid.*, p. 259.

[69] Frainnet, pp. 141-45.

[70] *Œuvres*, IV, 524.

[71] *Ibid.*, IV, 52.

[72] Ampère, "Ballanche," pp. 100-101.

[73] Entretien xvii, pp. 360-62.

[74] A similar resemblance may be found in Jules Romains' account of his vision of October, 1903, seen while walking up the rue d'Amsterdam with his friend,

George Chennevière (Cuissenier, *Romains et l'unanimisme*, p. 17).

[75] *Œuvres*, IV, 435-37.
[76] *Ibid.*, IV, 434.
[77] *Ibid.*, IV, 444.
[78] *Cf.* Enid Starkie, *Arthur Rimbaud*, p. 251 and chapter entitled "Ballanche."
[79] Lemaître, *From cubism to surrealism in French literature*, p. 30.
[80] *Œuvres*, IV, 363-64.
[81] *Ibid.*, IV, 401.
[82] *Ibid.*, IV, 306.
[83] *Ibid.*, IV, 391-92.
[84] *Ibid.*, IV, 388.
[85] *Ibid.*, IV, 287.
[86] *Ibid.*, IV, 498-99.

CHAPTER VII

[1] Herriot, *Madame Récamier*, II, 249-50.
[2] Ampère, *Correspondance*, II, letter of November 22, 1829.
[3] Paris: J. Barbezat, 4 vols. in-8°.
[4] Buche, *Ecole mystique*, pp. 54-55.
[5] E. V., "Variétés," *Revue de Paris*, June 27, 1830.
[6] Herriot, *Madame Récamier*, II, 263-64.
[7] *Ibid.*
[8] Rastoul, *Ville des Expiations*, Intro., p. xlix.
[9] Sainte-Beuve, "Ballanche," p. 32, note.
[10] Lady Morgan, *France en 1829 et 1830*, I, 195.
[11] Viatte, *Victor Hugo et les illuminés de son temps*, p. 104.
[12] Ampère, "Ballanche," pp. 181-83.
[13] Ch. Lenormant, "Ballanche," p. 825.
[14] Mme Lenormant, *Mme Récamier and her friends*, p. 142.
[15] Moreau, "Ferdinand Denis et les romantiques," p. 545.
[16] Jean Larat, *La Tradition et l'exotisme dans l'œuvre de Charles Nodier*, p. 311.
[17] *Ibid.*, pp. 309-10.
[18] Rastoul, *Ville des Expiations*, Intro., p. li.
[19] Moreau, *Ferdinand Denis et les romantiques*, p. 533. Ballanche returned Nodier's friendship heartily, even spreading it to all Nodier's family. In 1836, he published in the *Biographie des femmes auteurs contemporaines françaises*, a "Notice sur Mme Mennessier-Nodier," that shows his deep feeling for the Nodier family.
[20] Sainte-Beuve, "Ballanche," pp. 43-44.
[21] *Œuvres de Saint-Simon et d'Enfantin*, I, 39-41.
[22] *Ibid.*
[23] Marquiset, *Ballanche et Mme d'Hautefeuille*, p. 21.
[24] Le Bol de punch.
[25] P. iv.

[26] *Lettres à sa mère,* II, 302-3.

[27] *Ibid.,* II, 139.

[28] Buche, *Ecole mystique,* p. 219.

[29] *Œuvres,* ed. Dorchain, III.

[30] Buche, *Ecole mystique,* p. 219.

[31] Dupuy, *Alfred de Vigny,* II, 104-6.

[32] *Lettres de Frédéric Ozanam,* I, 32-33.

[33] Ozanam, *Mélanges,* I, 91.

[34] Buche, *Ecole mystique,* 291-94. Buche summarizes W. Koslowski's *Hœne Wronski et Ballanche.*

[35] Herriot, *Madame Récamier,* II, 273-74.

[36] Bonnerot, *Bibliographie des œuvres de Sainte-Beuve,* p. 99.

[37] Sainte-Beuve, *Correspondance générale,* I, 182.

[53] Bonnerot, *Bibliographie,* pp. 102-3.

[39] *Ibid.,* pp. 105-6.

[40] 1835, tome III.

[41] Bonnerot, *Bibliographie,* pp. 107-8.

[42] Sainte-Beuve, *Correspondance générale,* I, 531.

[43] *Ibid.,* II, 109.

[44] *Causeries du lundi,* XIV, 309-10.

[45] Karénine, *George Sand,* II, 219.

[46] *Ibid.,* II, 345.

[47] Denis, *Journal,* p. 60.

[48] Sainte-Beuve, *Correspondance générale,* III, 286.

[49] *Ibid.,* III, 285.

[50] Karénine, *George Sand,* II, 187.

[51] *Cours familier,* IX, entretien xlix, 29-30.

[52] *Cf. Jocelyn.*

[53] Hunt, *Epic in nineteenth century France,* pp. 171-72.

[54] Marquiset, *Ballanche et Mme d'Hautefeuille,* p. 50.

[55] Sainte-Beuve, *Correspondance générale,* II, 30.

[56] Marquiset, *Ballanche et Mme d'Hautefeuille,* p. 123.

[57] *Ibid.,* p. 204, July 16, 1842.

[58] *Ibid.,* p. 217, March 7, 1843.

[59] *Ibid.,* p. 259, June 3, 1847.

[60] *Cours familier,* entretien 1, pp. 122-24.

[61] Calippe, "Essai de rapprochement entre l'Eglise et l'etat," p. 311.

[62] Moreau, "Denis et les romantiques," p. 553.

[63] Marquiset, *Ballanche et Mme d'Hautefeuille,* p. 25.

[64] *Ibid.,* p. 26, May 18, 1834.

[65] D'Haussonville, *Sainte-Beuve,* letter dated October 6, 1834.

[66] *Ibid.,* December 6, 1835.

[67] Marquiset, *Ballanche et Mme d'Hautefeuille,* p. 115, December 22, 1837.

[68] *Journal,* p. 72.

[69] Marquiset, *Ballanche et Mme d'Hautefeuille*, pp. 123-24. January 20, 1839.

[70] *Ibid.*, p. 211, December 3, 1842.

[71] Vaudon, "Ballanche," p. 555.

[72] Moreau, "Denis et les romantiques," p. 545.

[73] *Ibid.*

[74] Pascal, "Un Prophète de l'avenir," p. 269.

[75] *Causeries du lundi*, XIV, 310.

[76] *Ibid.*

[77] Ch. Lenormant, 'Ballanche," p. 825.

[78] Vaudon, "Ballanche," p. 555.

CHAPTER VIII

[1] Paris: J. Didot, 1831. In-8°, 123 pp. *Cf.* Avertissement, V. In March, 1843, Ballanche actually came near preparing a second edition of the *Vision*, but never carried out the project.

[2] *Vision*, pp. 7-10.

[3] *Ibid.*, pp. 10-11.

[4] *Ibid.*, p. 15.

[5] *Ibid.*, pp. 18-19.

[6] *Ibid.*, p. 96.

[7] *Ibid.*, pp. 103-4.

[8] *Ibid.*, p. 107.

[9] *Ibid.*, p. 108.

[10] *Ibid.*, pp. 109-10.

[11] "Ballanche," pp. 24-25.

[12] *Ibid.*, p. 39.

[13] *Vision*, p. 110.

[14] Marquiset, *Ballanche et Mme d'Hautefeuille*, p. 32.

[15] "La Vision d'Hébal," tome LIII, janvier-mars, 1832, p. 602.

[16] *Ibid.*

[17] *Ibid.*, pp. 600-601.

[18] Ampère, "Ballanche," pp. 161-62.

[19] *Ibid.*, pp. 162-63.

[20] In a note to the 1830 edition of the *Œuvres* (I, 30), Ballanche commented that his description of the monastery and several of the statements made in the *Grande Chartreuse* later were expanded into the *Ville*.

[21] Herriot, *Madame Récamier*, II, 87-88.

[22] Viatte, *Bredin*, p. 212.

[23] "Charité chrétienne, base d'un nouveau régime pénitentiaire," 1834, tome xi; "Abolition de la peine de mort," *ibid.;* "Organisation de la ville," 1835, tome xix. These three episodes were also published separately in April, 1832.

[24] Marquiset, *Ballanche et Mme d'Hautefeuille*, p. 20.

[25] *Ibid.*, p. 48.

[26] Finally, in 1907, the *Ville* was published by the *Entretiens idéalistes*, then,

again, in 1926, as a part of the *Bibliothèque Romantique*.

[27] *Œuvres*, III, 217.

[28] *Ibid.*, pp. 220-21.

[29] *Ville*, pp. 16-17.

[30] *Ibid.*, p. 30.

[31] *Ibid.*, p. 63.

[32] *Ibid.*, p. 17.

[33] *Ibid.*, p. 72.

[34] *Ibid.*, p. 71.

[35] *Ibid.*, p. 107.

[36] *Ibid.*, p. 98.

[37] Marquiset, *Ballanche et Mme d'Hautefeuille*, p. 75.

[38] Paris: Delloye, 1837. The book ran through at least eight editions and was even translated into Spanish.

[39] Marquiset, *Ballanche et Mme d'Hautefeuille*, pp. 83-84.

[40] *Œuvres complètes*, IX, 41-42.

[41] Herriot, *Madame Récamier*, II, 291.

[42] *Ibid.*, II, 294.

[43] Volume 45, 1832.

[44] *Ibid.*, p. 229.

[45] *Ibid.*, p. 232.

[46] Karénine, *George Sand*, I, 414.

[47] Viatte, *Bredin*, pp. 289-90.

[48] Paris: Bureau de l'Encyclopédie des Connaissances Utiles.

[49] "Chronique littéraire," *Premiers lundis*, II, 183-84.

[50] "Un Mot sur les confiscations exercées en Pologne," p. 266.

[51] *Ibid.*

[52] "Un Mot sur la question d'Orient," *Polonais*, July, 1834, III, 37.

[53] "Pologne et Russie," *Polonais*, February, 1834, II, 109.

[54] "Le Providence et le destin," *Polonais*, IV, 181.

CHAPTER IX

[1] Marquiset, *Ballanche et Mme d'Hautefeuille*, p. 139.

[2] Durry, *Vieillesse de Chateaubriand*, I, 350.

[3] Louise-Adélade de Bourbon Condé, dite Mlle de Condé. *Lettres écrites en 1786 et 1787*. Paris, 1834.

[4] Lamennais, *Correspondance inédite avec le baron de Vitrolles*, p. 274.

[5] Paris: Didot, 1835.

[6] *De la publication*, p. 23.

[7] Frainnet, p. 317.

[8] Tome XI, 1834, pp. 15-16.

[9] Marquiset, *Ballanche et Mme d'Hautefeuille*, pp. 41-42, letter of March 25, 1835.

[10] *Ibid.*, p. 52.

[11] Tome XXV, janvier-février 1836.
[12] Marquiset, *Ballanche et Mme d'Hautefeuille*, p. 69.
[13] *Ibid.*, p. 71, October 15, 1836.
[14] *Ibid.*, p. 74, November 10, 1836.
[15] Herriot, *Madame Récamier*, II, 333.
[16] Sainte-Beuve, *Correspondance générale*, II, 198.
[17] Marquiset, *Ballanche et Mme d'Hautefeuille*, p. 99, June 23, 1837.
[18] *Ibid.*, p. 100.
[19] *Œuvres*, III, 79.
[20] Marquiset, *Ballanche et Mme d'Hautefeuille*, pp. 144-45, August 15, 1839.
[21] *Ibid.*, p. 146, September 29, 1839.
[22] *Ibid.*, p. 167, September 10, 1840.
[23] *Ibid.*, pp. 173-74, October 15, 1840.
[24] *Ibid.*, pp. 189-90, August 22, 1841.
[25] *Cf.* Ampère, "Ballanche," pp. 192-93.
[26] Marquiset, *Ballanche et Mme d'Hautefeuille*, p. 115, April 3, 1838.
[27] Levaillant, *Chateaubriand, Mme Récamier et les Mémoires d'outre-tombe*, pp. 284-88.
[28] Mme Lenormant, *Souvenirs de Mme Récamier*, II, 497.
[29] Harriot, *Madame Récamier*, II, 343.
[30] Marquiset, *Ballanche et Mme d'Hautefeuille*, pp. 190-91, September 18, 1841.
[31] Pp. 776-77.
[32] Sainte-Beuve, *Correspondance générale*, I, 487.
[33] Marquiset, *Ballanche et Mme d'Hautefeuille*, p. 36, January 16, 1835.
[34] *Ibid.*, pp. 38-39, January 23, 1835.
[35] *Ibid.*, p. 48, June 2, 1835.
[36] Sainte-Beuve, *Correspondance générale*, II, 22-23.
[37] Pp. 190-91.
[38] III, 225.
[39] Marquiset, *Ballanche et Mme d'Hautefeuille*, p. 200, February 5, 1842.
[40] Herriot, *Madame Récamier*, II, 349.
[41] *Discours de réception*, p. 253.
[42] *Ibid.*, p. 264.
[43] *Ibid.*, p. 266.
[44] *Réponse à M. Ballanche*, p. 275.
[45] Herriot, *Madame Récamier*, II, 352-53.
[46] Durry, *La Vieillesse de Chateaubriand*, I, 392.
[47] Marquiset, *Ballanche et Mme d'Hautefeuille*, p. 210, November 4, 1842.
[48] III, 2-3.
[49] Herriot, *Madame Récamier*, II, 358.
[50] *Ibid.*, II, 386.
[51] Ampère, *Correspondance*, II, 129, July 17, 1843.
[52] Marquiset, *Madame Récamier*, II, 249.
[53] *Ibid.*, p. 235, January 1, 1844.

[54] Blum, "Un Sociologiste inconnu," p. 414.

[55] Marquiset, *Ballanche et Mme d'Hautefeuille*, p. 245, October 16, 1845. The article hinted that Ballanche proposed to write a book on Julian the Apostate, but the project never went beyond the stage of pleasant expectations.

[56] *Ibid.*, p. 259, June 3, 1847.

[57] Edmond Biré, *Les Dernières Années de Chateaubriand*, pp. 386-87.

[58] Marquiset, *Ballanche et Mme d'Hautefeuille*, p. 260.

[59] Mme Lenormant, *Mme Récamier and her friends*, pp. 242-43.

[60] Herriot, *Madame Récamier*, II, 399.

CONCLUSION

[1] *Causeries du lundi*, X, 252, note 1.

[2] Buche, *Ecole mystique*, pp. 295-96.